Nicolas Vandeput
Inventory Optimization

Nicolas Vandeput

Inventory Optimization

Models and Simulations

DE GRUYTER

ISBN 978-3-11-067391-3
e-ISBN (PDF) 978-3-11-067394-4
e-ISBN (EPUB) 978-3-11-067399-9

Library of Congress Control Number: 2020939662

Bibliographic information published by the Deutsche Nationalbibliothek
The Deutsche Nationalbibliothek lists this publication in the Deutsche Nationalbibliografie;
detailed bibliographic data are available on the Internet at http://dnb.dnb.de.

© 2020 Walter de Gruyter GmbH, Berlin/Boston
Cover image: ZU_09 / DigitalVision Vectors / gettyimages.de
Typesetting: VTeX UAB, Lithuania
Printing and binding: CPI books GmbH, Leck

www.degruyter.com

I think that there is only one way to science—or to philosophy, for that matter: to meet a problem, to see its beauty and fall in love with it; to get married to it, and to live with it happily, till death do you part—unless you should meet another and even more fascinating problem, or unless, indeed, you should obtain a solution. But even if you obtain a solution, you may then discover, to your delight, the existence of a whole family of enchanting though perhaps difficult problem children for whose welfare you may work, with a purpose, to the end of your days.

Karl Popper, *Realism and the Aim of Science*

Acknowledgments

I would like to thank the many friends, practitioners and academics who have helped me reach the level of excellence I was pursuing throughout the writing of this book.

First and foremost, I would like to warmly thank my friend Gwendoline Dandoy for her help. Chapter after chapter, she carefully hunted down mistakes and inconsistencies, allowing the content of this book to be clearer, simpler and more consistent. Thank you, Gwen.

I would like to thank the publishing team at De Gruyter: Jeffrey Pepper, Jaya Dalal, as well as Mary Sudul for their incredible work, support and trust.

The help of many experts and practitioners was essential to the writing of this book. I am particularly grateful to three of them for their invaluable help, reviews, advice and corrections. Koen Cobbaert (Director at PwC) for our discussions about backorders, lost sales and multi-echelon inventory optimization. Stefan de Kok (Wahupa CEO & Founder) for our discussions about safety stock and probabilistic forecasts (his book *An Introduction to Probabilistic Planning and Forecasting* will be available by the end of 2020). Steven Pauly (Research Scientist at Slimstock) for our discussions about various inventory models, the tremendous number of models and papers he advised me about and his careful review of all the math included in this book.

I also had the great pleasure of discussing concepts with Professors Ton de Kok (Eindhoven University of Technology), Stephan Graves (MIT) and Sean Willems (Haslam Chair in Supply Chain Analytics at University of Tennessee). Ton de Kok for his help on single-echelon inventory policies; Stephan Graves and Sean Willems for their help on multi-echelon inventory policies.

Special thanks goes to the whole Qalinca research unit (Université Libre de Bruxelles) and in particular Professor Alassane Ndiaye, for his advice and kind support. I am also grateful to my colleagues: Alexis Nsamzinshuti, Haingo Rabarijaona, Yasin Tadayonard and Carole Biloé, and to my previous students Lynda Dhaeyer and Fanny Marcelis, who all provided me with continuous support and numerous reviews.

I would also like to extend my sincere thanks to my friends Romain Faurès, François Grisay and Charles Hoffreumon for their numerous reviews and invaluable advice. Romain for his dedicated reviews and spot-on remarks, François for his consultant point of view (usually shared in cafés and restaurants) and Charles for his statistician point of view (usually shared in his office at the university).

A special thanks goes to Joannes Vermorel (Lokad CEO) who has been a constant source of inspiration to me since we first started working on Bridgestone inventory optimization models in 2017. You can see Joannes and myself discussing inventory and forecasting on YouTube.[1] Joannes published his book *The Quantitative Supply Chain* in 2018.[2]

---

1 See Lokad TV episodes 30 and 33 https://www.youtube.com/channel/UC5r43_A7T7qXAty-uvNuJ5Q
2 Vermorel (2018).

https://doi.org/10.1515/9783110673944-201

I can also always count on the LinkedIn supply chain community. I would like to especially thank Niels De Smet (PhD researcher at Solventure & UGent) for his help on multi-echelon models, Suraj Vissa, Steve Frampton and Guillaume De Bruycker for their help, corrections and reviews. The reliability of the supply chain community on LinkedIn is impressive: no matter the question, there will always be someone there to help you.

I also had the great pleasure of working with my Bridgestone colleagues Jon San Andres, Niek Vaessen and Henri-Xavier Benoist. Year after year, our team managed to consistently deliver new models by pushing data science in supply chains further.

Last but not least, my friend Nathalie Dufour for her reviews—she allowed me to make the first part of the book more clear. Finally, special thanks to my family Veronique and Pierre Vandeput-Dellis, Caroline and Quentin Vandeput-Mortier as well as my friends Bruno and Emmeline Deremince-Everaert and Nicolas and Flore Pary-D'Argent for their support throughout 2019.

Nicolas Vandeput
February 2020
nicolas.vandeput@supchains.com

About the Author

Nicolas Vandeput is a supply chain data scientist specialized in demand forecasting and inventory optimization. He founded his consultancy company SupChains in 2016 and co-founded SKU Science—a smart online platform for supply chain management—in 2018. He enjoys discussing new quantitative models and how to apply them to business reality. Passionate about education, Nicolas is both an avid learner and enjoys teaching at universities: he has taught forecasting and inventory optimization to master students since 2014 in Brussels, Belgium. He published *Data Science for Supply Chain Forecasting* in 2018 and *Inventory Optimization: Models and Simulations* in 2020.

Foreword

What makes a supply chain great? As supply chains are made of people, a frequent answer is *great leadership* is what it takes. Indeed...but *great* is vague. More specifically, what sort of qualities and competencies should a company seek to foster among its supply chain management? The 20th century answer to this question has primarily been reliable, diligent, energetic if not charismatic leaders, capable of organizing the work of thousands of workers, and literally creating the *mass production* supply chains as we know them today.

Yet, with the advent of the barcode reader, supply chains had, by the end of the 20th century, already outgrown the *direct* capabilities of the human mind, even the most talented ones. There are too many SKUs, too many suppliers, too many clients, too many channels to expect management to sort it all out through sheer willpower. Instead of *directly* controlling fine-grained supply chain decisions, companies transitioned toward *indirect* management through software.

In this respect, supply chain management has been lagging behind. Factories have been heavily automated for over two decades—a few verticals such as textiles aside. Warehouses are getting there and will be almost exclusively automated by the end of the 2020s. Transportation still faces the *last mile* problem that resists automation, but within one decade—two at most—autonomous vehicles will be commonplace and deliver the last major productivity gains to be ever observed in supply chains. Beyond this point, blue collar jobs will have almost completely disappeared from supply chains.

Yet, software-driven supply chain management takes a fairly distinctive skill set compared to people-driven supply chain management. Being great at software takes a *hacker* mindset that emphasizes tinkering with programs or machines, experimenting for fun and profit, and treating reverse engineering as much as a learning opportunity as a way to hack your way into a better system. This hacker mindset wasn't part of the recipe for 20th century leadership, and yet, I firmly believe it will be the cornerstone of 21st century leadership.

In this book *Inventory Optimization: Models and Simulations*, Nicolas Vandeput hacks his way through the maze of quantitative supply chain optimizations. This book illustrates how the quantitative optimization of 21st century supply chains should be crafted and executed. This book is based on many years of experience, earned the hard way from the supply chain trenches of large companies.

With usually no more than 10 lines of Python, Nicolas Vandeput revisits classic models and turns mathematical models into actionable pieces of software. Doing so, Nicolas demystifies the discourse of (most?) large software vendors in supply chain who—under the guise of Big Data/AI/Demand Sensing (pick your buzzword)—end up delivering *less* than what Nicolas achieves with highly accessible tools, be it Excel or Python.

https://doi.org/10.1515/9783110673944-202

Also, after revising the classics, the last five chapters, starting from "Beyond Normality," venture into hard problems that do not have nice, closed-form, analytical solutions. Yet, once again, the book delivers the hands-on demonstration that even tough problems can be brute-forced to some extent with histograms, kernels or Monte Carlo algorithms.

The optimization of the 21st century supply chain will be driven by hackers. Hackers share insights, but more importantly, they share *code* as well. Nicolas Vandeput is at the forefront of a new and better way of doing supply chains, and thanks to a richly illustrated book, where every single situation gets its own illustrating code snippet, *so could you.*

Joannes Vermorel
March 2020

Contents

Part III: Advanced Stochastic Models

Introduction

Supply chains are complex.

In the current business landscape of our global economy, supply chains and businesses are made of international networks of suppliers and clients. As the competition became fiercer on quality and price, the pressure increased on supply chain execution. And its management only grew more complex. The catalog of products each company is offering is ever expanding—despite their best efforts to keep it limited. This is mainly due to an increased (global) competition pressure; and a wave of customization and product innovation that started during the second half of the 20th century. As businesses are dealing with more products, the average life-cycle is becoming shorter and the demand variability is increasing. On top of this, international supply chains result in longer lead times, imposing more constraints on operational planning.

The complexity of supply chains is also due to all the humans—us!—interacting with each other over long distances, with different tools, capabilities and information. More importantly, even if business leaders strive to align their teams, each actor is pursuing its own objectives often resulting in divergent actions.

For better or for worse, inventories lie at the bottom of these complex supply chains. The central question of **how much inventory is needed**, and **where it is needed**, is often an endless debate among colleagues. Especially when the game of politics drives decisions.

Inventory Done Right

Stocking products is helping companies around the globe to supply their clients on time and provides a buffer against any unforeseen event (we'll discuss this in the second part of the book). Since holding inventory disconnects the production process from the sales process, it allows planners to produce longer production batches decreasing the production costs (we'll discuss this in Chapter 2). In other words, inventory optimization done right reduces overall costs, while optimizing the service level.

Inventory Done Wrong

Nevertheless, holding inventory comes with two drawbacks. The first one is of course its cost: inventory is nothing more than sleeping cash that is depreciating over time. It costs money to store products, and it comes with risks. The more you keep, the higher the cost, and the riskier it gets. Will you really be able to sell all these products? There is always the risk of ending up with dead stock. Keeping less inventory might partially prevent the risk of dead stock, but won't help to provide adequate service levels to your clients. Actually, in some cases, inventory management is so flawed that supply chains face *both* low service levels *and* dead stock.

https://doi.org/10.1515/9783110673944-203

Too much inventory will also prevent companies from improving their processes because they don't see any of the process fluctuation anymore. Too much protection against unforeseen events won't incentivize the different process-owners to improve.

Impact of Inventory

Based on the 30th Annual Council of Supply Chain Management Professionals State of Logistics Report,[1] inventory **yearly costs** accounted for around $500 billion in the US in 2018 (around 2% of US GDP). These are more or less equally spread between financial costs, storage costs and other costs (like obsolescence, handling, insurance). We will discuss holding costs in detail in Chapter 2.

As shown in Figure 1, the U.S. Census Bureau (2019) reports that the amount of inventory for manufacturers, wholesalers and retailers has been rather flat for the last four years at around 1.4 months of sales (their all-time low was in 2010, with inventory levels 10 to 15% lower).

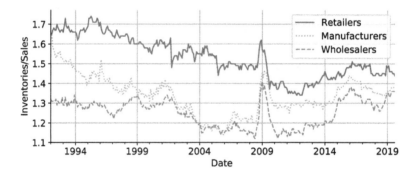

Figure 1: Seasonally Adjusted Inventories/Sales. Source: U.S. Census Bureau (2019).

Inventory is here to stay. We should therefore be serious about optimization—avoiding the trap of bad service levels and dead stock, and reaping the benefits of a properly orchestrated inventory policy. In this book you will see how to optimize your own inventory policies based on various tools and models.

---

1 Ward et al. (2019).

Inventory Modeling

All models are wrong, but some are helpful.

George Box (1919–2013)

As the amount of inventory grows, so does the need for optimization. Unfortunately, the science of optimizing inventories—keeping the *right* amount of inventory—can become as complex as the different modern supply chains. Even if an inventory policy seems simple—"Buy 4 when you have 5 left"—the models behind these can easily become *massively* complex. In order to solve these policies we have two methods at our disposal: mathematical models (i. e., equations) and simulations.

Models

Since the first inventory optimization model was published in 1913 by Harris, academics have published an ever-growing list of mathematical models to optimize **how much inventory should a supply chain hold**, and **where it should be stored**. Each new set of equations would tackle a supply chain under another set of assumptions. A model would discuss supply chains with perishable products; another one with multiple warehouses; or with a specific seasonality and production constraints; and so on. Unfortunately, even the cutting-edge models won't be enough to *perfectly* describe a supply chain.[2] As explained by Ton de Kok—professor at the Eindhoven University of Technology—*"Inventory models are abstractions that cannot capture all possible actions to balance supply and demand."* We are only at the beginning of our journey of inventory optimization and yet we already know that perfection is out of reach. And most likely will be forever.

Simulations

An equation can't handle the complexity of a modern supply chain, but we can nevertheless *try* to simulate it. Simulations can either be used to test the outcome of a mathematical model; or they can be used to find a *good-enough* policy when no equations are up to the challenge. In the final part of the book, **you will learn to use simulations to optimize inventory policies**. Simulations will allow you to cope with much more complexity than equations, but this will come at a cost: longer computation times and variable results. We will discuss in Chapter 13 how to overcome these limitations.

Limitations and Assumptions

Throughout the book we will pay careful attention to the assumptions (read *limitations*) behind the models (and simulations) we use. We won't be able to create perfect

---

2 Immanuel Kant (1724–1804), a German philosopher during the Age of Enlightenment, prognosticated that, *"From such crooked wood as that which man is made of, nothing straight can be fashioned."* Can we then really expect our models to be perfect?

simulations or models, but as we understand their weaknesses, we will be able to assess when it is right to use them (and when we should go for another model).

Model Accuracy and Sustainability

Does it make sense then to continue on this path of optimizing inventory policies despite the impossibility to be absolutely correct? Yes. Being correct 95% of the time should be enough to bring substantial savings to any supply chain.[3]

In this book, we will discuss models that deal with enough complexity to properly understand what drives supply chain inventory levels, costs and profits. We will also discuss the assumptions we make, and how we can refine them with some hacks and fit them to reality, while keeping them practical. As supply chain scientists, we have to make trade-offs for our models between complexity and accuracy on one side, and simplicity and practicality on the other. As Jordan Ellenberg explained in his book *How Not to Be Wrong: The Power of Mathematical Thinking*: *"If the universe hands you a hard problem, try to solve an easier one instead, and hope the simple version is close enough to the original problem that the universe doesn't object."*[4] This is exactly what we will do. A complex model will most likely be more accurate resulting in fewer costs and more profits; but less understandable and usable for different users. A simple model, on the other hand, will be less accurate, resulting in higher costs and waste; but might be more usable and sustainable for a business process. At some point, it is better for a model to be 80% accurate but trusted and always used; rather than be 95% accurate and never used nor well understood.

There is a Latin saying, "Vires acquirit eundo," which means, "We gather strength as we go." This represents perfectly the path we will follow in this book: as shown in Figure 2, we will start with a simple model and, as we apply it, we will learn new things. These will allow us to build a stronger model. And so on. We will gather insights and intuitions about supply chains as we go.

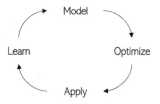

Model

Learn   Optimize

Apply

Figure 2: Inventory optimization journey.

Book Organization

The book is divided into four parts:

I **Deterministic Supply Chains** where our journey starts by discussing common inventory policies (Chapter 1) and then creating the first simple deterministic model (Chapters 2 and 3). This part will be mostly theoretical, but will lay the necessary ground for the next parts.

II **Stochastic Supply Chains** where you will create your first *stochastic* model:[5] first based on stochastic demand only (Chapters 4 and 5), then all together with stochastic lead times (Chapter 6). **You** will code in Chapter 5 your first inventory simulation. Going forward, it will help you to assess the accuracy of each of your models.

III **Advanced Stochastic Models** where you will refine the stochastic model from part II. We will first discuss the expected backorders and fill rate (Chapter 7). Then you will learn to minimize the cost of your inventory policies in Chapter 8, and create policies for non-normal demand (Chapter 9). These three chapters are the most technical of the book, nevertheless they should help you to optimize and refine your inventory policies **beyond** what is usually done in the industry. Finally, you will answer the question "where should we locate inventory" as you will create a model to optimize a *multi-echelon inventory policy*[6] (Chapter 10).

IV **Discrete Inventory Optimization** where you will learn to use simulations to optimize inventory policies. We discuss first a simple newsvendor model (Chapter 11), then we model custom demand probability distributions (Chapter 12) to finally optimize inventory policies with regard to simulations (Chapter 13).

Of course, inventory modeling is not an end. The real goal is to analyze your supply chain, optimize your inventory policy, minimize your costs and maximize your profits. We will often discuss the business implications of the various models, shifting from a scientific mindset to a business one.

Inventory Confusion

Throughout the book we will also discuss major sources of confusion and suboptimalities in inventory policies.

Vocabulary and definitions First and foremost, inventory management suffers from major confusion due to its terminology: "safety stock," "reorder point," "stock target," "expected inventory"… These might all refer to different concepts depending

---

5 Stochastic is a fancy word for random. In a stochastic model the outcome is not know in advance but can be estimated by statistical distributions; whereas you always know what will happen in a deterministic model.

6 Multi-echelon inventory policies refer to inventory policies that deal with complex warehouse networks with multiple layers (echelons) of stocking points.

on the software vendor, consultant or colleague you are talking to. We will take the time to define each of these in Parts I and II.

Long lead times As the lead times get longer, the spread between the order up-to level of an inventory policy and the expected average inventory gets bigger. We will discuss these in Chapters 3 and 5.

Review period Often practitioners forget to include the review period of their policies into the computation of safety stock targets (and only look at the lead time). You will see how to include the review period in Chapter 5.

Fill rate vs. Cycle service level A major confusion for practitioners is how to measure the service level of an inventory policy. Most of the safety stock models use the cycle service level whereas most companies record the fill rate. We will define both in Chapter 4 and learn to fit our inventory policies to a fill rate target in Chapter 7.

Optimal service level Finally, the service level targets are often set as arbitrary numbers. You will see in Chapter 8 how to set the optimal service level that will minimize your costs.

Other Resources

In order to help you with the various concepts presented in this book, there is a glossary and a list of symbols at the end of the book. Please note that throughout the book you will see that boldface is used to highlight important text for emphasis.

We will discuss many models, and refer whenever possible to their initial authors as well as current research and helpful resources. You can also check the following general resources about inventory and supply chains:

- *Inventory and Production Management in Supply Chains* by Edward Silver, David Pyke and Douglas Thomas.[7] The authors are well-known professors in the field of inventory management and operation management; their book is most likely one of the main reference for PhD students as it includes a thorough literature review and covers many topics in-depth.
- *Matching Supply with Demand: An Introduction to Operations Management* by Gérard Cachon and Christian Terwiesch.[8] The book offers an introduction to many supply chain subjects: it is great as a textbook for students.
- *Inventory Control* by Sven Axsäter.[9] This (mathematical) reference book covers in detail various inventory models (mainly continuous ones).

---

7 Silver et al. (2016).
8 Cachon (2018).
9 Axsäter (2015).

- Next to these reference books, you can also check the shorter *Inventory Management in Supply Chain Networks* from Horst Tempelmeier.[10] It also focuses on mathematical models.
- You can also register to the excellent online class *Supply Chain Fundamentals* proposed by MIT on the online platform edX.[11] It covers various inventory optimization models as well as forecast models.
- MIT also offers the online class "Supply Chains for Manufacturing I" on edX.[12] This class covers inventory and forecast models and is given by Stephen Graves and Sean Willems—known for their research work in the field of inventory optimization (we will discuss their models in Chapter 10).

Tools

As a painter needs the proper brush, the inventory analyst needs the proper tools to create her or his model. We will use two tools to build our models, experiment and share our results.

Excel

Excel is the data analyst's Swiss knife. It will allow you to easily perform simple calculations and plot data. The big advantage of Excel, compared to any programming language, is that you can **see the data**. It is much easier to debug a model or to test a new one if you see how the data is transformed by each step of computation. Therefore, Excel can be a first go-to to experiment with new models or data.

Excel also has many limitations. It won't perform well on big datasets and will hardly allow us to automate difficult tasks. It is therefore a good tool to test ideas and models on small datasets, or to visualize data, but it is not our preferred tool to create complex or massive models.

Python

Python is a programming language initially published in 1991 by Guido van Rossum, a Dutch computer scientist. If Excel is a Swiss knife, Python is a full army of construction machines awaiting instructions from an analyst. Python will allow you to perform computations on huge datasets in an automated, fast and simple way. It also comes

---

10 Tempelmeier (2011).

11 www.edx.org/course/supply-chain-fundamentals

12 www.edx.orgns-and-manufacturing-systems-planning-1

with many libraries dedicated to data analysis (pandas), data visualization (Seaborn and Matplotlib), scientific computations (NumPy and SciPy) and machine learning (scikit-learn). These will soon be your best friends, if they aren't already.

Why Python?

We chose Python over other programming languages because it is both user-friendly (it is easy to read and understand) and one of the most used programming languages in the world. In 2019, it was the programming language that was the most googled and it is the most commonly used for machine learning and deep learning.

Should You Start Learning Python?

Yes, you should.

Excel will be perfect to visualize results, perform some simple computations and simple data cleaning tasks. But it won't allow you to scale up your models to bigger datasets nor to easily automate any data cleaning. Excel will also make your life difficult if you want to define customized statistical functions, such as those we will need in the second half of the book.

Many practitioners are afraid to learn a coding language. Everyone knows a colleague who uses some macros/VBA in Excel—maybe you are this colleague—and the complexity of these macros might be frightening to the uninitiated. **Python is much simpler than Excel macros and much more powerful**. As you will see yourself in the following chapters, even the most advanced models won't require so many lines of code or complex functions. It means that you do not have to be an IT genius to use Python. **You can start to use it yourself, today, on your own computer, for free**. Python will give you a definitive edge over anyone using Excel.

Today is a great day to start learning Python. Many resources are available: videos, blogs, articles, books... You can, for example, look for Python courses on the following online platforms:

www.edx.org
www.coursera.org
www.udemy.com
www.datacamp.com

I personally recommend the MIT class: *"Introduction to Computer Science and Programming Using Python,"* available on edX.[13] This will teach you everything you need to know about Python to start using the models presented in this book.

---

13 www.edx.org/course/introduction-to-computer-science-and-programming-7

You can also look at the Appendix A, where I briefly introduce the most useful Python concepts (and how to install it) in order to help you out with the first code extracts.

Python Libraries

We will use throughout the book some of Python's very well-known libraries. As you can see below, we will use their usual import conventions. And, for the sake of clarity, we won't show the `import` lines over and over in each code extract.

```python
import numpy as np
import pandas as pd
import scipy.stats as stats
from scipy.stats import norm, gamma
import matplotlib.pyplot as plt
```

Simplicity vs. Efficiency

The various Python code extracts throughout the book are made with the objective of simplicity and clarity. Simple code is much easier to understand, maintain, share and improve than complex one. This simplification was sometimes done at the expense of efficiency or speed. This means that the codes are not as fast as an experienced Python user could produce, but the implementations are easy to understand—which is the primary goal here.

> *Perfection is finally attained not when there is no longer anything to add, but when there is no longer anything to take away.*
>
> Antoine de Saint-Exupéry (1900–1944)

Other Resources

You can download the Python codes shown in this book on supchains.com/resources-invopt (password: SupChains-IO). There is also a glossary (and an index) at the end of the book where you can find a short description of all the specific terms we will use. Do not hesitate to consult it if you are unsure about a term or acronym.

Part I: **Deterministic Supply Chains**

1 Inventory Policies

An inventory policy determines **how much** and **when** a product should be ordered (or produced).[1] Inventory policies determine how the products flow through a supply chain. We can categorize them into two types, based on when the inventory review is done:

- Continuous review policies: an order can be made at any time.
- Periodic review policies: the orders can only be made at specific times.

Let's discuss in detail three of the main inventory policies used in practice.

1.1 Policy #1 – Continuous Review and Reorder Point

In this first inventory policy, we order our products based on a fixed threshold: **as soon as the net inventory reaches the threshold (or goes below), we order a pre-determined number of units from our supplier** (or launch a production batch). This threshold is called the **reorder point** or ROP.

> **On-hand inventory**
>
> Inventory physically available for a client to buy.

> **Backorders**
>
> Backlog of open orders that are not yet fulfilled. This happens when you do not have enough on-hand inventory to fulfill orders directly and the orders are not lost.

> **Net inventory**
>
> Inventory level including: available on-hand inventory and *in-transit* inventory, minus backorders, orders not yet shipped, etc.

---

1 We will discuss **where** to keep inventory in Chapter 10.

https://doi.org/10.1515/9783110673944-001

> ### In-transit inventory
>
> Goods ordered from a supplier but not yet available in our warehouse for our clients to buy. These goods are considered to be in-transit between two warehouses (or in pipeline). See Section 3.1.

With a continuous review policy, the elapsed time between two consecutive orders will vary (as the demand fluctuates), but the order quantity will always be the same (as you can see in Figure 1.1).

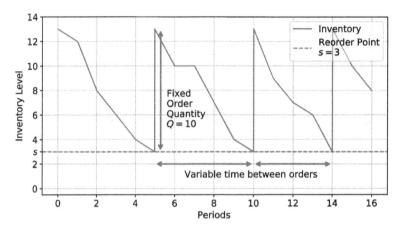

Figure 1.1: Fixed reorder point policy (with immediate replenishment): "Order 10 when less than 3 left."

Typically, with such a policy, you could say that:
– *When the stock level reaches 3 pieces, I order 10.*
   Here the fixed reorder point is 3, and the order quantity is 10 (see Figure 1.1). Note that, even if you only have 2 pieces in stock, you will still only order 10 pieces. Remember: with the fixed reorder point, the order quantity (10 in this case) is always fixed.
– *As soon as I am left with 2 bottles of milk in my refrigerator, I'll go to the supermarket and buy 6.*
– *When my printer says that I am left with only 10% of ink, I'll order a new set of cartridges.*

Advantages
This policy is safe (i. e., the risk of being out-of-stock is low) as it assumes you can make an order whenever you need to. It is therefore a good policy for expensive and/or important items that need to be monitored closely.

Another important advantage of this policy is that you can optimize the order quantity based on some (often obvious) constraints or costs. For example, you might get a rebate if you order a full pallet or a truckload. With such a policy you are sure to get the reduction each time you make an order.

Limitations

First, **it won't allow you to group into a single order different items with a single supplier**. Imagine that you supply a hundred different products from a single-favorite supplier: you might want to simplify your operations and buy all these products at once (in one single order) instead of doing different orders multiple times a day, when each one of your items needs to be replenished.

Then, we assume that **a client can make an order with its supplier at any time**. In reality, this might not be the case. For example, a supplier might only accept orders once a month (or only send one shipment a month—which is the same). In such a case, it is foolish to think that you would follow a fixed reorder point policy, as the supplier is actually following its own calendar.

Finally, the pure theoretical mathematical model of this policy (that we will discuss in the following chapters) assumes that **each client can only buy one product at a time**, so that the reorder point will always be perfectly reached.

In practice, these assumptions are not often respected. A pure continuous policy is therefore exceptional (some fully automated production processes, or internal processes, could follow these assumptions). It is therefore used as a (useful) theoretical simplification.

Notation

The fixed reorder point policy is noted (s, Q), with s the reorder point and Q the fixed order quantity.

1.2 Policy #2 – Periodic Review and Order Up-to Level

For this second inventory policy, we will order products periodically, based on a **fixed schedule** and on an **up-to level**. At the beginning of any review period, we will order enough products to bring our net inventory to the up-to level. As you can see in Figure 1.2, with this fixed periodic schedule, we will order a different quantity each time. The order quantity depends on how much inventory we have at the time we make the order, and is therefore variable. On the other hand, the orders are made following a fixed schedule: the elapsed time between two consecutive orders will always be the same (but the order quantity will always change).

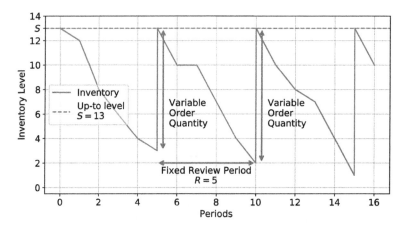

Figure 1.2: Fixed review period policy (with immediate replenishment): "Order up to 13 every 5 days."

Here are some typical examples:
- *We make an order every Friday evening to our supplier, so that they can prepare our order on Monday morning and deliver it on Tuesday.*
- *We make an order every third business day of the month with our supplier in China.*
- *I go to the supermarket every Saturday morning. I buy enough bottles of milk in order to have a total stock of 6 liters.*

Advantages
This periodic replenishment policy (with an order up-to level) is actually the most common inventory policy because it allows businesses to group their orders with each of their suppliers. This will help both clients and suppliers to streamline their operations as they can plan orders and workload in advance, and define a periodic review process.

A periodic replenishment policy is also often forced onto supply chains by the use of a MRP/DRP.[2] These tools follow a predefined schedule—often daily or weekly—resulting in the implicit use of a periodic review policy.

Limitations
As we will discuss later in Chapter 4, "Safety Stocks," this policy is riskier, due to the blind spot it creates: you cannot order in-between two review periods. If you make an order every Friday with your supplier, but are out-of-stock on Monday evening,

---

2 MRP stands for Materials Requirements Planning, it is a software/methodology that is used to plan the sourcing and production of goods. DRP stands for Deployment Requirement Planning, it is also a software/methodology used to plan the delivery of goods. Due to running time motives, these tools often run daily or weekly, imposing therefore a periodic review policy.

you will have to wait four more days before making a new order. You will possibly suffer lost sales due to being out-of-stock in the meantime. That is riskier than the fixed reorder point policy, where you would have made a new order directly on Monday evening.

Another issue is that the order quantity will vary at each order. This might disrupt a smooth operational flow. If you have a palletized product, you might not want to remove the packaging around an entire pallet in order to get a single unit.

Notation

The fixed review period policy is often noted (R, S), with R being the fixed review period and S the up-to level. Don't get confused by the notation: academics usually use s to denote the reorder point and S to denote the order up-to level. As a mnemonic device, **lowercase s denotes a minimum amount of stock**, and **uppercase S a maximum**.

1.3 Policy #3 – Periodic Review, Reorder Point and Fixed Order Quantity

We just discussed a first inventory policy that offered us the convenience of a fixed order quantity, and a second that gave us the convenience of a fixed review period. We can then create an inventory policy combining the best of both worlds in terms of operational convenience. This policy will consist of making orders of fixed quantity Q, based on a fixed schedule, if the inventory level reaches a threshold s (see Figure 1.3).

Here are some examples:

– *Every Saturday, if I have less than 2 bottles of milk in my refrigerator, I go to the supermarket to buy 6 bottles of milk.*

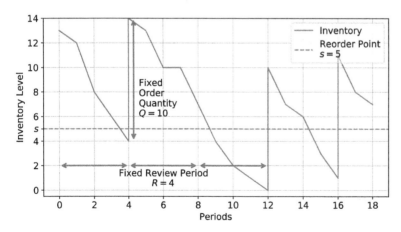

Figure 1.3: Period review with reorder point and fixed order quantity: "Order 10 pieces every 4 days only if inventory level reaches 5 pieces."

- *Every Friday evening, if our net inventory reaches 10 units (or below), we make an order of 10 pieces to our supplier (we order 10 pieces due to the packaging). We place the order on Friday, so that the supplier can prepare the order on Monday morning and deliver it on Tuesday.*

Advantages

This policy has two strong advantages:
- The order quantity is always constant, allowing transportation and packaging to be optimized (e. g., full pallet, full truckload).
- The order is always made at a predefined time slot (e. g., at the end of the day/week), allowing smooth operations and the ability to group orders with a supplier.

Limitations

The risk is high with this kind of policy: we have a review period possibly blocking us from making an order when we need it; on top of that, we will only make an order if the stock reaches a certain threshold. This extra risk will need to be compensated for by an extra amount of safety stock, resulting in higher inventory levels and costs. Besides, this policy is also much more difficult to optimize mathematically, and therefore less discussed in the academic literature.[3] As the models become too complex (and based on too many assumptions), we will optimize this policy with simulations in Chapter 13.

Notation

We will note this policy (R, s, Q), where R denotes the fixed review period, s the fixed reorder point, and Q the fixed order quantity. This policy is also sometimes noted $(R, s, n \cdot Q)$ if we can order a multiple of Q units at once (typically in the case of truckload or packaging constraints).

1.4 Other Policies

Of course, a supply chain can be piloted with other policies.

(R, s, S) Policy

We can imagine an (R, s, S) policy, where the inventory is reviewed periodically and, if the inventory level reaches a threshold s, an order is placed up-to a certain level S.

---

3 See Tempelmeier (2011), Tijms (1994) for more information.

Again, such policies are more difficult to optimize mathematically—yet analyzed since at least the 1960s—and are, therefore, out of scope for this book.[4]

Multi-Sourcing

We can also create even more complex policies. For example, in order to reduce the supply risk, it is rather common for a supply chain to have an emergency supply lane in addition to a regular supply lane with a preferred supplier. As the behavior of these policies become more complex, it will become *impossible* to solve them *perfectly* based on *tractable*[5] models.

That, of course, is not a reason not to use them. The question should be: how can we approximate these policies in order to get a useful and understandable model? Even if we cannot create such a model, we have another tool to optimize these: running simulations. We will discuss this technique in Chapter 13, "Simulation Optimization."

1.5 Confusion Curse: Inventory Target

Pay attention to the fact that supply chain practitioners—and software vendors—often use different terms to refer to the same policies. For example the term "reorder point" (or ROP) could define an order up-to level or a replenishment threshold. This means that a periodic review policy could be called an ROP policy as you set a "reorder point" (which is actually nothing more than the up-to level).

The term "stock target" is actually the most confusing. When a practitioner refers to a "stock target of 10," it is never clear what she refers to. Is it an order up-to target in a periodic review policy? Or the reorder point in a fixed reorder point policy? Or the average on-hand inventory they expect to have? We will discuss this confusion curse further in Chapter 3, "When Should I Order?" and Chapter 4, "Safety Stocks."

> **Important Point**
>
> When discussing with colleagues, software vendors or consultants, always define clearly what a "reorder point" and a "stock target" is.

---

4 See Veinott and Wagner (1965), Ehrhardt (1979), Tijms and Groenevelt (1984), Strijbosch and Moors (1999) for detailed models.

5 Tractable is a fancy word that mathematicians use to describe models or equations that are simple enough to be used or solved.

1.6 Recap

An inventory policy defines **when** an order needs to be made and **how many** units should be ordered. We can categorize them between continuous and periodic review inventory policies. A policy can be defined by different parameters:
- the order up-to level S
- the review period R
- the order quantity Q
- the reorder point s

We analyzed three policies:

(s, Q) A continuous review policy with a reorder point s and a fixed order quantity Q.
+ Pros: low amount of safety stock needed; optimized order quantity.
- Cons: continuous review needed; multiple items cannot be grouped in one order with one supplier.
  See Section 1.1.

(R, S) A periodic review policy following a review period R and an order up-to level S.
+ Pros: multiple items can be grouped in one order with one supplier.
- Cons: more safety stock needed; order quantity varies and can't be optimized.
  See Section 1.2.

(R, s, Q) A periodic review policy following a review period R, with a reorder point s and a fixed order quantity Q.
+ Pros: can group multiple items in one order with one supplier; optimized order quantity.
- Cons: even more safety stock needed; optimization is difficult.
  See Section 1.3.

2 How Much Should I Order?

The policies discussed in Chapter 1 come with questions:

- Fixed reorder point: *What is the optimal order quantity? What is the best reorder point?*
  We begin the discussion about these subjects in Chapter 2.
- Periodic replenishment and order up-to level: *What should be the up-to level? What is the optimal review period?*
  We will discuss these in Chapter 3.

In order to answer these questions, we will follow the *Model-Optimize-Apply-Learn* framework shown in Figure 2.1. We will first **model the costs** of our supply chain, based on the order quantity. Then we will optimize this model (i. e., find the optimal order quantity that minimizes costs) in order to find the **optimal order quantity**. We can finally apply this optimal order quantity in a supply chain to update its inventory policies.

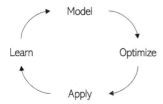

Figure 2.1: Inventory optimization journey.

2.1 Supply Chain Costs

Let's begin our first model with a simple supply chain in a deterministic world.

As shown in Figure 2.2, let's imagine, a supply chain with:

- A single stocking site.
- A single supplier.

Figure 2.2: Supply chain model.

https://doi.org/10.1515/9783110673944-002

- A single product that is reordered from the supplier instantaneously when the stock drops to zero (i. e., the lead time is 0).
- A deterministic, constant demand: we note the yearly demand D and the demand per period d.
- A fixed order quantity Q.

The attentive reader will notice that here we have a supply chain system that works thanks to a fixed reorder point policy (reorder point of 0 and a fixed order quantity of Q).

We will add new layers of complexity down the road:
- In Chapter 3, we will increase the lead time and discuss periodic review.
- In Chapter 4, we will use safety stock as a buffer against stochastic demand.
- In Chapter 6, we will discuss stochastic lead times.

Let's analyze the inventory level over time in our simple supply chain. The stock level of our unique product in our single location will follow a pattern similar to the one we can see in Figure 2.3.

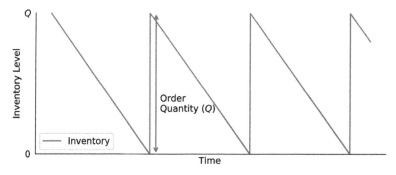

Figure 2.3: Simple inventory policy.

In this supply chain, the maximum inventory level we can have is Q and the lowest is 0. Because the demand is constant, the inventory will decrease uniformly from its maximum Q to its minimum 0: this means that we will have in stock $Q/2$ pieces on average. This is very interesting as, in other words, once the order quantity Q is set, the average inventory level is **independent** from the demand or the number of transactions per year. We will call this stock the **cycle stock.**

Cycle stock (C_s)

Average stock we have through an order cycle to fulfill the (expected) demand (or the forecast).

> **Order cycle**
>
> Time elapsed between two consecutive orders.

In such a simple supply chain we will have two types of costs:

Holding costs related to storing (or simply possessing) our products.

Transaction costs triggered by making an order (or a transaction) with our supplier (either internal or external).

Let's discuss these two costs in detail.

2.1.1 Holding Costs

These costs—incurred as we store or possess products—can be either variable (the more inventory, the more expensive) or fixed (constant no matter how much is stored). Here are some examples:

Variable holding costs —products' cost of capital, products' insurance, obsolescence, damages, losses, theft, spoilage (mostly for perishable goods), inventory control (i. e., periodically counting inventory).

Fixed holding costs —employees, warehouse insurance, warehouse cost of capital (or rent), warehouse security, warehouse lighting and heating, storage equipment (e. g., shelving, IT systems).

In order to simplify our model, and because the **fixed** holding costs are independent of the order quantity Q (i. e., we incur them no matter how much inventory we have in stock), we will take them out of the equation.

Let's define h as the **yearly holding costs for keeping one single piece in stock**. As we have $Q/2$ units in stock on average through the year, we can multiply the two to get the total yearly holding costs.

$$\text{(Yearly) Holding Costs} = h\frac{Q}{2}$$

$$= \text{holding cost per unit} \times \text{average cycle stock}$$

In this equation, h is expressed as a cost per year per unit $\left(\frac{€}{unit \cdot year}\right)$. In the literature h is typically expressed as a percentage of the cost $\left(\frac{1}{unit \cdot year}\right)$.[1] The holding costs equation becomes

$$\text{Holding Costs} = (h \cdot c)\frac{Q}{2}$$

where c is the product unit (or production) cost.[2]

---

1 Typically $10\% \leq h \leq 25\%$ depending on the industry.

2 Accountants often report it under the acronym COGS (cost of goods sold).

> **Important Point**
>
> Make sure to use a consistent unit of time. If D is the *yearly* demand, h should be also expressed as the *yearly* holding costs for one product.

What is important to understand here is that the holding costs are proportional to the order quantity Q (as you can see in Figure 2.4).

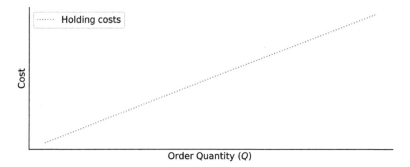

Figure 2.4: Yearly holding costs.

> **Example**
>
> You are a planner working to optimize orders with an external supplier. You want to minimize your total inventory costs, and therefore you will need to optimize your order quantity. You start by analyzing the holding costs. You collected the following information:
> - The purchasing cost of this product is 10€ per piece.
> - Due to the various warehousing expenses, it costs 2€ per year to stock a single piece.
> - You account for the cost of capital, the risk of obsolescence and the insurance as 15% of the purchasing price per year.
>
> If we assume that we order a quantity Q for each order (Q is still unknown), we can compute the yearly (variable) holding costs as:
>
> $$\text{(Yearly) Holding costs} = h\frac{Q}{2} = (15\% \cdot 10€ + 2€) \cdot \frac{Q}{2} = 1.75€ \cdot Q$$
>
> As expected, the yearly holding costs are proportional to the order quantity. This makes sense: the more product we order at once, the more we will have to stock.

> **Going Further**
>
> If h is expressed as a percentage of the product cost, the cost model is simplified but might be overly confident in the linear relationship between a product holding cost and its cost. The linearity between the two is mostly due to the cash tied up in the inventory and the cost of insurance (assuming the storage cost per m^2 is fixed at short/mid term). Nevertheless, non-linear costs exist as well (for example, the storage cost per m^2 can decrease as more m^2 are used). Investing time into a proper estimation of h is often worth it.

2.1.2 Transaction Costs

The transaction costs are all the costs incurred when we order a new batch of products. The order can either be made with an external supplier or trigger a production batch (in which case the production department can be seen as an internal supplier). As we did for the holding costs, we can split the transaction costs between variable and fixed. Let's take a look at some examples.

Variable transaction costs
    Supplier side: transport, packaging
    Client side: reception, inspection, unloading and storing

Fixed transaction costs
    Supplier side: fixed (administration) fee, change-over/set-up time
    Client side: working time (stock analysis, buying process, negotiations)

Naturally some of these costs might be partially fixed or fixed up to a certain point. For example, the transportation cost of a transaction could be considered as fixed as long as it is not more than a full truckload.

Change-over Time

In a production environment, the time it takes to do a change-over/set-up (i. e., the time it takes to switch production from one product to another) will often be the most important transaction cost we will face. Long change-over times can be due to many factors: need to cool down or clean a machine, need to move parts around, wasted time because of bad organization, etc. This change-over time has been the enemy of lean practitioners for a long time and they have developed many tools to reduce it.[3] As we will see later, if you reduce the fixed transaction costs, you can reduce the optimal

---

3 Don't hesitate to google "Single-minute exchange of die" to learn more about these techniques.

order quantity, which will result in less inventory. Lean practitioners know this very well.

Number of Yearly Transactions

Let's assume that we have a yearly demand of D pieces. During the year, one way or another, we will have to order these pieces from our supplier. If we assume that we will always order a fixed quantity of Q pieces with the supplier (same assumption as for the holding costs above), we know that we will have to do D/Q transactions throughout the year to cover the demand. The yearly number of transactions we will have to make with our supplier is **inversely proportional** to the order quantity Q. The more you order at once, the fewer transactions you will need.

Let's define k as the **fixed cost of a single transaction** and c_T as the **variable transaction costs**. The total yearly transaction costs will be equal to the fixed cost k multiplied by the number of transactions per year (D/Q), plus the variable costs c_T multiplied by the total yearly demand D.

$$\text{(Yearly) Transaction costs} = \text{Fixed costs} + \text{Variable costs}$$

$$= k\frac{D}{Q} + c_T D$$

Holding costs are proportional to the order quantity, but fixed transaction costs are **inversely proportional to the order quantity** (as shown in Figure 2.5). The intuition is: as you order more at once (Q is big), you will need to do fewer transactions with your supplier (or fewer different production batches), resulting in fewer transaction costs.

Figure 2.5: Yearly transaction costs.

> ### Example
>
> Let's go back to our earlier example. You now want to analyze the transaction costs. In order to do so, you gathered new information:
> - You have to pay 50€ of administrative cost per order to your supplier.
> - The supplier charges a delivery cost of 0.5€ per piece.
> - The unloading and storing cost is 0.5€ per piece.
> - You have an annual demand of 1000 pieces.
>
> Again, let's compute the expected yearly transaction costs based on the (yet unknown) order quantity Q:
>
> $$\text{Yearly transaction costs} = k\frac{D}{Q} + c_T D = 50€ \cdot \frac{1000}{Q} + (0.5€ + 0.5€) \cdot 1000$$
> $$= \frac{50000€}{Q} + 1000€$$
>
> The (fixed) transaction costs are inversely proportional to the order quantity: the more we buy at once, the fewer orders we will make.

2.1.3 Lost Sales and Backorders

For any product a business sells, being out-of-stock will result in, at best, backorders (frustrating the client), or, at worst, lost sales if the client doesn't maintain its order and decides to go to the competition.

Unfortunately, it is difficult (if not impossible) to evaluate the cost of lost sales and backorders, because of different factors:

Short term you do not know if the client will go to the competition or will just wait and come back later. This means that you do not know if you lost the sale or not. Your client could also decide to buy a similar product available in your inventory, and it could even be a more expensive item resulting in more profit for you.

Long term your brand image could be impacted and some of your clients may never come back. They could even spread the word and damage your reputation.

Moreover, it is hard for some companies to estimate the exact profit per product sold. Some companies do not even *want* to know the exact profit per product sold, as they fear it could be negative. We will discuss the impact of backorders on deterministic models in Section 2.5.2 and its impact on stochastic models in Chapters 8 and 11 when we will discuss costs and service level optimization.

2.2 Model Optimization

2.2.1 Supply Chain Costs

If we sum up the transaction and holding costs, we obtain this model of the supply chain costs:[4]

$$\text{Total Costs} = \text{Holding Costs} + \text{Transaction Costs}$$

$$C(Q) = h\frac{Q}{2} + k\frac{D}{Q} + c_T D$$

Where $C(Q)$ denotes the **total (holding and transaction) costs** based on Q. We observe that:

- Only the variable holding costs ($h\frac{Q}{2}$) and the fixed transaction costs ($k\frac{D}{Q}$) depend on the order quantity Q.
- The variable transaction costs ($c_T D$) only depend on the total demand D. No matter the order quantity, the total variable transaction costs will be the variable transaction cost per unit multiplied by the yearly number of units sold.

Since we are interested in minimizing the supply chain costs based on the order quantity, we can simplify our model by only keeping what is relevant for us. In our current model, we can remove everything that is not dependent on the order quantity. The costs are then expressed as:

$$C(Q) = h\frac{Q}{2} + k\frac{D}{Q} \tag{2.1}$$

Figure 2.6 shows how transaction and holding costs behave based on Q. **We are interested in the order quantity that minimizes the total costs.** We note the optimal

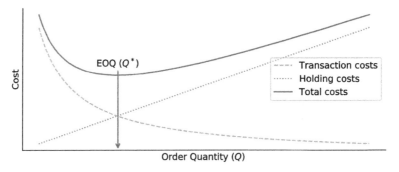

Figure 2.6: Supply chain costs.

---

[4] For the sake of simplicity, we abuse the convention here by discussing the "supply chain costs" whereas we keep only the *relevant* costs to our analysis; putting aside many other costs related to managing a supply chain (for example, the purchasing costs).

order quantity Q^* or EOQ (for Economical Order Quantity as it is historically called). We observe visually that Q^* is achieved when the holding and transaction costs are equal.

2.2.2 Order Quantity Optimization

Now that we have an equation that models the cost of our supply chain, we can look for the optimal order quantity Q^* that minimizes the costs. To do this we will compute the derivative of the total costs by Q and set it to zero.

$$\frac{\partial C(Q)}{\partial Q} = 0 \Leftrightarrow Q = Q^*$$

$$\frac{\partial C(Q)}{\partial Q} = \frac{\partial(h\frac{Q}{2} + k\frac{D}{Q})}{\partial Q}$$

$$= \frac{h}{2} - k\frac{D}{Q^2}$$

We have to set this derivative to 0 to find the optimal Q^* value.[5]

$$\frac{h}{2} - k\frac{D}{Q^{*2}} = 0$$

$$Q^* = \sqrt{\frac{2kD}{h}} \qquad (2.2)$$

This expression of Q^* is a very interesting first result as we see that **the optimal order quantity is proportional to the fixed transaction costs and inversely proportional to the holding costs**.

This makes sense:

- If you have high fixed transaction costs, you want to do fewer transactions to avoid paying these fees. To do so, you will increase the order quantity. This will result in a higher inventory level.
- If you have high holding costs per unit, you do not want to stock too much. To do so, you will reduce your order quantity but order more frequently.

---

5 The second derivative is positive—its computation is outside the scope of the book—assuring that we are looking at a minimum.

2.2.3 Cost Optimization

Based on the Q^* expression (eq. 2.2 in Section 2.2.2), we can compute the minimal cost C^* by replacing Q in the total costs equation (eq. 2.1 in Section 2.2.1).

$$C^* = h\frac{Q^*}{2} + k\frac{D}{Q^*}$$

$$= h\frac{\sqrt{\frac{2kD}{h}}}{2} + k\frac{D}{\sqrt{\frac{2kD}{h}}}$$

After some simplification, we obtain:

$$C^* = \sqrt{2kDh} \tag{2.3}$$

The expression of C^* is also interesting as we see that the optimal cost is proportional to the square root of the holding costs per unit and fixed transaction costs. This means that in order to reduce the inventory costs, it is of equal importance to reduce the fixed transaction costs as well as the yearly variable holding costs per unit. Of course, this relationship only applies based on the assumption of our simple model, specifically that there is no demand variation and therefore no safety stock.

2.2.4 A Question of Balance

We also observe that if we use Q^* in our supply chain, the total yearly holding costs will be equal to the yearly transaction costs (see Figure 2.6).

$$\text{Holding costs} = h\frac{Q^*}{2} = h\frac{\sqrt{\frac{2kD}{h}}}{2} = \frac{\sqrt{2kDh}}{2}$$

$$\text{Transaction Costs} = k\frac{D}{Q^*} = k\frac{D}{\sqrt{\frac{2kD}{h}}} = \frac{\sqrt{2kDh}}{2}$$

Both the total holding and transaction costs will be $\frac{\sqrt{2kDh}}{2}$. As shown in Figure 2.7, this confirms that, **at the optimal order quantity, the transaction and the holding costs are equal**.

There is actually a feedback loop between the transaction costs and the holding costs. An increase (or decrease) in either one of them will change the optimal order quantity so that **both** costs will be equal again: one will partially compensate the other's increase (or decrease).

For example, if your supplier increases the fixed transaction costs, the model would advise you to increase your order quantity in order to compensate for this with a reduced number of transactions. This will result in more inventory (as the order

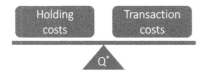

Figure 2.7: At the optimal order quantity, the transaction and the holding costs are equal.

quantity is higher) and therefore in higher inventory costs. In other words, if your supplier charges you more per order, you will want to order more at once to do fewer orders and, in the end, this increase of the transaction costs will impact your total holding costs as well.

Let's imagine that you managed to decrease the holding costs per unit—for example, thanks to a cheaper warehouse. The model will advise you to increase your order quantity so that you will do fewer transactions per year and thus keep more inventory. In other words, if you find a cheaper warehouse, you will want to use your new cheap asset to reduce your costs by placing bigger orders with your supplier to reduce the number of orders (but resulting in a higher inventory).

To sum up, based on our (simple deterministic) model, at the optimum, the total holding costs and the total transaction costs will always be equal.

Example

Let's follow upon our example. We have computed the expected holding and transaction costs based on Q:

$$\text{Yearly holding costs} = h\,Q = 1.75€ \cdot Q$$

$$\text{Yearly transaction costs} = \frac{k}{Q} + c_T D = \frac{50000€}{Q} + 1000€$$

And so $h = 1.75$ and $k = 50$. We can then compute the optimal order quantity and the optimal costs (see eq. 2.2 in Section 2.2.2 and eq. 2.3 in Section 2.2.3):

$$Q^* = \sqrt{\frac{2kD}{h}} = \sqrt{\frac{2 \cdot 50 \cdot 1000}{1.75}} \simeq 239$$

$$C^* = \sqrt{2kDh} = \sqrt{2 \cdot 50 \cdot 1000 \cdot 1.75} \simeq 418$$

This means that we can minimize our costs by ordering a fixed quantity of 239 units. By doing so, the total yearly holding costs and fixed transaction costs will amount to 418€.

2.2.5 Forecast or Historical Demand?

In the EOQ formula (eq. 2.2 in Section 2.2.2), we used the *historical* demand D. Actually, you can decide to use instead a (demand) forecast rather than historical numbers. That way, if a trend is observed (or is projected based on external insights), it can be used to improve the setting of the optimal order quantity. We then have

$$Q^* = \sqrt{\frac{2kF}{h}}$$

where F is the forecast (aligned with the periodicity of the holding costs h).

2.3 A Brief History of the EOQ Model

Ford Whitman Harris (1877–1962), an American engineer, published in 1913 his article *"How many parts to make at once,"* which introduced the idea of optimal order quantity. His initial article was followed-up by a second one, *"How much stock to keep on-hand"* that was published the same year.[6] Harris already explained a century ago that his model shouldn't be used as a silver bullet to model any complex supply chain but rather to be used as a practical tool.

Unfortunately, the story of Harris and his paternity of the EOQ model was forgotten. It was only in 1988 (75 years later!) that Donald Erlenkotter rediscovered it.[7] As Erlenkotter explained, even Ford Harris' grandson, who used the EOQ model from the 1960s until the 1980s in the US Air Force, where he was a supply officer, didn't know his grandfather was behind this model.

The EOQ model is in fact often referred to as the "Wilson model" based on R. H. Wilson's work. Wilson was a consultant who used the EOQ model in the first part of the 20th century. He published in 1934 an in-depth analysis of the model in his article: *"A Scientific Routine for Stock Control."*[8]

Over the years, many extensions to the EOQ model have been published.[9] Here are the main ones: in 1918, Taft analyzed the optimal production quantity;[10] in 1963, the first model to include a discount based on the order quantity was published by Hadley and Whitin;[11] in the 1980s and 1990s, models with backorders were solved, namely by

---

6 Harris (1913a,b).
7 Erlenkotter (1990).
8 Wilson (1934).
9 Andriolo et al. (2014) for a thorough analysis.
10 Taft (1918).
11 Hadley and Whitin (1963).

Grubbstrom and Erdem who proposed a model in 1999;[12] in 1995, Trietsch[13] optimized the order quantity with regard to the ROI instead of the usual cost minimization.

2.4 Sensitivity Analysis

Now that we have a model to optimize our order quantity, we will want to use it. To do this, we will first gather pieces of information about the holding and transaction costs to plug them in to our EOQ model. Of course, we can never achieve a perfect estimation of the holding and transaction costs. You will always have to make some simplifying assumptions (i. e., shortcuts) in your cost estimation. The risk is this: what if your cost estimation is really wrong? Will it have a big impact on the model's output—the optimal order quantity?

There are two ways to answer this question. A simple one, based on the graph of the supply chain costs; and a second, more rigorous, thanks to our EOQ mathematical model.

Graphical Intuition

As you can see in Figure 2.8, in the area close to the optimal order quantity, the total cost curve is rather flat. The intuition here is that, if you stay close to Q^*, you will achieve a total cost very close to the optimal one.

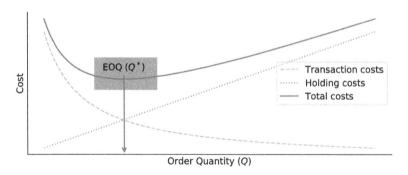

Figure 2.8: Supply chain costs.

Mathematical Demonstration

Let's now mathematically prove this graphical intuition. If you are not interested in this demonstration, don't hesitate to skip it and go directly to the paragraph starting with "Conclusion" below.

---

12 Grubbström and Erdem (1999).
13 Trietsch (1995).

Let's imagine we initially computed an optimal Q_{ini} and a C_{ini} based on an estimation of h, D and k. But we realize afterward that we missed a part of the transaction costs in our assumptions. So that we have,

$$k = \alpha k_{ini}$$

where k_{ini} is the initial estimation we made for the transaction costs; and k is the final estimation. Typically, we might have missed 20% or 50% of these costs. It seems to be a big mistake.

Let's take a look at the EOQ model to see how it behaves with this mistake. We need to compute the correct Q^* and C^* based on the initial estimations of Q_{ini} and C_{ini}.

$$Q^* = \sqrt{\frac{2kD}{h}} = \sqrt{\frac{2D\alpha k_{ini}}{h}} = \sqrt{\alpha}\, Q_{ini}$$

$$C^* = \sqrt{2kDh} = \sqrt{2D\alpha k_{ini}h} = \sqrt{\alpha}\, C_{ini}$$

We see that the actual optimal order quantity Q^* is equal to the initial (wrong) one multiplied by $\sqrt{\alpha}$. The same holds true for the actual optimal cost C^*.

If we assumed the transaction costs to be half of the actual value (i. e., $k = 2k_{ini}$), then our estimation of the optimal costs and order quantity was off by 41% ($1.41 = \sqrt{2}$). This might seems like a big difference, but using Q_{ini} as an operational order quantity in our supply chain will actually not result in a huge loss.

Let's take a look at what would happen to our operational costs if we chose an order quantity that is different than the optimal one.

$$\frac{C(Q)}{C(Q^*)} = \frac{k\frac{D}{Q} + h\frac{Q}{2}}{\sqrt{2kDh}}$$

$$= \frac{k\frac{D}{Q}}{\sqrt{2kDh}} + \frac{h\frac{Q}{2}}{\sqrt{2kDh}}$$

$$= \frac{\sqrt{kD}}{Q\sqrt{2h}} + \frac{Q\sqrt{h}}{2\sqrt{2kD}}$$

However, know that $Q^* = \sqrt{\frac{2kD}{h}}$, so

$$\frac{C(Q)}{C(Q^*)} = \frac{Q^*}{2Q} + \frac{Q}{2Q^*}$$

$$= \frac{1}{2}\left(\frac{Q^*}{Q} + \frac{Q}{Q^*}\right)$$

We now have a good relationship between the two different costs. We can solve it, as we know that $Q^* = \sqrt{\alpha}Q$, so we have:

$$\frac{C(Q)}{C(Q^*)} = \frac{1}{2}\left(\frac{Q^*}{Q} + \frac{Q}{Q^*}\right)$$

$$= \frac{1}{2}\left(\sqrt{\alpha} + \frac{1}{\sqrt{\alpha}}\right)$$

This ratio is actually rather limited, even for an impressive value of α. For example, if $\alpha = 2$, this ratio will only be 1.06. This is very interesting. It means that, even if you forgot half of the transaction costs (or the holding costs), and therefore wrongly estimated the optimal order quantity and total cost by 41%, your wrong assumption will only result in an extra cost of 6% compared to the optimal policy.

We also observe that the impact of α on the optimal cost is symmetrical: the impact of $\alpha = 1/2$ is the same as the one of $\alpha = 2$.

Conclusion

We can expand this conclusion by saying that **it is virtually inexpensive to round the optimal order quantity** to a close number in order to simplify order processing. This helps, for example, to order based on a packaging requirement, if any.

> **Example**
>
> Let's continue with our example. After a thorough analysis, we computed that $Q^* = 239$. Ordering a batch of 239 pieces is not always practical. So maybe we could round this optimal order quantity to 200 units. What is the extra cost of this rounding? The ratio between Q and Q^* is 1.195, so we have:
>
> $$\frac{C(Q)}{C(Q^*)} = \frac{1}{2}\left(\frac{Q^*}{Q} + \frac{Q}{Q^*}\right) = \frac{1}{2}\left(1.195 + \frac{1}{1.195}\right) = 1.004$$
>
> That's a cost increase of 0.4% (less than half of a percent). We conclude that it is virtually inexpensive to round the order quantity to 200 pieces from the optimal order quantity Q^*.

2.5 Extensions

Various extensions to the original EOQ model have been thoroughly discussed in the academic literature. Let's discuss in detail three of them—production rates, backorders and order discounts—and focus on the various insights and recommendations we can draw.

> **Important Point**
>
> The following pages will require a lot of math to optimize the (s, Q) inventory policy under varying assumptions. If you are not interested in these demonstrations, you can focus your reading the **Insights** paragraphs ending each subsection.

2.5.1 Production Rate

In most supply chains, the production process is not instantaneous but rather constrained to a maximum throughput. This constraint results in a (slow) ramp up of inventory level when production starts. If we need to optimize the EOQ for an internal production process (rather than optimizing the EOQ for an order with an external supplier) we should take this limit into account. The EOQ model with a production rate has been thoroughly discussed in the literature[14] since the first model was published by Taft (1918).

Here are the main findings.

Model

Let's note **r the production rate** expressed in units produced per period. We also note **d the demand per period**. We define the **production throughput ratio p** as:

$$p = 1 - \frac{d}{r}$$

This could be seen as a percentage of capacity available.

Example

Let's imagine we can produce 500 units per day and have a demand of 100 units per day. We have $r = 500$, $d = 100$. We compute the production throughput ratio p as

$$p = 1 - 100/500 = 0.8$$

Let's now update our EOQ cost model based on p. As shown in Figure 2.9, the maximum on-hand inventory is now pQ instead of simply Q, and the average inventory is $\frac{pQ}{2}$. We then have:

$$C_p = k\frac{D}{Q} + h\frac{pQ}{2}$$

$$Q_p^* = \sqrt{\frac{2kD}{ph}} = \frac{Q_{p=1}^*}{p}$$

$$C_p^* = \sqrt{2kDph} = \sqrt{p}\, C_{p=1}^*$$

This model is more general than the initial one we created without production rate (see Section 2.2.2):

$$C(Q) = k\frac{D}{Q} + h\frac{Q}{2}$$

---

14 It is often called the Economical Production Quantity model or EPQ.

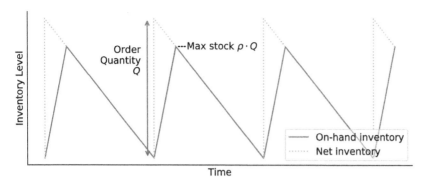

Figure 2.9: Order pattern with constrained production.

Insights

We observe that **if we limit the production rate, we actually reduce the costs**. It is rather exceptional that adding a constraint to a model helps to optimize it. We should actually conclude that having a lower production throughput helps to flatten production and align it to our needs (i. e., the demand). In other words, **producing too much too fast doesn't help to reduce the overall costs**. It is much better to produce a constant appropriated throughput rather than producing massive batches at once.

2.5.2 Backorders

Even if it seems counter-intuitive to many professionals, it is actually optimal for a supply chain to allow some backorders and not aim for 100% service level. In other words, it is optimal for a company to have *some* backorders instead of serving each and every order directly from the on-hand inventory. In B2B relationships, backorders can be allowed through negotiation with suppliers. The contract between a supplier and its client will then stipulate a backorder penalty (per order, or based on the waiting time).

Model

Let's define **B** as the **maximum number of backorders** we allow in our inventory policy (the model is shown in Figure 2.10). We then have an order pattern that looks like the one in Figure 2.11.

We can already note some interesting relationships:
- The maximum inventory level is $Q - B$.
- The minimum net inventory level is $-B$.
- An order cycle lasts $T = Q/D$ (remember D is the yearly demand) and is composed of two phases T^+ and T^-:

Figure 2.10: Supply chain model.

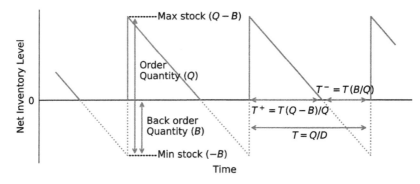

Figure 2.11: Order pattern with backorders.

- A first phase where on-hand inventory is available. This lasts for $T^+ = T\frac{Q-B}{Q}$.
- A second phase where the net inventory level is below 0. During this phase we have backorders because we can't serve the demand directly from the on-hand inventory. This lasts for $T^- = T\frac{B}{Q}$.

Using these relationships, we can estimate the average on-hand level and the average backorder level by computing the area of the positive and negative triangles in Figure 2.12.

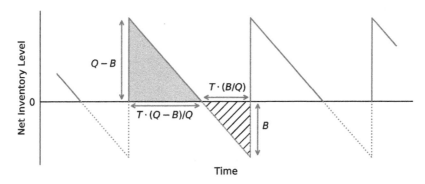

Figure 2.12: Inventory levels for backorders model.

$$\text{Average on-hand level (grey area)} = \frac{1}{2}\frac{T^+}{T}(Q-B) = \frac{(Q-B)^2}{2Q}$$

$$\text{Average backorder level (hatched area)} = \frac{1}{2}\frac{T^-}{T}B = \frac{B^2}{2Q}$$

Let's now look at the costs of the policy. We will note b_τ **the backlog costs per unit** (that is the cost per unit backordered per unit of time—similar to h).

The backlog costs are then,

$$\text{Backlog costs} = b_\tau \frac{B^2}{2Q}$$

The total costs are then,

$$\mathcal{C}(Q,B) = \text{Transactions} + \text{Holding} + \text{Backorder}$$

$$\mathcal{C}(Q,B) = k\frac{D}{Q} + h\frac{(Q-B)^2}{2Q} + b_\tau \frac{B^2}{2Q}$$

Cost Optimization

Now that we have defined the costs C, based on the order quantity Q, and the backorder quantity B, we can minimize them. The algebra is out of scope, see Grubbström and Erdem (1999), Robert et al. (2004) for the detailed computation.

$$Q_B^* = Q_{B=0}^* \cdot \sqrt{\frac{b_\tau + h}{b_\tau}} = \sqrt{\frac{2kD}{h}} \cdot \sqrt{\frac{b_\tau + h}{b_\tau}}$$

$$B^* = Q_B^* \cdot \left(\frac{h}{b_\tau + h}\right) = \sqrt{\frac{2kDh}{b_\tau(b_\tau + h)}}$$

$$C^* = C_{B=0}^* \cdot \sqrt{\frac{b_\tau}{b_\tau + h}} = \sqrt{2kDh} \cdot \sqrt{\frac{b_\tau}{b_\tau + h}}$$

We see that if we set $b_\tau = \infty$, B should be 0, and we are back to the initial $\mathcal{C}(Q)$ model (see eq. 2.3 in Section 2.2.3):

$$\mathcal{C}(Q) = k\frac{D}{Q} + h\frac{Q}{2}$$

Insights

We observe some interesting insights from allowing backorders:

- The average on-hand inventory is reduced, resulting in lower holding costs.
- The number of transactions per year is reduced (because the order quantity is increased) resulting in lower transaction costs.
- The total costs are reduced by a ratio $\sqrt{b_\tau/(b_\tau + h)}$.

We can conclude that **allowing (the right amount of) backorders in a supply chain is good and will bring down the total costs**.

In practice, very few supply chains use the EOQ model with backorders to optimize their inventory policy. Nevertheless, the insights we discussed here are a good starter for the discussion we will have later in Chapters 8 and 11, where we will optimize the costs of stochastic models.

2.5.3 Discounts

In order to incentivize buyers to increase their order quantities, many suppliers offer a discount depending on the order quantity (bulk orders). This can be incorporated into the EOQ model in order to update the optimal order quantity. In 1963, Hadley and Whitin published in their book *Analysis of Inventory Systems* the first model that dealt with such discounts.[15] They have been followed since by many other publications and models that deal with more complex discounts.[16]

As a general rule, let's imagine a supplier offers a volume discount δ (delta) as of a quantity threshold Q_δ. The volume discount δ is computed as such:

$$\delta = \frac{c_\delta}{c}$$

where c is the product purchase cost and c_δ is the discounted purchase cost. For example, a supplier could give you a 5% rebate if you buy at least 1000 units at once. δ is then 0.95 and $Q_\delta = 1000$.

We can find the optimal order quantity by following these rules:
1. Compute the Q_δ^* based on the volume discounted purchase cost c_δ.

$$Q_\delta^* = \sqrt{\frac{2kD}{c_\delta h}}$$

2. If Q_δ^* falls into the discount limits ($Q_\delta^* > Q_\delta$), this is the optimal order quantity.
3. If not, test if

$$C(Q^*) + cD < C(Q_\delta) + c_\delta D$$

if so, Q^* is the optimal order quantity (thus, without volume discount); otherwise you should order exactly Q_δ units (the minimal quantity to benefit from the discount).

---

15 Hadley and Whitin (1963).
16 See Nahmias (2015) for a complete overview of such models.

Example

You purchase electronic cards overseas. Your supplier gives you a unit price of
- 1 if you buy less than 2000 cards.
- 0.8 if you buy more than 2000 cards at once.

You have a yearly holding cost of 15%, a yearly demand of 2000 pieces and a fixed order cost of 100. Let's use the EOQ formula (eq. 2.2 in Section 2.2.2) for each of these offers.

$$Q^* = \sqrt{\frac{2kD}{ch}}$$

These are the results (see Figure 2.13):

$Q^* = 1633$ pieces if the price is 1;

$Q_\delta^* = 1826$ pieces if the price is 0.8. But Q_δ^* is outside of the bounds of the offer $(Q_\delta^* < Q_\delta)$;

Because Q_δ^* is lower than the discount limit (1826 < 2000), we have to compare the total cost of ordering 2000 pieces at once against the cost of ordering 1633 pieces:

$$C(Q) + c_\delta D = k\frac{D}{Q} + ch\frac{Q}{2} + c_\delta D$$

$$C(2000) + c_\delta D = 100\frac{2000}{2000} + 15\% \cdot 0.8\frac{2000}{2} + 0.8 \cdot 2000 = 1820$$

$$C(1633) + cD = 100\frac{2000}{1633} + 15\% \cdot 1\frac{1633}{2} + 1 \cdot 2000 = 2245$$

Since the total cost of ordering 2000 pieces at once is lower than the cost of 1633 units, we will order a batch of 2000 pieces to benefit from the volume discount.

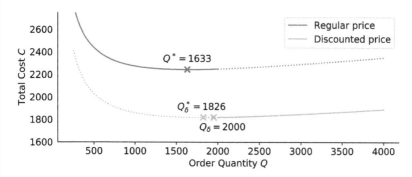

Figure 2.13: Total cost C based on purchasing cost and order quantity C.

You can easily solve this in Python:

```
def EOQ(k,D,h,p): #h is a percentage
    return np.sqrt(2*k*D/(h*c))

def Cost(k,D,h,Q,c): #h is a percentage
    return k*D/Q + h*c*Q/2 + c*D


#Case #1
c, k, D, h = 1, 100, 2000, 0.15
Q = EOQ(k,D,h,c)
C = Cost(k,D,h,Q,c)
print(round(Q),'\t',round(C))
#Case #2
c = 0.8
Q = max(2000, EOQ(k,D,h,c))
C = Cost(k,D,h,Q,c)
print(round(Q),'\t',round(C))
```

2.5.4 Other Extensions

Numerous other extensions to the EOQ model have been discussed by academics over time. Here, briefly, are two other extensions:

Return on investment The EOQ model is focusing on cost minimization whereas most businesses are actually looking to maximize their return on investment (ROI). In 1995, Trietsch looked at the order quantity optimization of multiple products with regard to the ROI.[17] His model shows that the EOQ that maximizes the company ROI will be lower or equal to the EOQ that minimizes the supply chain costs.

Batch size and set-up times In the case of production batch sizes, Cachon (2018) discusses an optimization model based on the various set-up times across a production line, prioritizing the process bottleneck.

---

17 Trietsch (1995).

2.6 Recap

In this chapter, we asked ourselves a simple question: *How much should I order?* We found an answer by optimizing the supply chain costs based on the order quantity. We obtained a set of equations known as the EOQ (Economic Order Quantity) model:

$$C = h\frac{Q}{2} + k\frac{D}{Q} \quad \text{(see eq. 2.1 in Section 2.2.1)}$$

$$Q^* = \sqrt{\frac{2kD}{h}} \quad \text{(see eq. 2.2 in Section 2.2.2)}$$

$$C^* = \sqrt{2kDh} \quad \text{(see eq. 2.3 in Section 2.2.3)}$$

This means that the optimal order quantity Q^* is proportional to the square root of the fixed transaction costs k, to the yearly total demand D; and inversely proportional to the square root of the variable holding costs per unit h.

We noted that a proper setting of the order quantity balances the ordering costs against the holding costs, and that high transaction costs will result in high inventory levels. We saw that the EOQ model is robust to a wrong evaluation of the transaction costs or the holding costs. This allows us to round the optimal order quantity (or the optimal time between two consecutive orders) to streamline our process with only a minimal impact on the total costs.

3 When Should I Order?

Now that we know **how much we should order**, we have to find **when we should order.** To do so, we will have to discuss two aspects of a supply chain: the supply (or order) **lead time** and the **review period** (as shown in Figure 3.1).

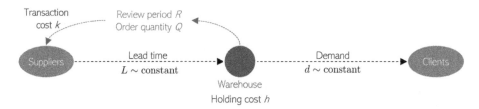

Figure 3.1: Supply chain model.

3.1 Lead Time

Until now, we assumed there was no wait time between the moment an order is made and its reception. In other words, we assumed that as soon as we want to make an order, we receive it.

It's time we remove this assumption—and replace it with a fixed lead time.[1] This means that if we place an order with our (internal or external) supplier, it will take a certain amount of time (fixed) before we receive our goods.

How does this influence our inventory policy? Remember that, in a continuous review policy with a reorder point, we order Q units when the on-hand inventory reaches the reorder point s. When we assumed no lead time, we ordered Q units when the on-hand inventory reached 0. With a lead time L (as shown in Figure 3.2), we will have to order Q units when the net inventory level will reach the demand over the lead time. We will note **the demand over the lead time $d_L = d \cdot L$.**

$$s = d_L \tag{3.1}$$

Pay attention to the units of measure: d is the demand per unit of time and L is the lead time expressed in the **same** unit of time. We could also compute d_L as D (the yearly demand) times L, if the lead time is expressed in years. So that we would have $d_L = D \cdot L$.

---

1 We will discuss stochastic lead times later in Chapter 6, "Stochastic Lead Times."

https://doi.org/10.1515/9783110673944-003

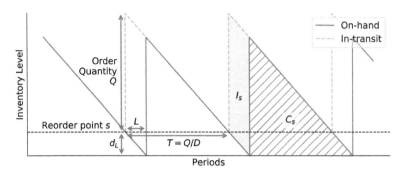

Figure 3.2: Reorder point policy (s, Q) with lead time L.

Example

If you have a supply lead time of 2 weeks and a weekly consumption of 3 units, you have a demand over the lead time d_L of 6 units (= 2 weeks $\times$ 3 $\frac{\text{units}}{\text{week}}$) so that you will have to make an order when you have 6 pieces left.

Once an order is made, it takes a lead time L to receive the goods. During this time L we have Q pieces of **in-transit inventory** (sometimes called *on-order inventory*).

In-transit inventory (I_s)

Goods ordered from a supplier but not yet available in our warehouse for our clients to buy. These goods are considered to be in-transit between two warehouses (or in pipeline).

As you can see in Figure 3.2, we can compute the expected average in-transit inventory I_s as the ratio between the lead time L and the cycle time T multiplied by the number of units ordered Q.

$$I_s = Q\frac{L}{T} = Q\frac{L}{Q/D}$$
$$I_s = D \cdot L = d_L \tag{3.2}$$

This identity is remarkable: **the expected amount of in-transit inventory is the demand over the lead time**. It will hold for any inventory policy (continuous or periodic), and for any demand (deterministic or stochastic). This means that, if you want to decrease the in-transit inventory, you should not try to reduce the number of orders (making fewer orders but ordering more at once will result in the same average amount of in-transit inventory), instead you should look at how to reduce the lead time.

Note that in-transit inventory might be owned by the supplier (shipper) or the client (receiver), depending on the agreement, resulting in holding costs for either one or the other.

3.2 Review Period

Apart from the lead time, the length of the review period also has an impact on any inventory policy following a periodic review (as shown in Figure 3.3). How does a review period R impact our policy?

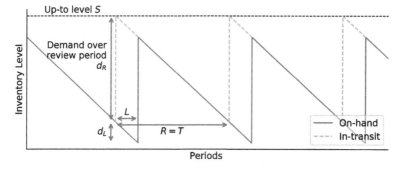

Figure 3.3: Review period and order up-to level policy (R, S) with lead time L.

1. **Order up-to level**
   The order up-to level is now defined as the demand over the lead time plus the demand over the review period (noted d_R):

$$S = d_L + d_R = d \cdot L + d \cdot R \tag{3.3}$$

   In other words, in the case of a periodic review policy, the up-to level will increase to cover both the demand over the lead time **and** the demand over the review period.

Example

If we take same circumstances as the first example in this chapter (demand of 3 pieces per week; lead time of 2 weeks) and we follow an inventory policy with a periodic review of 4 weeks, we have to make an order based on an up-to level of 18 pieces.

$$S = d_L + d_R = 3 \cdot 2 + 3 \cdot 4 = 18 \text{ units}$$

2. **Cycle stock**
   The amount of product ordered for each cycle is the demand over the review period d_R so that the expected cycle stock level is:

   $$C_s = \frac{1}{2}d_R$$

3. **In-transit inventory**
   Even if the length of an order cycle changes compared to the continuous review policy, we would still have the same expected level of in-transit inventory per cycle:

   $$I_s = d_R\frac{L}{R} = dR\frac{L}{R}$$

   $$I_s = d_L \tag{3.4}$$

4. **Review period**
   Let's note T^* **the optimal review period**, computed as (see eq. 2.2 in Section 2.2.2 for Q^* expression):

   $$T^* = \frac{Q^*}{D} = \frac{1}{D}\sqrt{\frac{2kD}{h}}$$

   Finally we have,

   $$T^* = \sqrt{\frac{2k}{hD}} \tag{3.5}$$

   What should we do if the optimal review period is not a round number? If you have an optimal review period of 1.23 days, should you *really* make an order every 29 hours, 31 minutes and 12 seconds?
   We discussed in Section 2.4 that we could round Q^* to a more appropriated number if needed. For example, if $Q^* = 2094.24$ pieces, we can order 2000 pieces for a marginal extra cost of only 0.1%. It would be much more convenient to order a batch of 2000 pieces rather than 2094.24 pieces.
   As we face the same issue with the optimal review period T^*, couldn't we round this 1.23 days to 1 day?

3.2.1 Rounding the Review Period

Let's discuss two methods to round the review period and the impact on the inventory policy costs.

Method #1 – Simple Rounding

With the first technique—a simple rounding—we set the review period T as a multiple of a **base time period** T_B like a day or a week. If you have the possibility to make an order every day—the base time period is a day—you would want to round the review period to an integer (1 day instead of 1.23). Thanks to our sensitivity analysis in Chapter 2, "How Much Should I Order?" (see Section 2.4 specifically), we know that the impact on the total cost will be marginal. This technique will work well for a supply chain with a single item. However, we might be missing another cost-saving opportunity.

As most supply chains deal with thousands of **stock keeping units (SKU)**, you probably want to avoid keeping track of thousands of different order schedules—even if they are all expressed in days. In order to reduce schedule complexity, couldn't we round the various review periods to specific values? Remember, we want to use the periodic review policy in order to group orders at specific points in time, in order to have the same periodic review for multiple products.

> **SKU**
>
> A stock keeping unit (SKU) refers to a specific material kept in a specific location. Two different pieces of the same SKU are indistinguishable.

Method #2 – Power-of-2 Policy

A practical way to round a review period is to use the **power-of-2 policy**. It was initially discussed in Maxwell and Muckstadt (1985). Their idea was to round the review period to a multiple of a base time period multiplied by a power-of-2:

$$R = 2^k T_B$$

For example, if the base period is 1 week, the optimal review period should be rounded to either 1, 2, 4, 8, 16... weeks. That way, products will fall into a smaller number of categories according to their respective optimal review period, therefore **reducing schedule complexity**. An example with a base time period of one week is shown in Table 3.1.

Table 3.1: Power-of-2 policy with a weekly base time period.

Review Period	k	2^k	W1	W2	W3	W4	W5	W6	W7	W8	W9	W10
Weekly	0	1	x	x	x	x	x	x	x	x	x	x
Bi-weekly	1	2	x		x		x		x		x	
Monthly	2	4	x				x				x	
Bi-monthly	3	8	x								x	

We choose k as the smallest fitting value:

$$\frac{T^*}{\sqrt{2}} \leq 2^k T_B \leq \sqrt{2}T^*$$

So **the ratio between T^* and T is at *worst* $\sqrt{2}$:**

$$\frac{T^*}{1.41} \leq T \leq 1.41 \cdot T^*$$

Example

In order to run your production facility, you are in charge of purchasing rubber overseas. You used the EOQ model to compute the best order quantity and review period, which is 29.12 days. Of course, this is not practical, so you want to round it to a workable schedule.

In order to find the best review period using the power-of-2 policy and a base time period of 1 day, we have to find the smallest k that satisfies $\frac{T^*}{\sqrt{2}} \leq 2^k T_B \leq \sqrt{2}T^*$. If we substitute T^* by its value (29.12) we have $20.59 \leq 2^k T_B \leq 41.18$, and $k = 5$ is the smallest value solving this equation (see Table 3.2). This means that you should make an order every 32 days.

Table 3.2: Example for determining k.

Review Period	k	2^k	$2^k T_B \leq 41.18 = \sqrt{2}T^*$	$\frac{T^*}{\sqrt{2}} = 20.59 \leq 2^k T_B$
1 Day	0	1	Yes	No
2 Days	1	2	Yes	No
4 Days	2	4	Yes	No
8 Days	3	8	Yes	No
16 Days	4	16	Yes	No
32 Days	5	32	Yes	Yes
64 Days	6	64	No	Yes

You could also decide to take a week (or 5 business days) as a base time period. You would then get an optimal review period of 8 weeks or 40 days.

Cost Impact

The power-of-2 policy is very useful to synchronize timing for different products across a supply chain. But what is the impact on the costs for not using the optimal review periods?

From the sensitivity analysis we did in Section 2.4 we know that:

$$\frac{C(Q)}{C(Q^*)} = \frac{1}{2}\left(\frac{Q}{Q^*} + \frac{Q^*}{Q}\right)$$

By extension, as $T = Q/D$, we have:

$$\frac{C(T)}{C(T^*)} = \frac{1}{2}\left(\frac{T^*}{T} + \frac{T}{T^*}\right)$$

Remember that the ratio between T^* and T is at worst $\sqrt{2}$. So the worst ratio between the actual cost and the optimal is:

$$\frac{C(T)}{C(T^*)} \leq \frac{1}{2}\left(\frac{\sqrt{2}}{1} + \frac{1}{\sqrt{2}}\right) \approx 1.06$$

This means that, by using the power-of-2 policy, we only take the risk of increasing the total cost by 6%. That's in theory. In practice, we are much more likely to reduce the total cost as we are able to group different orders into a single transaction.

Example

Let's take our previous example and compute the extra cost incurred if we use 32 days as a review period instead of the optimal one (29.12 days). Since we have a ratio of 1.067 between T^* and T, we then have:

$$\frac{C(T)}{C(T^*)} = \frac{1}{2}\left(\sqrt{1.067} + \sqrt{\frac{1}{1.067}}\right) = 1,001$$

This means that we incur an extra cost of 0.1% by rounding the order period from 29.12 days to 32 days. This is virtually nothing.

3.2.2 Forecast or Historical Demand?

In both policies, we used the demand per period to compute the reorder point s and the order up-to level S (see eq. 3.1 in Section 3.1 and eq. 3.3 in Section 3.2). You can decide to use a (demand) forecast rather than (demand) historical numbers. So that, if a trend is observed (or is projected based on external insights), it can be used to improve the setting of your inventory policies. You have then

$$s = F_L$$
$$S = F_L + F_R$$

where F_L is the forecast over the lead time and F_R the forecast over the review period.

Going Further

The order quantity optimization under a varying forecast per period is beyond the scope of this book. See Axsäter (2015), Silver et al. (2016) for more models.

3.3 Confusion Curse: Long Lead Times

Inventory policies with order up-to levels can be misleading for practitioners—especially when the supply chain faces long lead times. Often, practitioners assume that this order up-to level is the expected inventory level. The fact that the up-to level is often called "target stock" is not helping. The difference between the up-to level and the actual expected physical inventory will actually grow further as the lead time increases. This confusion can even get worse when orders need to be created while others are still waiting to be received.

Example

Let's imagine that you own a shop. You follow a simple inventory policy: you re-order daily your goods from your supplier, who delivers them in the morning of the following day. If, for a specific item, you have an up-to order level of 10, this means that you follow an (R, S) inventory policy with $R = 1$ and $S = 10$. So, each evening at the closure of your shop, you count the pieces of this product and order enough to have 10 pieces on your shelves by the next morning. Let's imagine that you sell on average 1 unit per day, so that you can expect your inventory to be around 9 to 10 units. Actually this up-to level (10 in our case) is a good proxy for estimating how much inventory you have on-hand (i. e., physically in your shop). For example, if you change S to 5, you can assume that the actual inventory in your shop for this item would be around 4 to 5 pieces.

Now let's imagine that your supplier changes its delivery policy: it will now take 5 business days to deliver the orders. If you keep the same inventory policy $(1, 10)$, your inventory will now fluctuate at around 4–5 pieces.

Let's assume that the demand is exactly 1 piece per day. If you start with an inventory of 10 pieces, it will decrease by 1 unit per day until it reaches a stock of 4 pieces, when you will receive your first order of 1 piece. Your stock level will then vary between 4 and 5 pieces. That is much lower than your up-to level of 10 pieces.

We will create a small simulation in Section 5.3 to show the impact of the review period, lead time and order up-to level on the expected inventory level.

3.4 Recap

We improved our EOQ model by taking into account the (supply) lead time as well as the review period (if any). Let's recap **how much we should order** and **when we should make an order** for the two main policies we discussed in Chapter 1:

(s, Q) Continuous review policy with a reorder point and a fixed order quantity.
(R, S) Periodic review policy with an order up-to level.

	Reorder point (s, Q)		**Review Period (R, S)**	
How much?	Order Quantity	$Q = \sqrt{\frac{2kD}{h}}$	Up-to level	$S = d_L + d_R$
When?	Reorder point	$s = d_L$	Review period	$R = 2^k T_B$
Expected inventory		$C_s = \frac{1}{2}Q \quad I_s = d_L$		$C_s = \frac{1}{2}d_R \quad I_s = d_L$

We saw that as the lead time grows bigger, the up-to level of a fixed review period policy can't be assumed to be the expected average stock on-hand. We will discuss this effect further in Section 5.2 for stochastic supply chains.

Part II: **Stochastic Supply Chains**

4 Safety Stocks

Buffer or suffer.

So far, we have discussed the EOQ inventory and have gained some insights into this model. It is suited for simple supply chains that don't face any kind of uncertainties. But, in reality, a supply chain does not have a steady flow and does not come without variation. Supply chains face many random events that simply cannot be predicted, leading ourselves to questions such as: *Are our clients going to buy as much as forecasted? Is the supplier going to be on time for its delivery? Will we have enough production capacity to produce these goods on time?* Safety stocks are a straightforward way **to create a buffer against these unforeseen events**. In this chapter and the next one, we will be discussing two potential causes of fluctuation in a supply chain:

1. **Demand side** The actual demand varies over time and is different from the forecasted demand.
2. **Supply side** Suppliers can be late compared to the announced (or negotiated) lead times.

In order to mitigate the risks resulting from these fluctuations, we will create, through the chapters in this second part, a first model that computes how much safety stock is needed. As usual, we will create our new model gradually. In this chapter, we will introduce stochastic demand and build our first stochastic model. Then, we will take the time to discuss in detail inventory policies and inventory analysis in Chapter 5, "Inventory Policies." Finally, we will introduce stochastic lead times in Chapter 6, "Stochastic Lead Times."

In order to make our first stochastic model, we will have to make a couple of simplifying assumptions:

- The demand and the lead time are **continuous random variables**. This means that the demand and the lead time can take any value, not just integers.
  We will discuss **discrete models** (where the demand can only take integer values) later, in Part IV, "Discrete Inventory Optimization."
- They both follow a normal distribution.
  We will discuss gamma-distributed demand in Chapter 9, "Beyond Normality," and custom discrete distributions in Chapter 12, "Discrete Probabilistic Demand."
- The demand that cannot be fulfilled by on-hand inventory is backordered until inventory is available (we will re-discuss this assumption in Section 5.3.2). In other words, the excess demand will not result in lost sales.
- We will stick to simple inventory policies:
  - Either a fixed review period with an order up-to level (R, S).
  - Or a continuous review with a fixed reorder point and an order quantity (s, Q).

https://doi.org/10.1515/9783110673944-004

More complex inventory policies such as (R, s, Q) or (R, s, S) have been studied by academics,[1] but solving them—even with many assumptions and simplifications—results in complex mathematical models that are difficult to implement in practice. We will discuss these later in Chapter 13, "Simulation Optimization."

4.1 Service Level

How should we determine the *right* amount of safety stock we need? On one hand, based on the **service level** that we want to deliver to our clients and, on the other hand, based on the magnitude of the demand and supply fluctuations that our supply chain is facing.

Let's first discuss the service level. Even though this seems to be a simple and straightforward concept, measuring it brings the same confusion as measuring the forecast error. As discussed in my previous book, *Data Science for Supply Chain Forecasting*, everyone agrees that a forecast qualifies as being perfect if the forecast error is 0.[2] Measuring the forecast error is trickier. What exactly is an accuracy of 60%, or an error of 25%? The same goes for the service level: everyone agrees that a perfect service level is achieved when all clients are served on time and in-full. The confusion comes when this is not the case. Let's review *some* possible ways to measure service levels:

Cycle service level α The probability of not having a stock-out during an order replenishment cycle. This is the probability that the inventory available at the beginning of an order cycle (that is just after we received the order from the previous order cycle) will be greater than (or equal to) the demand during this cycle. In other words, this is the probability that there is no stock-out between the time you receive a replenishment until the **next** replenishment arrives (*"Now that we have received an order, we have a 5% probability to run out-of-stock by the time we receive the next one"*).
This is also often called the "Type 1 service level."

Period service level α_p The probability that there is no stock-out during one arbitrary period (e. g., a day, a week). The period service level can be similar or different to the cycle service level depending on the length of an order cycle. It is also much easier to understand than the cycle service level (*"We only have a 5% probability to run out-of-stock by the end of any given business day"*). Due to the mathematical complexity, it is not common for inventory models to use this service measure. Nevertheless, we will track it in our simulations.

Client service level The probability that a client receives their full order (often containing multiple different products) from stock (often called On Time In Full or

---

1 See Strijbosch and Moors (1999), Tempelmeier (2011) for detailed models.
2 See Vandeput (2021).

OTIF). Due to its modeling complexity, it is not common to use it in inventory models. Nevertheless, business-wise it might be the most relevant.

Fill rate β The fraction of the demand (over the long term) that is supplied directly from the on-hand inventory. It is often called the "Type 2 service level."

Over the long term we should have (if we assume that a period is shorter than a cycle):

Fill rate β > Client service level > Period service level α_p > Cycle service level α

Other service level key performance indicators (KPIs) could also be tracked. For example, the average backlog per period could also be a relevant KPI. If you divide it by the average period demand you would get a KPI close to the fill rate (the amount of backorders/lost sales per period). However, it would be a more conservative approach since some backorders would stay for multiple periods in the backlog. You can also track how long on average an order stays in the backlog.

Example

Let's imagine that you manage a beer shop. Among other beers, you sell the famous Belgian beer Westvleteren—one of the best beers in the world. You store it based on the following inventory policy: you make an order every evening with the Westvleteren Abbey and receive your order the next day in the morning.[a] You order enough to always have 6 bottles on the shelf every morning. Your policy could be summarized as being an (R, S) policy with $R = 1$ and $S = 6$.

If you receive 10 tourists on the same day, all of them asking for one bottle of Westvleteren, you will be able to fulfill 60% of the demand. This is a fill rate of 60% but a period service level of 0%. Because the order cycle is one day—you make an order every evening—the period cycle service level is also 0%.

The very next day, if you receive the visit of one single tourist, buying a single bottle, you will fulfill 100% of the demand and achieve a cycle/period service level of 100%.

To measure your average cycle service level, you will count the number of days where you could fulfill all demand and divide by the number of days you were open. In this example you achieved a cycle service level of 50% (you had enough stock to cover all the demand only one day out of two), and a total fill rate of 64% (7 clients served directly from the on-hand inventory out of 11).

---

[a] That's a purely theoretical case, the brewing of Westvleteren is quite limited. Getting these beers is then relying more on luck than on anything else.

> **Important Point**
>
> Most inventory softwares optimize the cycle service level. But actually, most supply chain practitioners record the fill rate as the main Key Performance Indicator (KPI) to record service level. **This is a major source of confusion.** Inventory optimization software usually use the cycle service level for two reasons: it is (much) easier to optimize mathematically than the fill rate; and most supply chain textbooks discuss the cycle service level whereas only a few mention the fill rate.
>
> When negotiating with a software vendor, you should always take the time to define which service level metric you want to optimize.

Let's use, for now, the **cycle service level** as the metric to measure our service level. We will discuss the fill rate in Chapter 7, "Fill Rate." We will also assume, *for now*, that we know how much service level we want to reach. We will discuss later, in Chapter 8, how to optimize the service level.

> **Important Point**
>
> Practitioners usually start an inventory optimization exercise with a given service level target: "We want to set a service level of 95%." But this service level target is often arbitrarily set without any optimization. Is 95% really the *optimal* service level? We will answer this question later in Chapter 8, "Cost and Service Level Optimization."

4.2 Stochastic Demand

Once a service level target is defined by management, supply chain practitioners often translate this into overly simplistic rules like: "We take x weeks of average demand as safety stock." But these rules do not take into account each of the products, unique facets of demand variability and supply reliability. Some products might face volatile demand, while others could face stable demand but unreliable supply. For that reason, safety stocks should protect us against:
- The **demand variation** that could happen during the average (supply) lead time.
- The average demand over the **lead time variation**.

We will add these two new layers of insights to the EOQ model: suppliers will now have the possibility to be late (i. e., the lead times will no longer be constant) and clients won't order the exact same amount of products in each period. We will first tackle the issue of stochastic demand in this chapter and discuss the case of stochastic lead times in Chapter 6.

4.2.1 Normal Distribution

Let's start by looking at the demand variation. Let's note **d** the **demand per period** (day, week, month...). Until now, we assumed that this demand was constant in each period. Now, let's change this and assume that the demand follows a normal distribution, defined by a **mean μ_d** and a **standard deviation σ_d**.[3]

$$\text{Demand per period} \sim \mathcal{N}\left(\mu_d, \sigma_d^2\right)$$

The demand standard deviation is defined as:

$$\sigma_d = \sqrt{\frac{\sum (d_t - \mu_d)^2}{n-1}}$$

where n is the number of (historical) demand observations and d_t the demand at time t. If you are not familiar with the concept of a standard deviation, simple intuition says it is a measure of how the demand is spread around its mean. A high deviation will simply represent a demand that fluctuates a lot.

Sample Deviation

In our standard deviation formula, we divided the sum of the deviation by $n-1$ and not simply by n. The rigorous explanation of this trick is outside the scope of this book. Nonetheless, we can try to estimate the *true* standard deviation of the demand by looking at only a few observations: a *sample* of the true demand. Therefore we want to be conservative in our estimate by dividing the sum of deviation by $n-1$ instead of n, resulting in a higher estimate of σ_d than the actual standard deviation of the demand sample at hand.

> **DIY**
>
> You can compute the (sample) standard deviation of a range of cells in Excel by using =STDEV.S(range). In Python, with the famous NumPy library, you can compute the standard deviation of an array by using np.std(array,ddof=1).

Discrete vs. Continuous Distributions

We will discuss in Parts II and III inventory models based on continuous distributions. This means that we assume that the demand can take any value. In practice, this is

---

3 We will discuss normality further in Chapter 9, "Beyond Normality." Nevertheless, the exact mathematics needed to test demand normality are beyond the scope of this book, and unfortunately the assumption of normality is frequently not strictly respected. Nothing is normal in this world.

often not the case. Client can often buy products only in specific packaging (bottles, packs, pallets), and some products simply can't be cut into arbitrary pieces (selling 0.13 iPhones makes no sense). Nevertheless, we will first focus on continuous models since these are easier to implement in practice than discrete models. We will discuss the latter in Part IV, "Discrete Inventory Optimization."

Statistical Definitions
Before we go back to our demand analysis and inventory level, let's take some time to define some important statistical concepts.

Standard Normal Distribution
A standard normal distribution is a normal distribution with a mean of 0 and a standard deviation of 1, or $\mathcal{N}(0,1)$. It is also called a *Gaussian* distribution.

Probability Density Function
The intuition behind the probability density function (PDF) of a random distribution is that the higher the PDF is around a value, the higher the probability (likelihood) that an occurrence of the distribution is close to this value. In other words, if the PDF of a distribution is high around 1, it is likely that an occurrence of this distribution would fall close to 1. We note $f_{\mathcal{X}}(x)$ the **probability density function of distribution $\mathcal{X}$ expressed at a value x.**

Like any other statistical distribution, a normal distribution is also defined by a PDF. It is mathematically defined as:

$$f_{\mathcal{N}}(x;\mu,\sigma) = \frac{1}{\sqrt{2\pi\sigma^2}} \cdot exp\left(-\frac{(x-\mu)^2}{2\sigma^2}\right)$$

There is an exception to this notation: the **PDF of a standard normal distribution** is noted $\varphi(x)$ (*phi*). You can see in Figure 4.1 the PDF of such a Gaussian probability

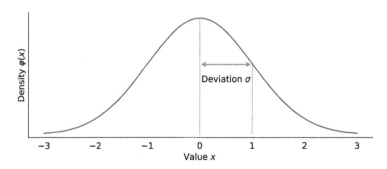

Figure 4.1: Probability density function of $\mathcal{N}(0,1)$.

function.

$$\varphi(x) = f_{\mathcal{N}}(x; 0, 1) = \frac{1}{\sqrt{2\pi}} \cdot exp\left(-\frac{x^2}{2}\right)$$

Cumulative Distribution Function

The cumulative distribution function (CDF) of a random distribution is the probability for an occurrence of this distribution to be less than or equal to a certain value. In other words, the CDF of a random distribution $\mathcal{X}$ will tell you how likely it is that an occurrence x of this distribution is lower than a threshold z. We note $F_{\mathcal{X}}(z)$ **the CDF of a distribution $\mathcal{X}$ evaluated at a threshold z.**

$$F_{\mathcal{X}}(z) = \text{Probability that } \mathcal{X} \leq z = \int_{-\infty}^{z} f_{\mathcal{X}}(x)\, dx$$

The CDF of a random distribution is expressed as a probability; it is therefore always between 0 and 1 (and can also be expressed as a percentage). We note α this percentage:

$$F_{\mathcal{X}}(z) = \alpha \quad 0 \leq \alpha \leq 1$$

Again we note $\Phi(z)$ (*phi*) **the CDF of a standard normal distribution** (see Figure 4.2).

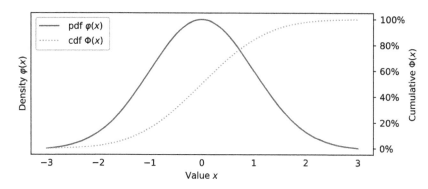

Figure 4.2: Cumulative distribution function of $\mathcal{N}(0, 1)$.

We have this relationship between the CDF of a normal distribution and the one of a standard normal distribution:

$$F_{\mathcal{N}}(x; \mu, \sigma) = \Phi\left(\frac{x - \mu}{\sigma}\right)$$

DIY

Excel You can easily compute the CDF of a normal distribution in Excel with the formula =NORM.DIST(z,mu,sigma,TRUE). You can do the same for a Gaussian either by =NORM.DIST(z,0,1,TRUE) or simply by =NORM.S.DIST(z,TRUE).

Python In Python we can use the library SciPy to compute the CDF of a normal distribution with the function stats.norm.cdf(z,mu,sigma). For the sake of simplicity we will import norm directly from scipy.stats:

```
from scipy.stats import norm
z, mu, sigma = 125, 100, 25
alpha = norm.cdf(z, mu, sigma)
print(alpha)
>> 0.8413
```

This means that an occurrence of a normal distribution with a mean of 100 and a standard deviation of 25 has an 84.13% chance to be lower than 125.

Inverse Cumulative Distribution Function

We note $F_X^{-1}(\alpha)$ the **inverse cumulative distribution function** (also known as the quantile function) of a distribution $\mathcal{X}$ evaluated at the probability α. It will give us the threshold z that will achieve a probability α for an occurrence of the distribution $\mathcal{X}$ to be below this threshold z.

$$F^{-1}(\alpha) = z \iff F_X(z) = \alpha$$

This threshold is often called the **quantile.**

We note $\Phi^{-1}(\alpha)$ the **standard inverse cumulative distribution.**

$$F_{\mathcal{N}}^{-1}(\alpha; 0, 1) = \Phi^{-1}(\alpha)$$

More generally, we have this useful relationship between the two:

$$F_{\mathcal{N}}^{-1}(\alpha; \mu, \sigma) = \mu + \sigma \cdot \Phi^{-1}(\alpha)$$

For example, there is a 95% probability that an occurrence of a random variable following a Gaussian distribution will be lower than 1.645: $\Phi^{-1}(0.95) = 1.645 \iff \Phi(1.645) = 0.95$. We say that the standard cumulative distribution of 1.645 is 95% and that the standard inverse cumulative distribution of 0.95 is 1.645.

Excel You can compute the inverse CDF of a normal distribution with the formula =NORM.INV(alpha,mu,sigma). You can do the same for a Gaussian either by =NORM.INV(alpha,0,1) or simply =NORM.S.INV(alpha).

Python You can compute the inverse CDF of a normal distribution with the function norm.ppf(alpha,mu,sigma) (read **p**ercent **p**oint **f**unction).

```
alpha, mu, sigma = 0.8413, 100, 25
z = norm.ppf(alpha, mu, sigma)
print(z)
>> 124.995
```

4.2.2 A Demand Assumed to Be Normal

You can see in Figure 4.3 the PDF and CDF of a *normal* demand where $\mu_d = 100$ and $\sigma_d = 25$. In other words, the probability density of a demand that varies around 100 units per period with a standard deviation of 25. We observe that there is a 10% chance for the demand during a period to be higher than 132 units (as $F_{\mathcal{N}}^{-1}(0.9; 100, 25) = 132$ there is a 90% probability for the demand to be below 132 units), and only 5% to be higher than 141 ($F_{\mathcal{N}}^{-1}(0.95; 100, 25) = 141$).

The CDF of our demand distribution is particularly useful as it tells us **the probability for the demand (during one period) to be below a threshold.**

We can then simply compute the inventory level ι (*iota*) needed at the beginning of a period to achieve a service level α:

$$\iota = F_{\mathcal{N}}^{-1}(\alpha; \mu_d, \sigma_d)$$

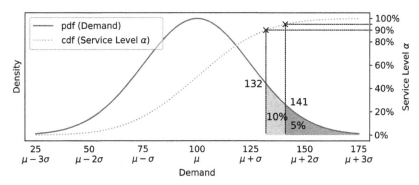

Figure 4.3: Demand probability density function with $d \sim \mathcal{N}(100, 25^2)$.

Similarly, we can compute the expected cycle service level during a period based on an initial inventory level.

$$\alpha = F_{\mathcal{N}}\,(\iota;\mu_d,\sigma_d)$$

In other words, this means that if we have an inventory of ι pieces at the beginning of a period, we can expect, with a probability α, to have enough inventory to fulfill all the demand during this period.

We show in Table 4.1 (for this specific demand distribution) the relationship between the inventory level at the beginning of a period and the expected cycle service level.

Table 4.1: Impact of the inventory level ι on the cycle service level α.

Inventory level	ι	100	106	113	121	132	141	149	158
Cycle service level	α	50%	60%	70%	80%	90%	95%	97.5%	99%

DIY

Let's assume that we have a normal demand with a mean mu and a standard variation sigma. We either want to compute the service level alpha we would achieve based on an initial inventory level inv, or the other way around: how much inventory we need to reach a service level alpha.

Excel You can compute alpha with the formula =NORM.DIST(inv,mu,sigma, TRUE); and you can get the required inventory level with the formula =NORM. INV(alpha,mu,sigma).

Python The expected service level will be given by norm.cdf(inv,mu,sigma) and the required inventory level by norm.ppf(alpha,mu,sigma).

The code below will reproduce the results of Table 4.1.

```
mu, sigma = 100, 25

alpha = [0.5,0.6,0.7,0.8,0.9,0.95,0.975,0.99]
inv = norm.ppf(alpha, mu, sigma)

inv = [100,106,113,121,132,141,149,158]
alpha = norm.cdf(inv, mu, sigma)
```

4.2.3 Safety Stocks

We can now compute how much inventory we need at the beginning of a period in order to reach a certain service level. Let's refine this by splitting the inventory between the cycle stock on one side and the **safety stock** on the other side.

> **Safety stock (S_s)**
>
> Inventory we need to have at the beginning of a cycle, on top of the cycle stock, in order to guarantee a service level against unexpected variations in supply and demand.

We have:

$$\text{Inventory} = \text{Cycle} + \text{Safety}$$
$$\iota = C_s + S_s$$
$$\iota = F_{\mathcal{N}}^{-1}(\alpha; \mu_d, \sigma_d)$$
$$\iota = \mu_d + \sigma_d\, \Phi^{-1}(\alpha) \tag{4.1}$$

where the cycle stock at the beginning of the period is μ_d (in other words, the expected demand over the period) and the safety stock is $\sigma_d\, \Phi^{-1}(\alpha)$.

$\iota = F_{\mathcal{N}}^{-1}(\alpha; \mu_d, \sigma_d)$ can be read as "ι is the inventory necessary to guarantee a cycle service level α if the demand follows a normal distribution $d \sim \mathcal{N}(\mu_d, \sigma_d^2)$."

> **Example**
>
> Let's imagine that we sell a product with a mean demand of 100 units and a deviation of 25 units per period. The inventory we need to reach a cycle service level of 95% is 141 units. You can compute this in Excel with =NORM.INV(0.95,100,25). We can virtually split this inventory into 100 units of cycle stock and 41 units of safety stock.

4.2.4 Service Level Factor

Usually the safety stock formula is noted as:[4]

$$\text{Safety} = \text{Service level factor} \cdot \text{Demand deviation}$$
$$S_s = z_\alpha \sigma_d \tag{4.2}$$

---

4 It is commonly accepted that Thomson Whitin (1923–2013) introduced stochastic inventory optimization—and the famous safety stock formula—with his book *The Theory of Inventory Management* that he published in 1953 while he was working as a professor at the MIT. See Whitin (1953).

We call z_α the **service level factor**, because it is the ratio that multiplies the demand deviation in order to compute the required safety stock and to obtain a desired service level. z_α is computed as $\Phi^{-1}(\alpha)$. Remember, this is the inverse cumulative *standard* distribution function, estimated at the probability α. Some examples are shown in Table 4.2 and Figure 4.4. Typically, with a service level factor of 1.64 we can expect to reach a service level of 95%.

Table 4.2: Service level factor.

Service level factor	z_α	0	0.25	0.52	0.84	1.28	1.64	1.96	2.33
Cycle service level	α	50%	60%	70%	80%	90%	95%	97.5%	99%

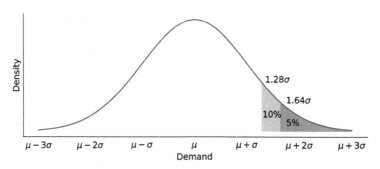

Figure 4.4: Demand level thresholds.

> **Example**
>
> In order to obtain a cycle service level of 95% we have to use a service factor of 1.64 since $z_{.95} = \Phi^{-1}(0.95) = 1.64$. In other words, if we start a period with an inventory level equivalent to the expected demand during this period plus 1.64 times its deviation, we have a 95% probability of not running out-of-stock by the end of this period.

> **DIY**
>
> **Excel** The service level factor can be easily computed in Excel with the formula =NORM.S.INV(service level).
>
> **Python** You can use the function norm.ppf(service level) to get the service level factor.

Impact of Service Level Factor

The relationship between the service level (that we want for our clients) and the amount of safety stock needed is not at all linear.

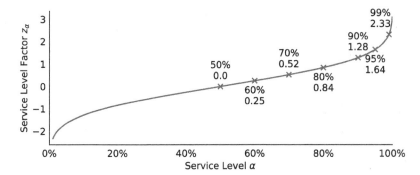

Figure 4.5: Impact of the service level α on the service level factor z_α.

As shown in Figure 4.5, in order to achieve a (cycle) service level of 60% you will need a service level factor of 0.25, but achieving 95% is already 1.64. And 99% is 2.33. This means that the marginal extra cost of guaranteeing an extra point of service level is growing fast. In other words, increasing service level by 1% from 98% to 99% is much more expensive than the increasing it from 60% to 61%. It means that, **the closer you approach a 100% service level, the faster your marginal extra cost grows**.

Actually, based on our model, a service level of 100%—which is a risk of 0.00% of being out-of-stock—will only be achieved thanks to an infinite amount of safety stock. In other words, there is no such thing as zero risk in our continuous normal model.

You will see in Chapter 8, "Cost and Service Level Optimization," how to optimize the service level in order to minimize the inventory policy costs.

> **Important Point**
>
> You might often see inventory managers working with a very high level of theoretical service level in their safety stock formula ($\gg$ 95%). This is a worrying hint that something is missing in the model. The service level factor z_α is often used to *hack* the model until the results look fine. In other words, the inventory manager would push the service level until the model provides an appropriate safety stock; not trying to fix the underlying cause of the mismatch between the model and the practitioner's expectations.
>
> Don't do this—fix the model, don't hack it.

4.2.5 Forecast or Historical Demand?

In the safety stock formula (see eq. 4.2 in Section 4.2.4), we use the **demand** standard deviation (σ_d). As for the EOQ formula, you can decide to use a (demand) forecast rather than (demand) historical numbers. That way, if a trend is observed (or is projected based on external insights), it can be used to improve the setting of the optimal order quantity. We then have

$$S_s = z_\alpha \, \sigma_e$$

where σ_e is the standard deviation of the forecast error.

The forecast error is defined as the forecast minus the demand.

$$e = f - d$$

And its standard deviation is computed as for any other statistical distribution:

$$\sigma_e = \sqrt{\frac{\sum (e_t - \mu_e)^2}{n - 1}}$$

We assume that the forecast is not biased,[5] so that we should have $\mu_e = 0$.

4.3 Demand Variation over Multiple Periods

We just made our first safety stock model, but we assumed that the demand variation was computed on the same period length as the lead time. For example, we assumed that we computed the demand variation per week **and** that we had a lead time of one week. But what happens if we have a lead time of two weeks but we compute the demand variation at a weekly level? Or the other way around, what if the lead time is only two days?

4.3.1 Demand Aggregation

If we look at the demand distribution over multiple periods at once (rather than a single period), the demand **coefficient of variation** should decrease, as the demand variation in each period might offset the others.

---

5 See my previous book *Data Science for Supply Chain Forecasting* for a detailed discussion about forecast accuracy and bias.

> ### Coefficient of variation (CV)
>
> The *coefficient of variation* of a dataset represents the ratio between its standard deviation and its mean. It is often expressed as a percentage.
>
> $$CV = \frac{\sigma}{\mu}$$

If we assume that the demand is normally and independently spread across each period (we'll discuss this in a moment), statistics teach us that the demand standard deviation is proportional to the square root of the number of periods τ (*tau*). Mathematically we have:

$$\tau \cdot \mathcal{N}\left(\mu_d, \sigma_d^2\right) = \mathcal{N}\left(\tau\mu_d, \tau\sigma_d^2\right)$$

So that the coefficient of variation is lowered by $\sqrt{\tau}$.

$$CV_{d\tau} = \frac{\sqrt{\tau\sigma_d^2}}{\tau\mu_d} = \frac{\sigma_d}{\sqrt{\tau}\mu_d} = \frac{CV_d}{\sqrt{\tau}}$$

A good illustration of this effect is to look at the difference between throwing one die or multiple dice. If you throw one die, you have as many chances of getting a 1 as a 6 (the two most extreme values)—you have a high variance. But the more dice you throw at once, the lower the probability of getting an extreme value. For example, if you throw 3 dice, the probability to get the maximum possible value (18) is only 1 out of 216; on the other hand you also have 1 chance out of 4 to get either a 10 or 11. In short, the probabilities at the extremes are very low and probabilities near the middle are high. The results are bunched closer together toward the middle, hence the coefficient of variation of throwing three dice is lower than that of throwing a single die.

The same effect will happen with the demand distribution. You have less chance to face an extreme month than an extreme day. Let's say that you track the daily demand in a shop, you then have these relationships between daily, weekly and monthly variations (as shown in Figure 4.6, assuming you have 5 business days per week and 22 per month):

$$\text{Daily demand} \sim \mathcal{N}\left(\mu_{day}, \sigma_{day}^2\right)$$
$$\text{Weekly demand} \sim \mathcal{N}\left(\mu_w, \sigma_w^2\right) = \mathcal{N}\left(5\mu_{day}, 5\sigma_{day}^2\right)$$
$$\Rightarrow \sigma_w = \sqrt{5}\sigma_{day}$$
$$\text{Monthly demand} \sim \mathcal{N}\left(\mu_m, \sigma_m^2\right) = \mathcal{N}\left(22\mu_{day}, 22\sigma_{day}^2\right)$$
$$\Rightarrow \sigma_m = \sqrt{22}\sigma_{day}$$
$$\text{Demand over multiple days} \sim \mathcal{N}\left(\tau\mu_{day}, \tau\sigma_{day}^2\right)$$
$$\Rightarrow \sigma_\tau = \sqrt{\tau}\sigma_{day}$$

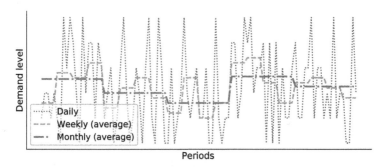

Figure 4.6: Simulated demand variation over different temporal aggregations.

4.3.2 Demand Disaggregation

Let's imagine now that we estimate the demand per week as $d_w \sim \mathcal{N}(\mu_w, \sigma_w^2)$, but we need to assess the demand at a daily level (we have a daily replenishment). We can then assume:

$$d_{day} \sim \mathcal{N}\left(\frac{\mu_w}{5}, \frac{\sigma_w^2}{5}\right)$$

so we see that the daily demand is five times lower than the weekly one but its deviation only got reduced by the square root of five.

We can then summarize these relationships by saying that, if we aggregate the demand over τ multiple periods, we have:

$$\tau \cdot d \sim \mathcal{N}\left(\tau\mu_d, \tau\sigma_d^2\right)$$

and, if we want to disaggregate it, we have:

$$\frac{d}{\tau} \sim \mathcal{N}\left(\frac{\mu_d}{\tau}, \frac{\sigma_d^2}{\tau}\right)$$

So that, if the demand over one period is assumed to follow $d \sim \mathcal{N}(\mu_d, \sigma_d^2)$, the required amount of safety stock S_s to guarantee a service level α is,

$$S_s = z_\alpha \sigma_d \sqrt{\tau} \tag{4.3}$$

which is a more general expression than what we had before: $S_s = z_\alpha \sigma_d$ (see eq. 4.2 in Section 4.2.4).

4.3.3 Demand Independence and Correlation

The safety stock model we created assumes that the demand during a period is **independent** of the demand during the next one. This independence is **not observed**

in practice most of the time. A high demand during one period can result in a lower demand during the following one, as your clients will already have bought what they needed. In other cases, a high demand during one period might be followed by... another high demand period. An external factor might be affecting the overall demand. For example, you can have a sunny weekend, so your sales are high both on Saturday and on Sunday. In this case of positive auto-correlation (i. e., a high demand period followed by another high demand period), our model will undershoot the required amount of safety stock to reach the desired service level.

The fact that this independence is not respected is, of course, an issue. It will only get worse if you use a demand deviation value estimated at a monthly level to compute the daily demand deviation by simply dividing it by $\sqrt{22}$. Or, stated differently, it is not a good idea to estimate the demand deviation at a monthly level by multiplying the one computed at a daily level by $\sqrt{22}$. There are too many assumptions present at once:
- The monthly demand is normally distributed.
- The daily demand is normally distributed.
- The daily demand is uniformly and independently distributed through a month.

We have to think of another solution.

The best way to get rid of this question of independence is to compute the demand variation at the same level of time aggregation as the lead time and the review period. Best practice is to generate a forecast at the same level of aggregation as the supply chain it is used to work on. For example, if your supply chain works with a weekly review period (i. e., with weekly replenishment), it is better to forecast the demand—and measure the forecast accuracy—in weekly buckets rather than in monthly buckets. If you can't do this (for example, due to the limitation of the forecast model) you can at least measure the forecast accuracy per week using a *flat split*[6] of the monthly forecast.

This becomes unfortunately more complex—too complex?—if you face a review period based on another scale than the lead time. As usual, we have to do a trade-off between usability and accuracy.

Correlation

When you need to combine the demand of multiple products into one (for example if you need to estimate the right amount of safety stock for raw materials) you need to pay attention to the correlation between the demand of these products.

We can measure the **correlation** between two variables with a mathematical expression.

---

6 A flat split means that you spread the monthly forecast equally over each day in the month.

> ## Correlation (ρ)
>
> The correlation ρ (*rho*) between two variables is an indicator of some coordinated behavior. If one goes up the other goes up and vice versa (a positive correlation); or the opposite as one variable goes down the other goes up and vice versa (a negative correlation).
>
> The correlation between two variables X and Y is computed as:
>
> $$\rho_{X,Y} = \frac{\sum (x_i - \mu_x)(y_i - \mu_y)}{\sigma_X \sigma_Y}$$
>
> It varies between –1 (straight negative correlation) and 1 (straight positive correlation). A correlation of 0 between two variables means that there is no linear relationship between the two.

> ## DIY
>
> **Excel**   You can use the formula =CORREL(Range1,Range2) to compute the correlation between two ranges.
>
> **Python**   You can use the function corrcoef(a,b) from NumPy. It returns the 2×2 correlation matrix of the two datasets, but we are only interested into the value on the top right (or bottom left).
>
> ```
> a = [1,2,3,4,5,6,7,8]
> b = [1,1,2,2,3,3,4,4]
> print(np.corrcoef(a,b)[0,1])
> >> 0.976
> ```

Sum of Correlated Variables

Once we know the correlation between two variables, we can compute the expected mean and deviation of their sum as below.

If we have X and Y defined as:

$$X \sim \mathcal{N}(\mu_X, \sigma_X^2) \qquad Y \sim \mathcal{N}(\mu_Y, \sigma_Y^2)$$

Then their sum is characterized as:

$$\mu_{X+Y} = \mu_X + \mu_Y$$

$$\sigma_{X+Y} = \sqrt{\sigma_X^2 + \sigma_Y^2 + 2\rho\,\sigma_X\sigma_Y}$$

These equations can be used to estimate the standard deviation when combining two products or markets into one. Remember if $\rho = 0$, then we say that X and Y are linearly uncorrelated (or, with slight abuse, independent). Unfortunately, it is much more complex to use it to properly estimate the demand deviation over multiple periods because some periods could be positively correlated and other negatively correlated.

Example

You are the owner of a famous car model of the early 20th century. You sell this car model in two different colors: red and blue. Your manager says the clients should choose "any color as long as it is black" and asks you to analyze the expected demand if a single color is offered.

You could gather the following information concerning the demand of both cars

$$\text{red} \sim \mathcal{N}(100, 25^2) \quad \text{blue} \sim \mathcal{N}(120, 75^2)$$

Based on an analysis of the demand data you could compute that the correlation ρ is 0.5.

You can then estimate the demand for the black car:

$$\text{black} \sim \mathcal{N}\left(100 + 120, 25^2 + 75^2 + 2 \cdot 0.5 \cdot 25 \cdot 75\right) = \mathcal{N}\left(220, 90.14^2\right)$$

Warehouse Centralization

Supply chain network analysts often look at the impact of warehouse centralization on the cycle and safety stock levels. This impact has been studied thoroughly since Maister (1976). The mathematical models used to assess the impact of centralization are similar to those we discussed here to aggregate or disaggregate the demand across different time buckets. See Wanke (2009) for a more recent literature review and detailed models. Warehouse centralization will help to reduce demand variability, but it won't help against supply variability (we will discuss this in Chapter 6, "Stochastic Lead Times"). On the other hand, adding a central warehouse to an existing inventory network will increase the handling costs and might result in longer total lead times.

4.4 Recap

We defined the cycle service level α as the probability of no stock-out within an order cycle. In order to achieve this cycle service level over τ periods of demand, we computed that we need a safety stock S_s:

$$S_s = z_\alpha \sigma_d \sqrt{\tau} \quad \text{(see eq. 4.3 in Section 4.3.2)}$$

where

z_α is the service level factor and is computed as $z_\alpha = \Phi^{-1}(\alpha)$

σ_d is the demand standard deviation per period

we assume that the demand observed in each period is independent from one another.

We will now to integrate this safety stock into our inventory policies.

5 Inventory Policies

5.1 Safety Stocks and Inventory Policies

We just created our first mathematical model that computed how much safety stock we need to achieve a desired cycle service level, over a certain period, and based on the demand variation. As we know, in order to run a supply chain (as modeled in Figure 5.1), we need a proper inventory policy—which is not the same as simply knowing how much safety stock we need. For our two main policies, (s, Q) and (R, S), let's see how much safety stock we need, and then answer the two questions needed to run an inventory policy: *how much* and *when* to order. We will answer the question *where* to keep inventory in Chapter 10, "Multi-Echelon Inventory Optimization."

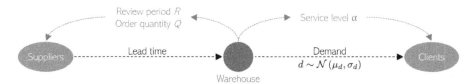

Figure 5.1: Supply chain model.

5.1.1 Policy #1 – Continuous Review and Reorder Point (s,Q)

Let's first discuss the fixed reorder point (s, Q) policy. Remember that, with this policy, we order a fixed amount Q when the stock on-hand reaches a threshold: the reorder point s. You can see in Figure 5.2 this kind of policy with a stochastic demand.

How Much Safety Stock?
We know from Chapter 4 (see eq. 4.3 in Section 4.3.2) that the required safety stock S_s to guarantee a service level α over τ periods, is computed as

$$S_s = z_\alpha \sigma_d \sqrt{\tau}$$

In a continuous (s, Q) policy, the required safety stock is based on the square-root of the supply lead time L:

$$S_s = z_\alpha \sigma_d \sqrt{L}$$

Indeed, the **risk-period x_τ** in an (s, Q) policy (as shown in Figure 5.2) is the lead time L: at any point in time, you can make an order and should get it within time L. Therefore, in order to guarantee a cycle service level of α over the order cycle, you need to keep a

https://doi.org/10.1515/9783110673944-005

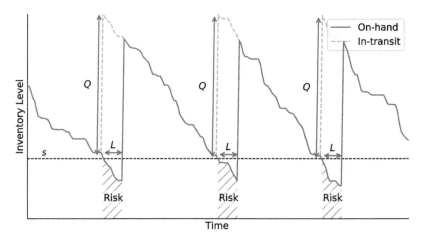

Figure 5.2: (s, Q) policy with stochastic demand $d \sim \mathcal{N}(\mu_d, \sigma_d^2)$.

safety stock to protect it against any demand variation that could happen during the lead time.

> ### Risk-period (x_r)
>
> Maximum period of time that you need to wait to receive an order. During this period your inventory is at risk of being depleted.

Reducing risk-periods (or lead times) should be a priority for supply chain managers. As the safety stocks are proportional to the square root of the lead time, it means that reducing the lead time is profitable for a supply chain. For example, if you divide the (total) lead time by 2, you can reduce the safety stock by $\sqrt{2}$ (= 1.41). This will also reduce the amount of in-transit inventory in the supply chain, resulting in less cash tied up in useless inventory.

How Much to Order?

We compute the order quantity, which we know from the EOQ model (see Chapter 2, specifically eq. 2.2 in Section 2.2.2):

$$Q^* = \sqrt{\frac{2kD}{h}}$$

When to Order?

The reorder point s is now computed as the sum of the demand over the lead time d_L and the safety stocks S_s (as discussed in Chapter 3).

$$s = d_L + S_s$$

5.1.2 Policy #2 – Periodic Review and Order Up-to Level (R,S)

As a reminder, a fixed review period policy (R, S) is an inventory policy where replenishment orders follow a specific schedule: every R periods we make an order to bring the *net inventory level*[1] to S. When computing the safety stock in such a policy, we have to take into account the review period R, as well as the up-to level S. You can see in Figure 5.3 an example of this kind of policy with a stochastic demand.

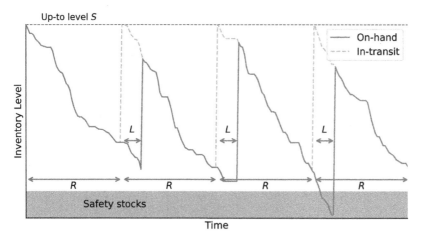

Figure 5.3: (R, S) policy with stochastic demand.

How Much Safety Stock?

As the length of the risk-period x_τ is $R + L$ in an (R, S) policy, we have:

$$S_s = z_a \sigma_d \sqrt{x_\tau} = z_a \sigma_d \sqrt{R + L} \tag{5.1}$$

The required safety stocks are proportional to the square root of the sum of the lead time and the review period. In order to understand why we have to compute the demand variation over the lead time plus the review period, we have to look at the risk-period of such a policy. As shown in Figure 5.4, when a supply planner places an order, at the time of the review R_1, the next time she will be able to make an order is at the time of the next review R_2. Even then, she will still have to wait the supply lead time L before receiving this second order. So when she makes the order at the review period R_1 she must keep enough safety stock in order to be protected during the total time of the risk-period $R + L$.

---

[1] Remember, the net inventory level is the available on-hand inventory and in-transit inventory, minus backorders, orders not yet shipped, etc.

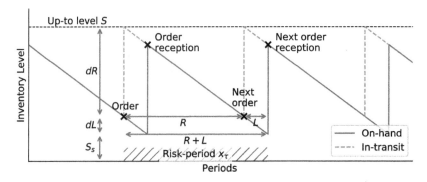

Figure 5.4: risk-period for (R, S) policy.

In other words, the risk-period is now $R + L$ (it was only L with a continuous review policy).

How Much to Order?

We order enough quantity to bring the net inventory level to the up-to level S (not to be confused with S_s the safety stock).

$$S = d_L + d_R + S_s$$
$$Q = S - \text{net inventory}$$

When?

We make an order at each review period. Remember, the optimal (but not practical) review period is based on the EOQ (see Section 3.2):

$$Q^* = \sqrt{\frac{2kD}{h}}$$
$$T^* = \frac{Q^*}{D}$$

From here, we can either round the optimal review period T^* to a practical number, or use the power-of-2 policy (see Section 3.2.1):

$$\frac{T^*}{\sqrt{2}} \leq R = 2^k T_B \leq \sqrt{2} T^*$$

Unfortunately, as the amount of safety stock required is impacted by the review period, the cost optimization of an (R, S) policy under stochastic demand is not as easy as with the deterministic EOQ model. We will discuss this cost optimization in detail in Chapter 8, "Cost and Service Level Optimization."

Similarities between (s, Q) and (R, S)

We can easily draw many similarities between an (s, Q) and an (R, S), and interchange their respective equations by replacing a few variables as shown in Table 5.1.

Table 5.1: Similarities between (s, Q) and (R, S).

Variable	Notation	(s, Q)	(R, S)
Inventory to cover the risk-period	l	s	S
Length of the risk-period	x_τ	L	$R + L$
Demand over an order cycle	d_c	Q	$d_R = dR$

We can express in a very general way the equations that set our policy:

$$S_s = z_\alpha \sigma_d \sqrt{x_\tau}$$
$$l = S_s + dx_\tau$$

5.1.3 Periodic Review and Order Quantity (R, s, Q)

In practice, many supply chains rely on both a periodic review R and a fixed quantity Q: *"We review the inventory once a week and order a full truck if needed."* These policies are (much) more difficult to optimize than (s, Q) and (R, S) policies due to the **undershoot U** (see Figure 5.5).

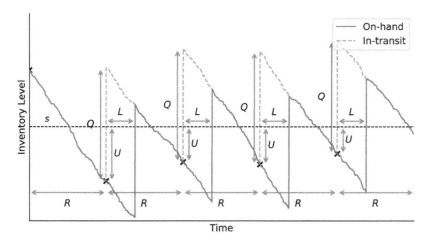

Figure 5.5: Undershoot U under an (R, s, Q) policy.

> **Undershoot (U)**
>
> Expected level of inventory below the reorder point s that is reached at the review period R when an order is made. It is random variable influenced by the inventory policy parameters as well as the demand distribution.

The mathematical optimization of this policy is complex due to the estimation of the undershoot U that gets rapidly complex—even under restrictive assumptions—and changes depending on the assumptions made about the lead time and the demand. Therefore, a *mathematical* optimization of (R, s, Q) is out-of-scope for this book. You can nevertheless check Tempelmeier (2011) and Johansen and Hill (2000) for more information.

Instead of using mathematical models to solve (R, s, Q) policies, we can optimize them—and even more complex ones—with simulations shown in Part IV, "Discrete Inventory Optimization."

5.2 Inventory Analysis

Now that we have updated our inventory policies with our new safety stock model, we can shift our mindset from that of a scientist working on a model to that of a business analyst looking at the inventory levels in a supply chain. Let's use our model and policies to answer some interesting business questions:
- Do we currently have the right amount of stock?
- What is the expected inventory level?
- How does my current (or expected) inventory level balance between safety, cycle and in-transit stock?
- How much impact does the safety stock level have on my total inventory?

Before we start to discuss these points, let's recap the different kinds of inventory we've covered so far:

On-hand This is the physical inventory available in a warehouse for clients to buy. We divided it into two types of inventory:

    Safety The stock kept to guarantee a service level if there is any demand or lead time fluctuation.

    Cycle The amount of inventory we need through an order cycle to cover the expected demand.

In-transit The amount of inventory that is currently in-transit from a supplier to the warehouse.

In practice we can also distinguish between other types of inventory such as:

On-hold The amount of inventory physically in a warehouse but waiting to be shipped to a client (who already booked it). In some cases, these goods can stay a couple of days in a warehouse before being shipped, resulting in extra *useless* inventory.

Anticipation Some inventory is produced in advance to prepare for a busy season and stored for when the production (or supply) capacity is not sufficient to produce on time what will be required.

Merchandising In some businesses, goods are required to fill shelves in stores. The purpose of this inventory is only related to merchandising, marketing or branding.

5.2.1 Theoretical Inventory Levels

Let's compute the theoretically expected inventory levels. We will look at the simulations later. With the safety stock model, we still have the same expected levels of cycle C_s and in-transit I_s inventory as with the regular deterministic EOQ model (as discussed in Chapter 3):

Policy		Cycle C_s	In-transit I_s	Safety S_s
Continuous review	(s, Q)	$\frac{1}{2}Q$	d_L	$z_\alpha \sigma_d \sqrt{L}$
Periodic review	(R, S)	$\frac{1}{2}d_R$	d_L	$z_\alpha \sigma_d \sqrt{R + L}$

The **expected on-hand inventory** is simply the expected cycle stock C_s plus the expected safety stock S_s. This means that the on-hand inventory should fluctuate between the bounds $[S_s, C_s + S_s]$. Of course, as the demand varies over time, the **actual on-hand inventory level** will fluctuate outside of these bounds (we will see that in Figures 5.6 and 5.7).

As an inventory analyst, you can estimate how much inventory is missing (if the on-hand inventory is lower than S_s) or how much short-term excess there is (if the on-hand inventory is higher than $C_s + S_s$). In an (R, S) policy, the net inventory level should never exceed the up-to level S—except if S decreased abruptly (for example, if the demand decreases resulting in a lower inventory target).

> **Important Point**
>
> As already discussed in Section 3.3, you should never expect an (R, S) policy to end up having an average inventory of S units. Remember: don't get misled by the proliferation of supply chain jargon such as "target stock," "reorder point" or "maximum level." You should always take the time to discuss what these terms refer to.

Inventory Zones

Now that we have computed the expected theoretical inventory levels, we can use these to assess the quality of our actual inventory. In order to do so, you can use a color-system to flag inventory. A proposition of thresholds is presented in Table 5.2.

Table 5.2: Inventory thresholds and color-codes.

Status	Color-code	On-hand inventory level
Shortage	Red	$\iota \le 0$
Under-stock	Orange	$0 < \iota < S_s$
Perfect	Green	$S_s \le \iota \le C_s + S_s$
Over-stock	Orange	$C_s + S_s < \iota \le C_s + S_s + I_s$
Excess	Red	$C_s + S_s + I_s < \iota$

Of course, these can be defined differently. For example, the red zone could be defined as below 25% of the safety stock theoretical level. The thresholds are also defined based on the on-hand inventory, but you could do the same with the net inventory level.

We can also easily estimate—based on the actual on-hand level—how much safety, cycle, excess or missing inventory there is.

Example

You are in charge of a product under an (R, S) policy with $R = 1, S = 250, d = 40$ and $L = 4$. You currently have 30 pieces available in stock. Your theoretical level of safety stock is:

$$S_s = S - d_L - d_R = 250 - (40 \cdot 4) - (40 \cdot 1) = 50$$

As your cycle stock varies between 0 and 40 pieces ($C_s = d_R = 40 \cdot 1$), a healthy level of inventory should be between 50 and 90 pieces ($[S_s, C_s + S_s]$). This means that you are missing (currently) 20 pieces of safety stock.

5.3 Simulation

Nullius in verba – Take nobody's word for it.

Royal Society motto, originally from the Roman poet Horace

5.3.1 Stock Levels

Now that we discussed the theoretical expected inventory levels, let's make a simulation of these policies to see how the inventory level would behave.

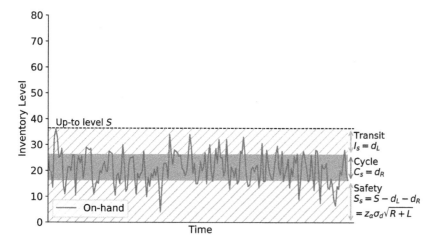

Figure 5.6: (R, S) policy with $R = 1$; $L = 1$, $d = \mathcal{N}(10, 5^2)$ and $\alpha = 99\%$.

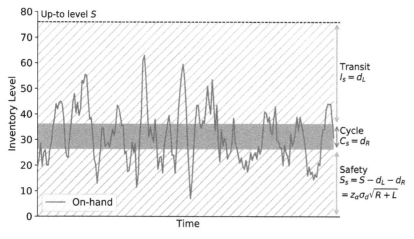

Figure 5.7: (R, S) policy with $R = 1$, $L = 4$, $d = \mathcal{N}(10, 5^2)$ and $\alpha = 99\%$.

You can see in Figures 5.6 and 5.7 how a change in lead time impacts the inventory level, remember that $S = d(R + L) + z_\alpha \sigma_d \sqrt{L + R}$. We clearly see that, as the lead time gets bigger (Figure 5.7), the difference between the up-to level and the average inventory gets bigger. We also see that, with a longer lead time, the on-hand inventory level fluctuates much more around the expected average on-hand level.

Another important finding is that it is common for the on-hand inventory level to be below the safety stock. In other words, it is common to consume part of the safety stock. This might seem obvious, but it can be confusing for some practitioners. Some see the "safety" stocks as being there for emergency situations only. This is obviously not the case here. If you need to have an emergency-only inventory it should be determined out of the current safety stock model.

We will discuss further the estimation of the on-hand inventory levels in Chapter 8 (see specifically Section 8.4.1).

> **Important Point**
>
> As discussed, a model is not a *perfect* representation of the reality. It is unfortunately the same for a simulation: it is not a perfect representation of the reality. It might be close to reality, but it still contains many assumptions. The reality is still much more complex. In our simulations, for example, the demand is assumed to be perfectly normally distributed and independent from one period to another. Is that *really* the case?

5.3.2 Service Levels

Since we used simulations to compare actual and theoretical inventory levels, we can do the same to compare expected and simulated cycle service levels.

Table 5.3: Simulated cycle service level (%) over 1,000,000 periods for an (R, S) policy with $R = 4$.

	L	CV_d	CV_x	Theoretical cycle service level (%)				
				70	80	90	95	99
$d \sim \mathcal{N}(100, 25^2)$	1	.25	.11	70.1	80.3	90.2	95.1	99.0
	4	.25	.09	70.2	80.4	90.1	95.0	98.9
	10	.25	.07	69.9	80.0	90.2	95.0	99.0
$d \sim \mathcal{N}(100, 50^2)$	1	.50	.22	70.1	80.0	90.0	95.0	99.0
	4	.50	.18	69.7	79.8	89.9	95.0	99.0
	10	.50	.13	69.5	79.6	89.9	95.1	99.0
$d \sim \mathcal{N}(100, 100^2)$	1	1.00	.45	66.4	77.9	89.3	94.7	99.0
	4	1.00	.35	64.1	76.3	88.3	94.2	98.9
	10	1.00	.27	60.9	73.6	86.7	93.4	98.7

> **Important Point – How to read a simulation table**
>
> In Table 5.3 you can see simulated results for various inventory policies with different period demand ($d \sim \mathcal{N}(100, 25^2)$ for example), different lead times ($L = 1, 4$ or 10), and different cycle service level **targets** ($\alpha = 70, 80, 90,$ 95 or 99).

For example, you can see that, for a period demand $d \sim \mathcal{N}(100, 25^2)$, a lead time $L = 1$, a review period $R = 4$ and a cycle service level target of 70% we obtain a simulated cycle service level of 70.1%.

You will see later in this section how to create your own simulations. Note that as the simulations are stochastic in nature, the results might vary slightly from one table to another.

As you can see in Table 5.3, the theoretical and simulated cycle service levels are very close when the demand coefficient of variation CV_d is rather low. Remember you can compute CV_d as:

$$CV_d = \frac{\sigma_d}{\mu_d}$$

And CV_x (the risk-period coefficient of variation) as

$$CV_x = \frac{\sigma_x}{\mu_x} = \frac{\sigma_d \sqrt{R + L}}{\mu_d(R + L)} = \frac{\sigma_d}{\mu_d \sqrt{R + L}} = \frac{CV_d}{\sqrt{R + L}}$$

Long lead times $(L > R)$ and low cycle service levels also drive the gap between the theoretical expected cycle service level and the actual one.

Negative Demand?

Our model assumes that the demand follows a normal distribution. As the demand coefficient of variation grows, so does the probability that the demand during a period is negative. Negative demand is not realistic, so in our simulations, we set the minimum demand to be 0. This results in a gap between the theory (a normal demand) and the simulation (a *truncated* normal demand). As the average demand in the simulation is higher than in the theoretical model, therefore, our simulation shows a lower-than-expected cycle service level.

With a CV_d of 100%, there is a 16% chance for the demand during a period to be lower than 0.[2]

In the (common) case of highly variable demand, we should look into new statistical distributions such as gamma (see Chapter 9, "Beyond Normality") or custom distributions (see Chapter 12, "Discrete Probabilistic Demand").

Backorders or Lost Sales?

One of the main assumptions we made in our model is that the **excess demand** would result in backorders until new stock is available. In other words, if a client comes with

---

2 You can compute the probability that the demand during one period is negative as $F_{\mathcal{N}}(0, \mu_d, \sigma_d)$, which can be computed in Excel with =NORM.DIST(0,mu_d,sigma_d,TRUE).

an order and there is no stock available, her order will be put in the backlog and served as soon as new stock is available. The client's demand is not lost but backordered.

> **Excess demand**
>
> Demand that cannot be served directly from the on-hand inventory.

Backorders

In many businesses—especially in B2B—this assumption is correct. If you have some excess demand during one order cycle, at least part of it will be pushed to the next cycle.

Lost Sales

In other businesses, this assumption is not correct. Clients won't wait or simply will go to the competition, resulting in lost sales. The mathematics to compute the required safety stock under the assumption of lost sales are out of our scope,[3] but we can include this effect in a simulation and see its impact on the service level. Note that, in a lost sales model, the net inventory can never be negative, because there are no backorders.

As shown in Table 5.4, if the excess demand is lost (and not backordered), the cycle service level increases. This is normal, as the incoming orders are not used to fill previous orders but are only used to deliver to new clients in subsequent periods. The spread between an inventory policy with backorders, and one with lost sales, grows as the cycle service level decreases because it results in more and more stock-outs (so that the backorder policy needs to keep more stock aside to fill the backlog rather than new clients).

Table 5.4: Simulated cycle service level (%) over 1,000,000 periods for an (R, S) policy with $R = 4$ and $d \sim \mathcal{N}(100, 25^2)$ and lost sales.

	L	Theoretical cycle service level (%)				
		70	80	90	95	99
Backorders	1	70.0	80.1	90.2	95.1	99.0
Lost sales	1	74.8	82.6	91.0	95.4	99.0
Backorders	4	69.6	80.0	90.0	94.9	98.9
Lost sales	4	75.5	83.5	91.5	95.5	99.0
Backorders	10	70.4	80.4	90.2	95.2	99.1
Lost sales	10	81.2	86.9	93.0	96.3	99.2

---

3 See Nahmias (1979), Silver et al. (2016), Axsäter (2015) for detailed lost sales models.

Period Service Level

Our model is setting a safety stock to achieve a cycle service level α, but many supply chains record (and are interested in) the period service level α_p

As a reminder,

- The cycle service level α is the probability not to have a stock-out **during a cycle order** (which can contain multiple periods).
- The period service level α_p is the probability not to experience a stock-out **during a single period** (e. g., a day, a week).

Our safety stock model is based on the cycle service level. It does not provide us a prediction about α_p, so we need to simulate it.

Table 5.5: Simulated cycle and period service levels (%) over 1,000,000 periods for an (R, S) policy with $L = 4$ and $d \sim \mathcal{N}(100, 25^2)$.

Service level	R	Theoretical cycle service level (%)				
		70	80	90	95	99
Cycle α	1	70.2	80.3	90.3	95.1	99.0
Period α_p	1	70.2	80.3	90.3	95.1	99.0
Cycle α	4	69.8	80.2	90.1	95.0	99.0
Period α_p	4	92.1	94.9	97.5	98.7	99.7
Cycle α	10	69.8	79.8	90.0	95.0	99.0
Period α_p	10	96.5	97.7	98.9	99.5	99.9

As you might expect, when the review period R grows (i. e., more time elapses between two consecutive orders), so does α_p. You have multiple periods in one cycle order, so that even though you could be out-of-stock by the end of the order cycle, most of the periods during this cycle could still have had enough inventory. The impact is especially impressive for small values of α. In Table 5.5, you can read the case where $R = 10$ and the theoretical cycle service level is 70% as follows (let's say each period is a working day): *"If we make an order every 2 weeks (10 days) and aim for a cycle service level of 70%, we can expect a probability of only 3.5% of stocking out on any given day."* We conclude that it makes no sense to use cycle service level as a service level KPI if the supply order cycles are long compared to the daily activities of a supply chain. To overcome the limitation of the cycle service level, we will discuss the fill rate later in Chapter 7.

> **Important Point**
>
> The cycle service level should not be used as a service level KPI if order cycles are spread over long periods.

Let's create a small simulation in Python in order to confirm our model and get a graph similar to Figures 5.6 and 5.7. Let's start by defining the variable `time` which will be the length of our simulation. We can then populate a demand array that follows a normal distribution.

```
time = 200
d_mu = 100
d_std = 25
d = np.maximum(np.random.normal(d_mu,d_std,time).round(0).astype
    (int),0)
```

We can then define the remaining inputs of our policy and compute the various parameters.

```
L, R, alpha = 4, 1, 0.95
z = norm.ppf(alpha)
x_std = np.sqrt(L+R)*d_std
Ss = np.round(x_std*z).astype(int)
Cs = 1/2 * d_mu * R
Is = d_mu * L
S = Ss + 2*Cs + Is
```

You can see in Figure 5.8 how our example would behave over the first timesteps. The order made at the end of timestep 0 will be available in period timestep 5.

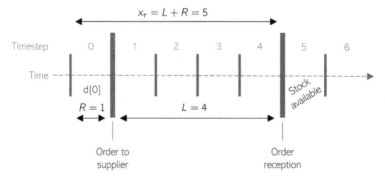

Figure 5.8: Supply chain flow for $R = 1$ and $L = 4$.

We define 2 arrays to keep track of the on-hand and in-transit inventory per period.

```
hand = np.zeros(time,dtype=int)
transit = np.zeros((time,L+1),dtype=int)
```

Lead Times and In-Transit Inventory   In order to represent the fact that the orders can stay in-transit for multiple periods (in our example, 4 periods), we will define transit as a 2-dimensional array. As you can see in Table 5.6, a new order will start at the end of the 2nd dimension (transit[time,-1]) and then make its way through the 2nd dimension as time passes by (one layer per period) until it reaches the last slot (transit[time,0]). The last slot means that this in-transit inventory will be received at the end of the current period (in other words, be available as of the next period).

Table 5.6: Example of df for d_mu, d_std, R, L, alpha = 100, 25, 1, 4, 0.95 and S=592.

time	Demand	On-hand	In-transit (at the end of the timestep)				
0	88	504	[0,	0,	0,	0,	88]
1	91	413	[0,	0,	0,	88,	91]
2	125	288	[0,	0,	88,	91,	125]
3	92	196	[0,	88,	91,	125,	92]
4	107	89	[88,	91,	125,	92,	107]
5	107	70	[91,	125,	92,	107,	107]
6	55	106	[125,	92,	107,	107,	55]
7	109	122	[92,	107,	107,	55,	109]

We now have to initialize these arrays for the first timestep. The initial on-hand and net inventories are S minus the demand during the first period. The in-transit inventory is initialized for the second period as the demand in the first period.

```
hand[0] = S - d[0]
transit[1,-1] = d[0]
```

We also have to create two objects to track the service level of our policy:
- stock-out_period will contain a Boolean that flags if there is a shortage during a period.

- stock-out_cycle will contain a Boolean for each order cycle (i. e., review period) that flags if we had a shortage at any time during the last cycle.

```
stock-out_period = np.full(time,False,dtype=bool)
stock-out_cycle = []
```

We can now start our simulation. These are the main steps performed at each timestep t:

1. Check whether we received an order at the beginning of the period (transit[t-1,0] > 0). If so, we need to compute the cycle service level by checking if there was a stock-out last period. Remember, we define the cycle service level as the probability that there is no stock-out just before an order is received.

2. Update the on-hand inventory by subtracting the demand d[t] and adding the received inventory transit[t-1,0]

3. Indicate in stockout_period[t] whether we had a shortage.

4. Update the net inventory position net[t]. Remember that it is the total in-transit inventory transit[t].sum() plus the on-hand inventory hand[t] Note that you can exclude backorders (i. e., excess demand will be lost) by uncommenting the line hand[t] = max(0,hand[t]).

5. Update the in-transit array by offsetting the values of the previous timestep by 1: transit[t,:-1] = transit[t-1,1:]. This represents the fact that the orders move through the supply pipeline.

6. If we are at the review period (t%R==0), we make an order based on the current net inventory position net[t] and the up-to level S. The order is then stored at the extreme of the in-transit array transit[t,L].

```
for t in range(1,time):
    if transit[t-1,0]>0:
        stockout_cycle.append(stockout_period[t-1])
    hand[t] = hand[t-1] - d[t] + transit[t-1,0]
    stockout_period[t] = hand[t] < 0
    #hand[t] = max(0,hand[t]) #Uncomment if excess demand result
        in lost sales rather than backorders
    transit[t,:-1] = transit[t-1,1:]
    if 0==t%R:
        net = hand[t] + transit[t].sum()
        transit[t,L] = S - net
```

Finally, we can create a DataFrame df (see an example in Table 5.6) to hold our simulation results and plot them on a graph similar to Figure 5.7.

```
df = pd.DataFrame(data= {'Demand':d,'On-hand':hand,'In-transit':
    list(transit)})
df = df.iloc[R+L:,:] #Remove initialization periods
print(df)
df['On-hand'].plot(title='Inventory Policy (%d,%d)' %(R,S), ylim
    =(0,S), legend=True)
```

We can also print cycle and period service levels.

```
print('Alpha:',alpha*100)
SL_alpha = 1-sum(stockout_cycle)/len(stockout_cycle)
print('Cycle Service Level:',round(SL_alpha*100,1))
SL_period = 1-sum(stockout_period)/time
print('Period Service Level:',round(SL_period*100,1))
```

Of course, these code extracts are just a simple example on how to create a simulation. Feel free to add new elements.

5.4 Recap

We have created an initial safety stock model where the safety stocks are meant to protect us against the demand variation.

$$S_s = z_\alpha \sigma_d \sqrt{R + L} \quad \text{(see eq. 5.1 in Section 5.1.2)}$$

These safety stocks are proportional to:
- The demand standard deviation σ_d (in other words, the more the demand fluctuates, the more safety stocks we'll need)
- To the cycle service level α we want
- To the square root of the lead time plus the review period (if any)

We took the following assumptions to make our model:
- The demand is independently distributed in each period.
- The demand is assumed to be normally distributed and continuous.
- Excess demand is backordered (no lost sales).
- The lead time is deterministic.

Let's recap our two favorite inventory policies so far:

	Reorder point (s, Q)		Review Period (R, S)
How much?	Order Quantity $\quad Q = \sqrt{\frac{2kD}{h}}$	Up-to level	$S = d_L + d_R + S_s$
When?	Reorder point $\quad s = d_L + S_s$	Review period	$R = 2^k T_B$
Safety	$S_s = z_\alpha \sigma_d \sqrt{L}$		$S_s = z_\alpha \sigma_d \sqrt{R + L}$
Cycle	$C_s = \frac{1}{2} Q$		$C_s = \frac{1}{2} d_R$
In-transit	$I_s = d_L$		
Cycle Service Level	$\Phi^{-1}(z_\alpha)$		

6 Stochastic Lead Times

So far we have created a safety stock model—$S_s = z_a \sigma_d \sqrt{R + L}$ (see eq. 5.1 in Section 5.1.2)—that is able to deal with stochastic demand and deterministic lead times. That was a good improvement from the EOQ model where both the demand and the lead time were assumed to be determined and known in advance. But most of the *real* supply chains actually face stochastic lead times: you never know if your supplier—or your (production) process—will deliver your order on time. Therefore, we want our safety stocks to protect us against longer-than-expected lead times, as well as against variable demand.

We will improve our model in two steps:
1. First, we will assume that the demand is fixed and the lead time varies.
2. Then, we will assume that **both** the demand and the lead time vary.

By the end of this chapter we will model our supply chain as shown in Figure 6.1.

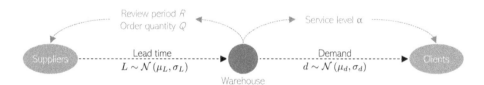

Figure 6.1: Supply chain model.

6.1 Lead Time: What Is It Made of?

Before jumping into the mathematical models, an important point to realize is that the lead time in the safety stock model **is not limited to the transportation time**. It does actually include all kinds of other waiting times that accumulate along the supply chain and result in the need for more safety stock. It is therefore a pity that most supply chain practitioners confuse lead time and transportation time. The time it takes for a truck (or boat, train, plane) to move goods from point A to point B is **not** the only delay between the time a planner places an order and the time the goods are available in her warehouse.

Let's review one-by-one all the possible delays and waiting times.

Review period In a periodic review policy (as discussed in Chapter 1) this is the time between two consecutive orders. Typically a day, a week or a month.

Production frequency Time between each production batch. Typically, you might want to produce some goods once every 6 months or so. So when a production order is made, you might want to produce enough to cover 6 months of demand.

https://doi.org/10.1515/9783110673944-006

The production frequency is a specific case of the review period where you set the review period based on production cycles.

Frozen period Period during which production planning is frozen: no changes are allowed. This frozen period is forcing production planners to fix the production schedule for subsequent weeks in order for the operational teams to properly plan their different agendas.

Production time Time needed to produce the goods. The products currently under production are called **work-in-progress** (WIP).

Planning time Time needed for production planning and/or to plan the transportation of the goods (in or out of a warehouse for example).

Preparation time Time needed to pick the goods and prepare the order (can also include administrative tasks).

Transportation time Time needed to move stock from one location to another. This is what most practitioners consider as being the (total) lead time. We call the inventory being transported from one warehouse to another the **in-transit inventory**. Computing the transportation time is not always straightforward:

- In the case of multimodal shipments, you might need to include some extra handling time on top of the transportation time.
- Sometimes suppliers deliver the goods up to a port (or an external warehouse). Their quote will only include the transportation time up to this point. You will then need to take into account additional transportation time to include the transportation of the goods from this external warehouse to your main warehouse.
- You might also have to take custom time into account.

External events External (unexpected) events like strikes, thefts, storms, earthquakes or black swans like the coronavirus can also impact total lead time.

Important Point

The concept of lead time is often confusing for many supply chain practitioners and consultants. Do not hesitate to explicitly define what the lead time consists of, in order to avoid confusion between "lead time" and "transportation time."

Lead Time Variability

The total lead time is often variable. You can never know exactly when a specific order will be delivered. These fluctuations can be due to many factors: process variability, production constraints, lack of raw materials, mistakes, defects, planning constraints and so on.

Example

Let's imagine that you review your production planning once a week. During the review, you need to plan production 4 weeks in advance. It takes 1 week for your production facility to produce a batch of goods and 1 week to ship it to your warehouse. Your total lead time is $1 + 4 + 1 + 1 = 7$ weeks. Therefore, your safety stock should be evaluated as $S_s = z_\alpha \sigma_d \sqrt{7}$.

Example

You work as a supply chain analyst for a manufacturing industry. You have different warehouses in multiple countries and one production facility. You know the production process very well.
- You review the production tickets once every 4 weeks together with the production manager.
- The production planning has a frozen period of 4 weeks. This means that you can't change the production planned for the following 4 weeks.
- It also takes 1 week for your production facility to actually manufacture your goods.
- Once the goods are ready, the shipment planning takes 1 week (it takes time to find a slot for a truck to come and pick up the goods).
- Finally, it takes 1 week to transport the goods from the manufacturing plant to the regional warehouses.

A consulting company comes in and proposes to reduce the production frozen period from 4 weeks to 2 weeks. A junior consultant asserts that this will reduce the total amount of safety stock by 29% ($\simeq 1 - \frac{\sqrt{2}}{\sqrt{4}}$).

Is this correct? Should we launch this project with the business based on the potential savings of the 29% reduction of our safety stocks?

Let's compute the safety stock required before and after the frozen period reduction.

Before We have a total lead time of $4 + 4 + 1 + 1 + 1 = 11$ weeks so that $S_s = z_\alpha \sigma_d \sqrt{11}$.

After If we reduce the frozen period from 4 to 2 weeks, we will have a total lead time of 9 weeks and therefore $S_s = z_\alpha \sigma_d \sqrt{9}$. The safety stock reduction will be 9.5% $\simeq 1 - \frac{\sqrt{9}}{\sqrt{11}}$.

The consultant forgot that the lead time is not only made of the production frozen period but by many other waiting times. By doing this, she overestimated the cost reduction impact.

6.2 Stochastic Lead Time and Fixed Demand

Let's assume that we have a product that we sell consistently the same amount every day. Because the supplier is not as reliable as we wish it to be, we will model its lead time as a normal distribution.[1] Mathematically, we can express this as:

$$\text{Lead time} \sim \mathcal{N}\left(\mu_L, \sigma_L^2\right)$$

This means that a supplier can be late or early compared to its announced time of arrival.[2]

If it is late, we have a potential issue with our on-hand inventory at risk of being depleted.

If it is early, we would have too much inventory on-hand resulting in higher (useless) holding costs.

You can see in Figure 6.2 the probability density function of our supplier lead time if the supply process follows a random normal distribution with a mean of 20 and a deviation of 5.

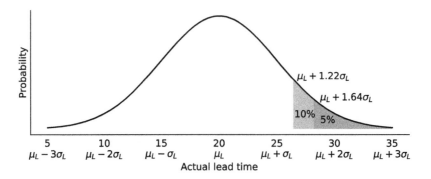

Figure 6.2: Expected lead time.

Just as for the stochastic demand (see Table 4.2) we can estimate the probability for the demand during the (stochastic) lead time to be below a certain threshold thanks to its cumulative distribution function (CDF). For example, as shown in Figure 6.2, there is a 10% probability that the lead time is longer than $\mu_L + 1.22\,\sigma_L$ resulting in a 10% probability that the demand during the lead time is higher than $d(\mu_L + 1.22\,\sigma_L)$.

---

[1] In practice, the lead time is often not normally distributed. We will discuss gamma distribution in Chapter 9, "Beyond Normality," and custom distributions in Chapter 13, "Simulation Optimization."

[2] We suppose that its announced time of arrival, or expected time of arrival, is its average lead time μ_L. If this isn't the case, your policy should account for a lead time bias.

If you have a supplier with a lead time that can be described as $L \sim \mathcal{N}(5, 2^2)$, and a daily demand of 20 pieces, you can expect that if you place an order today, there is a 10% chance that the supplier will take at least 7 days ($\approx 5 + 1.22 \times 2$) to deliver your order. In the meantime you will have sold at least 149 pieces ($\approx 20 \times (5 + 1.22 \times 2)$). This means that if you want to be 90% sure to have enough stock on-hand when making an order, you should make an order once you have 149 pieces left in your inventory.

Let's generalize our findings to compute the amount of safety stock we need to protect our supply chain against lead time variations. This safety stock will be computed as:
- the service level factor z_α (as discussed in Section 4.2.4),
- times the lead time standard deviation σ_L,
- times the average demand μ_d.

We finally obtain:

$$S_s = z_\alpha \, \mu_d \, \sigma_L \tag{6.1}$$

You run a factory that produces scooters. You have a specific supplier that provides you steel. Unfortunately you can't trust its estimated delivery dates. When your supplier is late, you face the risk of being out-of-stock for one of your raw materials which would result in stopping the production line. You want to avoid this and therefore will have to keep some safety stock aside. Here are the pieces of information you could gather:
- You have a daily production of 50 scooters (let's assume there is no variation).
- On average it takes 30 days for your supplier to delivery an order.
- The *actual* lead time has a standard deviation of 10 days.
- You want to be sure at 99% that you won't be out-of-stock of steel to be sure that your production line can run smoothly. You can compute $z_{.99}$ in Excel by using the formula =NORM.S.INV(0.99).

Let's feed our safety stock model ($S_s = z_\alpha \sigma_L \mu_d$) with the different values: $\mu_d = 50$; $z_{.99} = 2.33$ and $\sigma_L = 10$. We obtain:

$$S_s = z_{.99} \, \sigma_L \mu_d = 2.33 \cdot 10 \cdot 50 = 1165$$

This means that you should keep a safety stock of steel big enough to produce 1165 scooters in order to protect your production line against supplier delays.

6.3 Stochastic Lead Time and Demand

We now have two different safety stock models:
- One for **stochastic demand** and fixed lead times: $S_s = z_\alpha \sigma_d \sqrt{R+L}$ (see eq. 5.1 in Section 5.1)
- Another for fixed demand and **stochastic lead times**: $S_s = z_\alpha \sigma_L \mu_d$ (see eq. 6.1 in Section 6.2)

In order to deal with both variable demand and lead times, we have to bring these two models into a single unified model. In other words, we have to define the probability function of the demand over the lead time while both are random.

6.3.1 The Sum of a Random Number of Random Variables

The demand over the lead time is now defined as
- the sum,
- of a random number (the lead time),
- of random variables (the demand).

As an analogy, you can imagine throwing a first die (representing the random lead time), then, based on the result obtained, throwing an equivalent number of dice. Each die of the second throw represents the (random) demand during one period. We are interested in the probability distribution of this second throw.

To compute this, let's define C as $C = A \cdot B$ where A and B are random variables. In other words, C is a random distribution equal to the sum of a random number A of random variables B. Now we have to define the expected value of C ($E[C]$) as well as its variance ($V[C]$). Assuming A and B are independent[3] we have,

$$E[C] = E[A]E[B] \tag{6.2}$$

$$V[C] = E[A]V[B] + V[A]E[B]^2 \tag{6.3}$$

The proof is given in Appendix B.1. Note that, if A and B are normally distributed (as assumed), so is C.

---

3 In most cases, the lead time variation can be assumed to be independent of the demand variation. There are exceptions of course. For example, during periods of global high demand you could face a supply shortage. Wang et al. (2010) provides mathematical formulations for such cases.

6.3.2 Fixed Reorder Point (s, Q)

If we replace (in eq. 6.2) A by the lead time, B by the demand and C as the demand over the lead time, we obtain:

$$E[C] = E[A]E[B] \Rightarrow \mu_{dL} = \mu_L \mu_d$$

$$\sqrt{V[C]} = \sqrt{E[A]V[B] + V[A]E[B]^2} \Rightarrow \sigma_{dL} = \sqrt{\mu_L \sigma_d^2 + \sigma_L^2 \mu_d^2}$$

So the demand over the lead time behaves as $\mathcal{N}\left(\mu_L \mu_d, \sigma_L^2 \mu_d^2 + \mu_L \sigma_d^2\right)$. Specifically, as the *risk-period*[4] is the lead time in an (s, Q) policy, the standard deviation of the demand over the risk-period is:

$$\sigma_x = \sigma_{dL} = \sqrt{\mu_L \sigma_d^2 + \sigma_L^2 \mu_d^2}$$

You can see in Figure 6.3 how a stochastic lead time impacts an (s, Q) policy.

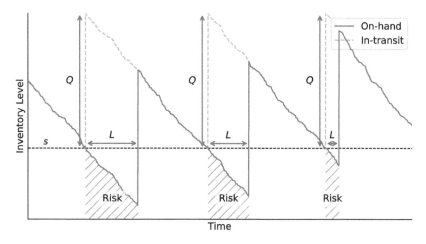

Figure 6.3: (s, Q) policy with stochastic demand and lead time.

We can then compute the required safety stock as:

$$S_s = z_\alpha \sigma_x$$

$$\sigma_x = \sqrt{\mu_L \sigma_d^2 + \sigma_L^2 \mu_d^2}$$

$$S_s = z_\alpha \sqrt{\mu_L \sigma_d^2 + \sigma_L^2 \mu_d^2} \tag{6.4}$$

---

4 Risk-period (x_τ): maximum amount of time you need to wait to receive an order (from your supplier). During this period your inventory is at risk of being depleted. $x_\tau = R + L$ in an (R, S) policy and $x_\tau = L$ in an (s, Q) policy. See Section 5.1.1.

6.3.3 Fixed Review Period (R, S)

In the case of a periodic review policy (R, S), we have to refine this model one step further by taking into account the periodic review. We have to protect ourselves against the demand variation over the lead time **plus** the review period. As shown in Figure 6.4, the elapsed time between when we make an order and the reception of the **next** order is:

$$R + L \sim R + \mathcal{N}\left(\mu_L, \sigma_L^2\right) = \mathcal{N}\left(R + \mu_L, \sigma_L^2\right)$$

See Section 5.1.2 for a detailed explanation of the case where both R and L are deterministic.

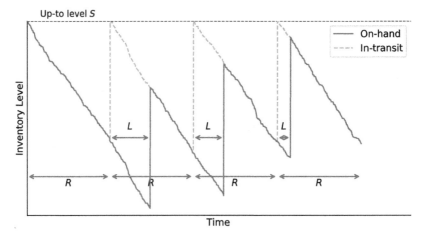

Figure 6.4: (R, S) policy with stochastic demand and lead time.

The demand deviation over the risk-period is:

$$\sigma_x = \sqrt{(\mu_L + R)\sigma_d^2 + \sigma_L^2 \mu_d^2}$$

We can then update our safety stock model by taking into account the review period:

$$S_s = z_a \sigma_x$$

$$S_s = z_a \sqrt{(\mu_L + R)\sigma_d^2 + \sigma_L^2 \mu_d^2} \tag{6.5}$$

Example

You are working for a bicycle shop. You have a supplier in Asia who produces the bicycles you sell. The supplier has a long lead time (the bicycles are shipped in containers by sea) and your sales vary from one week to another. On top of this, in order to reduce your order costs and to simplify your ordering process, you only place one order per month (or every four weeks) with your supplier.

Due to all the possible sources of variation in the long lead time and review period, you want to keep safety stock to guarantee a decent service level for your clients.

Let's note the different pieces of information you gathered:

- You have a weekly demand of around 350 units with a standard deviation of 100 units.
- The expected lead time is 13 weeks with a deviation of 3 weeks.
- You want to achieve a cycle service level of 95%. You can easily compute in Excel and Python that $\Phi(0.95) = 1.645$.
- You make an order every 4 weeks.

Let's compute the safety stock by applying our new model:

$$S_s = z_{.95} \sqrt{(\mu_L + R)\sigma_d^2 + \sigma_L^2\mu_d^2} = 1.645\sqrt{(13 + 4) \cdot 100^2 + 3^2 \cdot 350^2} = 1855$$

This means that we need to keep a safety stock of 1855 pieces to compensate for the lead time, its variation, the review period and the demand variation.

6.4 Simulation

The model we created to compute the required safety stock is not a perfect representation of reality. However, we can test it further through simulations. In order to do so, let's return to the simulation we created in Chapter 5 and add random lead times.

DIY

These are the changes compared to the code given in Section 5.3.2. We define L_std as the lead time deviation and include it into the safety stock computation.

```
L, L_std = 4, 1
x_std = np.sqrt((R+L)*d_std**2+L_std**2*d_mu**2)
Ss = np.round(x_std*z).astype(int)
```

Each time an order is made, a random lead time will be computed so that the transit array is now defined as arbitrary number of columns (in the example L + 5*L_std+1). We still initialize transit with a first shipment.

```
transit = np.zeros((time,L+5*L_std+1),dtype=int)
transit[0,L] = d[0]
```

We update our main loop by computing an actual lead time for each order. This lead time must not be negative.

```
for t in range(1,time):
    if transit[t-1,0]>0:
        stockout_cycle.append(stockout_period[t-1])
    hand[t] = hand[t-1] - d[t] + transit[t-1,0]
    stockout_period[t] = hand[t] < 0
    transit[t,:-1] = transit[t-1,1:]
    if t%R==0:
        actual_L = int(round(max(np.random.normal(L,L_std),0),0))
        net = hand[t] + transit[t].sum()
        transit[t,actual_L] = S - net
```

6.4.1 Results and Limitations

We now have a powerful model that can allocate safety stocks based on both the lead time variation and the demand variation.

As usual, our model makes some assumptions about the lead time. These are necessary in order to obtain tractable mathematical models; but these assumptions might not be realistic, resulting in over- or under-estimation of the expected service level. Let's review them one by one.

Continuous Lead Time

The model assumes the lead time to be a **continuous** normal random variable. However, in practice, the lead time will often be a **discrete** variable since an order can only be received and stored at fixed periods (e. g., at the start/end of the day/shift) or can only be shipped at certain point in time (e. g., the supplier makes one delivery per day). This is also what we do in our simulations where orders can only be received at the end of a timestep.

As you can see in Table 6.1, the stochastic lead times model often deviates from the expected cycle service level target. The actual service level is close to the target in cases where:

$$R \gg L \gg \sigma_L$$

We see this for example when $R = 50$, $L = 20$, $\sigma_L = 5$.

Table 6.1: Simulated cycle service level (%) over 1,000,000 periods for an (R, S) policy with $d \sim \mathcal{N}(100, 25^2)$.

| μ_L | σ_L | Theoretical cycle service level (%) | | | | | | | | | |
| | | $R = 1$ | | | | | $R = 50$ | | | | |
		70	80	90	95	99	70	80	90	95	99
	1	45.9	58.5	73.5	83.1	93.1	69.8	79.7	89.8	94.7	98.9
10	5	59.4	81.2	95.5	98.9	99.9	70.5	80.0	89.6	94.9	99.0
	10	67.7	92.0	99.5	100.0	100.0	70.2	79.8	90.0	94.9	99.0
	1	49.1	61.5	76.0	85.0	94.5	69.8	80.0	89.9	94.9	98.9
20	5	59.3	80.6	95.1	98.7	99.9	70.1	79.8	90.0	94.8	98.9
	10	69.7	91.8	99.4	100.0	100.0	69.9	80.1	90.2	95.0	99.0
	1	52.5	65.0	78.8	87.3	95.9	70.3	80.1	89.5	95.0	98.9
40	5	59.3	79.6	94.4	98.5	99.9	69.8	80.1	89.7	94.9	99.0
	10	69.3	91.4	99.3	99.9	100.0	70.1	79.9	89.9	95.0	98.9

In many other cases, the actual cycle service level is much lower than expected. Especially when the lead time coefficient of variation and the cycle service are low ($CV_L < 25\%$). Generally, the shorter the lead time variation, the bigger the spread is between the discrete values in the simulation and the continuity assumption of our model, resulting in a discrepancy between the expected service level and the observed level.

To summarize, we have to conclude that the stochastic lead time model is not robust and will only achieve the expected results in a few cases. If you face random lead times, you should rely on policy optimization via simulation rather than models. We will do this in Chapter 13, "Simulation Optimization."

We will see later in Chapter 7, "Fill Rate," (specifically in Section 7.5.1), that our stochastic lead time model gives more appropriate results when measuring the fill rate rather than the cycle service level.

Lead Time Independence

Just as for the demand, our model assumes that the lead times of different orders are independent from each other. Again, in practice, this is not true. If a supplier is late to deliver an order one week, it is likely to be late the next week as well—maybe it is currently overloaded.

Our model also assumes—implicitly—that two orders can cross each other. This means that a first order O_1 could be delivered after a second order O_2 (that was ordered afterward). In practice these cases are rather exceptional: orders should be delivered in the sequence they were ordered. This limitation has been discussed since the 60s at least,[5] but modeling mathematically this sequencing results in complex models.

DIY

In order to prevent orders from crossing each other in the simulation, you can define the actual lead time `actual_L` of each order as the minimum between a new random value and any current order plus one:

```
actual_L = int(round(max(np.random.normal(L,L_std),0),0))
try:
    max_L = int(max(np.argwhere(transit[t]>0)))
except:
    max_L = 0
actual_L = max(actual_L,max_L)
```

We use Python exception handlers `try` and `except` to compute `max_L` for cases where there is no in-transit inventory (i. e., there is currently no order in the pipeline).[a]

———

a See www.w3schools.com/python/python_try_except.asp for more details.

Normality

In practice, the lead time probability distribution is not normal but often looks like a right-curved bell: the supplier is most of the time on-time, only a few times late and nearly never early.

We have to refine our model further. We will discuss skewed probability functions in Chapter 9, "Beyond Normality," and discrete optimization with custom distributions in Part IV, "Discrete Inventory Optimization."

———

5 Hadley and Whitin (1963).

6.5 Recap

We have created a unified safety stock model that protects us against two different sources of variation:

1. The demand over the lead times variation.
2. The demand variation over the average lead time.

We compute the safety stock as:

$$S_s = z_\alpha \sqrt{(\mu_L + R)\sigma_d^2 + \sigma_L^2 \mu_d^2} \quad \text{(see eq. 6.5 in Section 6.3.3)}$$

where

$\mu_L + R$ are the average lead time and the review period (if any)
σ_d is the demand standard deviation
μ_d is the average demand
σ_L is the lead time standard deviation
z_α is the service level factor

We now have the ability to create two much stronger inventory policies which can deal with a variable lead time, a review period (if any) and a stochastic demand.

	Reorder point (s, Q)		Review Period (R, S)
How much?	Order Quantity $\quad Q = \sqrt{\frac{2kD}{h}}$		Up-to level $\quad S = d_L + d_R + S_s$
When?	Reorder point $\quad s = d_L + S_s$		Review period $\quad R = 2^k T_B$
Safety	$S_s = z_\alpha \sqrt{\mu_L \sigma_d^2 + \mu_d^2 \sigma_L^2}$		$S_s = z_\alpha \sqrt{(\mu_L + R)\sigma_d^2 + \mu_d^2 \sigma_L^2}$
Cycle	$C_s = \frac{1}{2}Q$		$C_s = \frac{1}{2}d_R$
In-transit		$I_s = d_L$	
Cycle Service Level		$\alpha = \Phi(z_\alpha)$	

This model still makes some strong assumptions about the demand and the lead time:

–   They are both continuous and normally distributed.
–   The demand is independently distributed in each period and independent from the lead time.
–   Excess demand is backordered.
–   Different orders can cross each other.

Part III: **Advanced Stochastic Models**

7 Fill Rate

7.1 Service Level Definition

Until now we have used the **cycle** service level α as the metric to measure the service level. Remember that the cycle service level is the expected probability that during an order cycle there is no stock-out. For example, for a supply chain with a weekly order cycle, a cycle service level of 95% means that you will have enough stock to fulfill your demand 19 weeks out of 20.[1]

But the cycle service level does not say how much in backorders (or lost sales) you can expect during a cycle. In the example above, you know you can expect to run out-of-stock once every 20 weeks, but you do not know **how much excess demand** you will face due to lack of stock. Remember, the excess demand is the demand that cannot be served directly from the on-hand inventory. Actually, you might be able to fulfill 99% of the demand on-time through the year, achieving a very high fill rate even if your cycle service level is lower. The **fill rate β** is defined as the expected part of the demand you will be able to serve directly from your inventory (it is also often called *volume* fill rate in order to avoid any confusion with the *order* fill rate). Mathematically, we compute it as 1 minus the expected excess demand divided by the expected total demand over an order cycle.

$$\beta = 1 - \frac{\text{excess demand (over the order cycle)}}{\text{demand (over the order cycle)}}$$

We can also express the fill rate based on the number of **units short** noted U_s:

$$\beta = 1 - \frac{U_s}{d_c}$$

Where d_c is the **expected demand over an order cycle** (remember, an order cycle is the period between two consecutive orders), it is computed based on the inventory policy:

$$d_c = \begin{cases} Q & \text{if } (s, Q) \\ d_R & \text{if } (R, S) \end{cases}$$

---

[1] Note that this is even different than a metric such as "number of days without stocking out" because here we are measuring the probability to be out-of-stock during one week. The stock-out could happen on Friday or on Wednesday, it still counts as one stocking out event.

https://doi.org/10.1515/9783110673944-007

> **Unit short (U_s)**
>
> Number of units missed to be able to fulfill the demand entirely. Equal to the excess demand, it is the difference between the demand and the inventory available to serve it. Units short will result either in lost sales (the excess demand is lost) or in backorders (the excess demand is backordered).

As you can see in Figure 7.1, the expected fill rate is actually higher than the cycle service level (assuming a stationary normal demand)—especially for low service levels. In the example shown in Figure 7.1 (and the following Example box), when $\alpha = 21\%$, $\beta = 77\%$. That's a difference of 56 points!

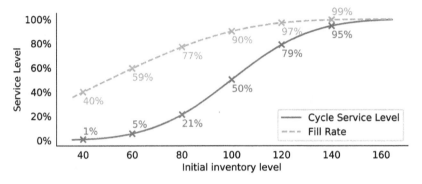

Figure 7.1: Service levels for $d_c = 100$ and $\sigma_x = 25$.

> **Example**
>
> You expect a (normally distributed) demand of 100 pieces over the next week. You decide to store 100 pieces in advance. By doing so, you can expect that there is one chance out of two that you won't have enough inventory to fulfill all the demand (i. e., cycle service level expected to be 50%). But on the other hand, you can also expect that most of the demand will be served directly from the inventory (i. e., fill rate expected to be around 90%). For example, if the demand is 110 units, you can serve the first 100 units (91% of the demand) from the stock on-hand, achieving a fill rate of 91%; but you failed to entirely fulfill the cycle demand resulting in a cycle service level of 0%.

As a metric for a supply chain service level, the fill rate often makes more sense than the cycle service level. Especially when the order cycles are long (we will discuss this in Section 7.4). On the other hand, the fill rate is more difficult to record than the cycle service level:

- In order to compute the cycle service level, you just have to see if your stock goes to zero during an order cycle (assuming that some demand is unmet as soon as the item is out-of-stock, which is not always true).
- In order to properly record the fill rate, you need to be able to **record the excess demand**.
  - If the excess demand is **backordered** (i. e., the excess demand is kept in a backlog until inventory is available) this is easy since the total demand is known (as shown in Figure 7.3). This is usually the case in B2B.
  - If the excess demand is **lost**, measuring the fill rate can become difficult. This is usually the case in B2C. For example, a client who doesn't find a product on a shelf won't *always* mention it to the retailer.

7.1.1 Curse of Lost Sales

As shown in Figure 7.2, not being able to measure lost sales will result in a vicious circle. Because you can't measure the true demand, you will use the sales as a proxy and therefore will most likely under-evaluate the demand.[2] As you start to underestimate the demand in your forecast, you will produce or deploy fewer products resulting in a bigger part of lost sales (that is not measured), resulting in a lower forecast. And so on. A virtuous circle between demand and inventory can be achieved when all the demand is properly recorded as shown in Figure 7.3.

This effect is also called the "Spiral-down effect" in field of *revenue management*[3]—a discipline where it has been observed and analyzed.[4]

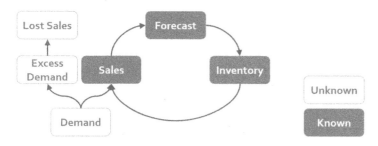

Figure 7.2: Lost sales vicious circle.

---

2 During each inventory cycle you risk missing part of the demand. Over the long term you will eventually undershoot the average demand estimation—since you missed some—resulting in a lower inventory target. Less inventory means lower service level, resulting in missing a greater part of the demand. And so on.

3 Revenue management is the field of management science that optimizes price and revenue for service industries such as hospitality and air traffic.

4 See Cooper et al. (2006).

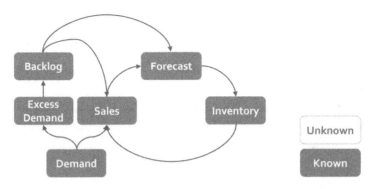

Figure 7.3: Backorders virtuous circle.

Measuring lost sales is unfortunately not possible for every business. Just think about a grocery store: the customers won't go to the cashier to mention they couldn't find the chocolate bar they wanted to buy. They'll simply buy another snack instead.

> **Important Point**
>
> Many ERP allow sales representatives to record the initial (unconstrained) client demand thanks to the order initial "requested delivery date" and "order quantity." This should then be used as the demand rather than the actual sales. The difference between the initial order quantity and the final sales quantity is then the amount of lost sales.

Unconstraining the Demand

Instead of *recording* the lost sales, you can try to *estimate* them. This is called *unconstraining* the demand. One simple—but not perfect—way to do this is to use a smart forecast model.[5] When you are out-of-stock during a certain period, instead of using the sales as a proxy for the demand, you can estimate the demand as the initial forecast for this period. Your forecast is then used as a proxy for the lost sales—it is actually your best guess. In other words, when you are out-of-stock, your forecast is a better estimation of the demand than the actual sales. Of course, in order to apply this technique, you will have to record your inventory level over time to track out-of-stocks.

---

5 See Nahmias (1994) for a discussion about unconstraining normal demand in a lost sales environment.

You are the owner of a tea shop. You usually sell 10 bags per day of your best-selling mint tea. So you forecast a demand of 10 bags per day.

Due to your supplier delay, you have been out-of-stock for five days. You can easily assume that you lost a demand for 50 bags.

Always discuss how the lost sales are recorded when you start an inventory or forecast model.

7.2 Expected Unit Shorts

7.2.1 Normal Loss Function

Let's model the expected fill rate that we are looking for (see Figure 7.4, our current supply chain model). The question we ask ourselves is the following: *"If I have ι pieces at the beginning of the risk-period,[6] what is the expected amount of excess demand (or units short) I am likely to face?"*

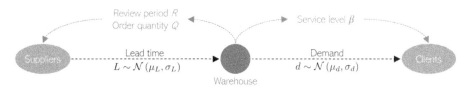

Review period R
Order quantity Q

Service level β

Suppliers

Lead time
$L \sim \mathcal{N}(\mu_L, \sigma_L)$

Demand
$d \sim \mathcal{N}(\mu_d, \sigma_d)$

Clients

Warehouse

Figure 7.4: Supply chain model.

Before looking at an equation, let's try to express in plain English how to compute the **expected amount of units short over the risk-period**. This is the same as the **expected excess demand** over this risk-period.

The expected excess demand (or number of units short) over the risk-period is the sum of:

---

6 Risk-period (x_τ): maximum amount of time you need to wait to receive an order (from your supplier). During this period your inventory is at risk of being depleted. $x_\tau = R + L$ in an (R, S) policy and $x_\tau = L$ in an (s, Q) policy. See Section 5.1.1.

- Each possible value of the demand d, that is higher than the initial inventory level ι,
- times the probability $f(d)$ of the demand d to materialize,
- times the number of units short $d - \iota$ (i. e., the difference between the demand d and the inventory ι).

As we model the demand as a continuous distribution function *"over each value of the demand d that is higher than inventory level ι,"* is translated into an integration over d from $d = \iota$ to $d = \infty$, so that we obtain this elegant formulation:

$$U_S = \mathcal{L}(\iota) = \int_{d=\iota}^{\infty} (d - \iota) f(d) \, dd$$

where $\mathcal{L}(\iota)$ is the **demand loss function** evaluated at ι, and $f(d)$ is the *demand probability density function*[7] of d (over the risk-period). For the sake of clarity, we simplify the notation, by using $f(d)$ instead of $f_{Dx}(d)$.

If we assume $d \sim \mathcal{N}(\mu_x, \sigma_x^2)$ over the risk-period, we have:

$$U_S = \mathcal{L}_{\mathcal{N}}(\iota; \mu_x, \sigma_x) = \int_{d=\iota}^{\infty} (d - \iota) \cdot f(d) \, dd$$

$$= \int_{d=\iota}^{\infty} d \cdot f(d) \, dd - \iota \int_{d=\iota}^{\infty} f(d) \, dd$$

$$= \sigma_x^2 f(\iota) + \mu_x (1 - F(\iota)) - \iota (1 - F(\iota))$$

$$\mathcal{L}_{\mathcal{N}}(\iota; \mu_x, \sigma_x) = \sigma_x^2 f(\iota) + (\mu_x - \iota)(1 - F(\iota))$$

where $f(d)$ and $F(d)$ are respectively the PDF and CDF of the demand d over the risk-period (assumed to be normally distributed).

The proof is shown in Appendix B.2. Note that this solution to the loss function only applies to a **normal** distribution (we call $\mathcal{L}_{\mathcal{N}}(\iota; \mu, \sigma)$ the normal loss function).

DIY

Excel You can compute the expected loss in Excel with the formula:

`=std^2*NORM.DIST(inv,mu,std,FALSE)+(mu-inv)*(1-NORM.DIST(inv,mu,std,TRUE))`

Python You can also easily compute the expected loss in Python. Let's create our own function `normal_loss(inv,mu,std)` that will return the expected

---

7 See Section 4.2.1 for a refresher about probability density functions.

number of units short based on an initial inventory level `inv` and a normal demand defined by `mu` and `std`.

```
def normal_loss(inv,mu,std):
    return std**2*norm.pdf(inv, mu, std) + (mu - inv)*(1-norm.cdf
        (inv, mu, std))
```

We can then test it.

```
inv = 120
mu = 100
std = 50
print(normal_loss(inv,mu,std))
>> 11.52
```

This means that if we start a period with an inventory of 120 pieces and have a demand $\sim \mathcal{N}(100, 50^2)$, we can expect the demand to be 11.52 pieces higher than our inventory.

7.2.2 Standard Normal Loss Function

Usually, academics prefer to use the **standard normal loss function $\mathcal{L}_N(x)$**:

$$\mathcal{L}_N(x) = \mathcal{L}_{\mathcal{N}}(x; 0, 1)$$
$$= \sigma^2 f(x) + (\mu - x)(1 - F(x))$$
$$= 1^2 \varphi(x) + (0 - x)(1 - \Phi(x))$$
$$\mathcal{L}_N(x) = \varphi(x) - x(1 - \Phi(x))$$

You can use the standard normal loss function $\mathcal{L}_N(x)$ to compute the expected units short of any normal distribution. It can be shown that:

$$\mathcal{L}_{\mathcal{N}}(x; \mu, \sigma) = \sigma \cdot \mathcal{L}_N\left(\frac{x - \mu}{\sigma}\right) \tag{7.1}$$

DIY

Excel You can compute the standard normal loss function in Excel with
`=NORM.S.DIST(x,FALSE)-x*(1-NORM.S.DIST(x,TRUE))`

Python We can also compute the standard normal loss function in Python. Let's create another custom `normal_loss_standard(x)` function.

```
def normal_loss_standard(x):
    return norm.pdf(x) - x*(1-norm.cdf(x))
```

Let's use our two functions `normal_loss_standard(x)` and `normal_loss(inv, mu, std)` to test the relationship from eq. 7.1.

```
inv = 120
mu = 100
std = 50
print(normal_loss(inv,mu,std))
>> 11.52
print(std*normal_loss_standard((inv-mu)/std))
>> 11.52
```

It's a match!

7.3 Fill Rate Model

7.3.1 Expected Fill Rate

We can now compute the expected number of units short U_s over the risk-period based on the initial on-hand inventory level ι.

$$U_s = \mathcal{L}_{\mathcal{N}} \left(\iota; \mu_x, \sigma_x \right)$$

where (see Table 7.1 for the exact expressions):
- μ_x is the demand during the risk-period
- σ_x is the demand deviation during the risk-period
- ι is the inventory at the beginning of the risk-period

Table 7.1: d_c, μ_x, σ_x and ι for (R, S) and (s, Q) policies.

Policy	d_c	μ_x	σ_x	ι
(s, Q)	Q	dL	$\sqrt{L\sigma_d^2 + \sigma_L^2 \mu_d^2}$	s
(R, S)	dR	$d(R + L)$	$\sqrt{(R + L)\sigma_d^2 + \sigma_L^2 \mu_d^2}$	S

We are actually interested in determining the expected amount of units short **over an order cycle** (an order cycle is the period between two consecutive supply orders).

During an order cycle, we assume we only witness units short during the risk-period.[8] It follows that the expected number of units short over the risk-period is the same as the expected number of units short over the full order cycle.

We can then compute the **expected fill rate over an order cycle** as:

$$\beta = 1 - \frac{U_s}{d_c} = 1 - \frac{\mathcal{L}_{\mathcal{N}}(\iota; \mu_x, \sigma_x)}{d_c}$$

where d_c is the expected demand during an order cycle.

Using eq. 7.1 (see Section 7.2.2) we can compute the fill rate based on the standard normal loss function.

$$U_s = \mathcal{L}_{\mathcal{N}}(\iota; \mu_x, \sigma_x) = \sigma_x \mathcal{L}_N \left(\frac{\iota - \mu_x}{\sigma_x} \right)$$

$$\beta = 1 - \frac{U_s}{d_c} = 1 - \frac{\sigma_x}{d_c} \mathcal{L}_N \left(\frac{\iota - \mu_x}{\sigma_x} \right)$$

This answers the question, *"If I have ι pieces at the beginning of the risk-period, what is the expected amount of excess demand (or units short) I am likely to face?"*

Example

You are in charge of a bakery next to a school. You sell sandwiches through the week and buy the ingredients during the weekend. The flour consumption varies around 250 kg per week with a deviation of 30 kg. Each weekend you buy enough flour in order to have 270 kg in stock at the beginning of the week. What fill rate can you expect?

Let's first compute the expected lost sales in Python, by using the functions defined above:

```
inv, x_mu, x_std = 270, 250, 30
lost = normal_loss_standard((inv-x_mu)/x_std)*x_std
print(lost)
>> 4.53
```

We obtain an expected amount of 4.53 kg short of flour each week. That's a fill rate of

$$\beta = 1 - \frac{\text{units short}}{\text{cycle demand}} = 1 - \frac{4.53}{250} = 98\%$$

---

8 This can be confusing but, in a periodic review policy, the risk-period $x_\tau = R + L$ is longer than the order cycle R. In a continuous review policy, we have $x_\tau = L$ which can be shorter or longer than the order cycle which is Q/D long. See Chapter 5, "Inventory Policies."

Safety Stocks

Let's imagine that you have a certain amount of safety stock S_s. What is the service level you can expect? We defined ι as *"the available quantity at the beginning of the risk-period,"* which is the sum of the expected demand over the risk-period μ_x and the safety stock S_s. We then have,

$$\iota = \mu_x + S_s$$

$$\beta = 1 - \frac{\sigma_x}{d_c} \mathcal{L}_N \left(\frac{\iota - \mu_x}{\sigma_x} \right)$$

$$= 1 - \frac{\sigma_x}{d_c} \mathcal{L}_N \left(\frac{(\mu_x + S_s) - \mu_x}{\sigma_x} \right)$$

$$= 1 - \frac{\sigma_x}{d_c} \mathcal{L}_N \left(\frac{S_s}{\sigma_x} \right)$$

So we have this relationship between the fill rate β and the amount of safety stock S_s:

$$\beta = 1 - \frac{\sigma_x}{d_c} \mathcal{L}_N \left(\frac{S_s}{\sigma_x} \right)$$

Remember that, by definition (see Section 4.2.4), the service level factor z is computed as:

$$z = \frac{S_s}{\sigma_x} = \frac{\iota - \mu_x}{\sigma_x}$$

Meaning that we can also compute the expected fill rate based on the service level factor:

$$\beta = 1 - \frac{\sigma_x}{d_c} \mathcal{L}_N(z)$$

Important Point

This model still assumes that the excess demand is backordered and not lost. Just as for the model created in Part II, "Stochastic Supply Chains." See Nahmias (1979), Silver et al. (2016), Axsäter (2015) for detailed lost sales models.

Example

Let's go back to our bakery example. We computed that we could expect a fill rate of 98% with our safety stock of 20 kg. What would then be the cycle service level?

First, we have to compute the service level factor z:

$$z = \frac{S_s}{\sigma_x} = \frac{l - \mu_x}{\sigma_x} = \frac{270 - 250}{30} = 0.66$$

We can then compute the expected cycle service level as $\alpha = \Phi(z)$. In Python, we can do this easily:

```
z = (inv - mu)/std
alpha = norm.cdf(z)
```

and we obtain $\alpha = 75\%$. That is rather low, even though we have a fill rate of 98%. It means we have a relatively high probability to be out-of-stock (25%) but the expected number of units short is low (2%). In other words, you will run out of flour one week out of 4 ($\alpha = 75\%$) but you will only miss (on average) 2% of the flour demand per week ($\beta = 98\%$).

Actually, the question is most often asked the other way around: *"If I want to get a fill rate of 95%, how much safety stock should I keep?"* We already answered a similar question with the cycle service level in Chapter 4, "Safety Stocks" (see Section 4.2.4). We had this relationship:

$$\text{Cycle service level} = \alpha \Leftrightarrow z_\alpha = \Phi^{-1}(\alpha)$$

We can do the same for the fill rate:

$$\text{Fill rate} = \beta = 1 - \frac{\sigma_x}{d_c} \mathcal{L}_N(z_\beta) \Leftrightarrow z_\beta = \mathcal{L}_N^{-1}\left(\frac{d_c(1 - \beta)}{\sigma_x}\right)$$

We want to achieve a fill rate β, and in order to do this we need to compute the service level factor z_β, based on the inverse of the normal loss function.

However, an issue remains. There is no mathematical formula to compute the inverse of the standard normal loss function. Should we then stop here? No, we have other tools at hand.

7.3.2 Inverse Loss Function

If we cannot compute the *exact* inverse standard normal loss function, we can nevertheless solve it by using either a solver or an approximation.

Solver

We can use a solver to minimize the difference between the desired number of units short and the expected number of units short.

The **desired** number of units short is simply derived from the fill rate β and the cycle demand d_c:

$$U_s = d_c(1 - \beta)$$

The **expected** number of units short based on z is:

$$U_s = \sigma_x \mathcal{L}_N(z)$$

Now, we want the expected and desired number of units short to be equal:

$$\sigma_x \mathcal{L}_N(z) = d_c(1 - \beta)$$

In other words, we have to find the value of z that minimizes the absolute difference between:

$$\mathcal{L}_N(z) \text{ and } \frac{d_c(1 - \beta)}{\sigma_x}$$

We express this mathematically as:

$$z = \arg \min_z \left[\left| \mathcal{L}_N(z) - \frac{d_c(1 - \beta)}{\sigma_x} \right| \right]$$

which means that z is the value that minimizes the absolute difference between $\mathcal{L}_N(z)$ and $d_c(1 - \beta)/\sigma_x$.

To compute this, we can use a solver (in Excel or Python).

DIY

Excel   You first need to activate Excel Solver.

Solver activation   Depending on your version of Excel, the process changes a bit, but it should be simple to do. Google will indicate the exact procedure for each version.

Usually you can do it by checking the `Solver` add-on box after following this path in starting an Excel window: `file/options/add-ins/excel add-ins`.

Once Excel Solver is activated, you have to define its objective as the absolute difference between the cell with the expected standard loss (cell `B5` in the example below) and the cell with the target (cell B6).

	A	B
1	d_c	100
2	x_std	50
3	beta	0,99
4		
5	Expected loss	=NORM.S.DIST(B9;FALSE)-B9*(1-NORM.S.DIST(B9;TRUE))
6	Target	=(1-B3)*B1/B2
7	absolute difference	=ABS(B5-B6)
8		
9	z	1,66303165816032

You can then use Solver with the objective of minimizing the difference between the expected loss and the target. In our example, we asked the solver to
minimize cell B7. The solver method should be set to GRG Nonlinear.

Python   Let's first define the standard target we want to get:

```
d_c, x_std, beta = 100, 50, 0.99
target = d_c*(1-beta)/x_std
```

We can then define a function f(x) that returns the difference between this
target and the standard normal loss function.

```
def normal_loss_standard(x):
    return norm.pdf(x) - x*(1-norm.cdf(x))
def f(x):
    return abs(normal_loss_standard(x) - target)
```

We can now use the function optimize.minimize_scalar from SciPy in order
to find the value that minimizes f(x).[a]

   minimize_scalar will return an object that contains—among other information—the value that minimizes the function.

   Be careful, the function minimize_scalar should take as a parameter a
function with a **single** numerical parameter. This is why we didn't provided
target as a parameter.

```
from scipy import optimize
result = optimize.minimize_scalar(f)
print(result)
>> fun: 3.771691292620005e-10
>> nfev: 28
```

```
>> nit: 23
>> success: True
>> x: 1.663
```

The value we are looking for is simply result.x:

```
z = result.x
```

---

a docs.scipy.org/doc/scipy/reference/generated/scipy.optimize.minimize_scalar.html

Approximation

In 2016 two researchers—Andrade and Sikorski—published a polynomial approximation to the inverse standard normal loss function.[9] This approximation works quite well and can be used to find z_β without using a solver. Nevertheless, it requires the evaluation of a 12th degree polynomial at the logarithm of the value we want to inverse. In other words, $\mathcal{L}_N^{-1}(x)$ is approximated as:

$$\mathcal{L}_N^{-1}(x) \approx a_0 + a_1 \log(x) + a_2 \log(x) + a_3 \log(x) + \dots + a_{12} \log(x) + \epsilon$$

Where the various coefficients a_0 to a_{12} are defined below.

DIY

Let's first define the coefficients given by Andrade and Sikorski.

```
coefficients = [ 4.41738119e-09, 1.79200966e-07, 3.01634229e-06,
        2.63537452e-05, 1.12381749e-04, 5.71289020e-06, -2.64198510
       e-03, -1.59986142e-02, -5.60399292e-02, -1.48968884e-01,
       -3.68776346e-01, -1.22551895e+00, -8.99375602e-01]
```

We can use np.polyval(coefficients,x) from NumPy to simply evaluate our polynomial at the value x.

```
def inverse_standard_loss(target):
    x = np.log(target)
    z = np.polyval(coefficients, x)
    return z
```

---

9 Andrade and Sikorski (2016).

We can then simply compute z:

```
d_c, x_std, beta = 100, 50, 0.99
target = d_c*(1-beta)/x_std
z = inverse_standard_loss(target)
print(z)
>> 1.663
```

The difference with the solver is usually lower than 0.01%.

Example

Let's consider again the bakery example where the weekly flour demand was assumed to follow $\mathcal{N}(250, 30^2)$. You decide to tackle the problem of ordering flour from another angle: how much flour should you buy during the weekend to only miss 2% of the demand during the following week?

Let's first compute the expected amount of flour short.

$$\beta = 0.98 \qquad U_s = (1 - \beta)d_c = (1 - 0.98) \cdot 250 = 5$$

We can then compute the standard target and use the function `inverse_standard_loss(target)` defined earlier.

```
d_c, x_std, beta = 250, 30, 0.98
target = d_c*(1-beta)/x_std
z = inverse_standard_loss(target)
print(z)
>> 0.61
```

We then have $z_\beta = 0.61$, this means that

$$S_s = z_\beta \cdot \sigma = 0.61 \cdot 30 = 18.3$$

You should keep a safety stock of 18.3 kg of flour on top of the expected weekly consumption of 250 kg (resulting in an initial inventory of 268.3 kg).

You do not feel fully reassured by this safety stock of 18.3 kg: you want to know the expected probability to run out-of-stock during a week.

Let's compute the cycle service level expected by our safety stock:

$$\alpha = \Phi(z)$$

We can compute this easily in Python: `alpha = norm.cdf(z)` and we obtain $\alpha = 0.73$. This means that we have a 27% probability of running out of flour each week. Again, we have a high probability of running out of flour (27%) by the end of week, despite the fact that the expected amount of flour short per week is low (2%).

7.4 Impact of Order Cycle Length

7.4.1 (R, S) Policy

The cycle service level is only linked to the safety stock. An increase of the review period (e. g., going from a weekly order to a monthly order) would always result in a lower cycle service level if the safety stock level is left constant. This is obvious: you face more volatility, so you need more protection.

But, this is no longer the case when using the fill rate. As we have seen, it has a very interesting property: it is impacted by both the cycle demand **and** the safety stock.

When Do We Take Risks?

When we have a simple inventory policy (as shown in Figure 7.5), we understand that the high-risk period is the one preceding the reception of an order. This is the time when the on-hand inventory is at its lowest point; this is when the risk of running out-of-stock is at its peak. In other words, it is when you are about to receive the order from your supplier, that your stock is at its lowest point: this is when you face the most risk to run out of stock.

As shown in Figure 7.6, if we make less frequent orders—but order more at once—we get a policy with less of these high-risk periods. This means that we are safe during

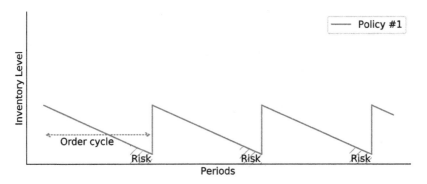

Figure 7.5: Policy with short review periods.

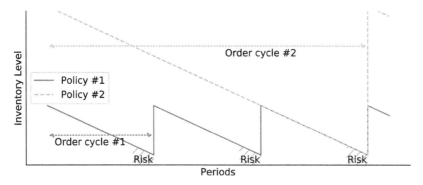

Figure 7.6: Policies comparison.

most of the order cycle since we have ample cycle stock left. It is only at the end of the order cycle that we are in a riskier situation.

For these long order cycles, the fill rate is guaranteed by the massive amount of cycle stock. The safety stock is only required to buffer the last period of the order cycle. On the other hand, the cycle service level is not guaranteed by the cycle stock; the only thing that matters is how likely the safety stock will be enough to resist the high-risk period at the end of the cycle.

> **Example**
>
> You buy food for your household once per month. By doing so, you have no risk of running out of food during the first 3 weeks of the month. But as you get closer to grocery shopping day (at the end of the month), the risk of running out of food gets higher.

Actually, if you analyze the fill rate and the cycle service level for varying review periods, *ceteris paribus*, you see that the fill rate virtually doesn't change whereas the cycle service level only decreases. As the order cycle gets longer, the difference between the fill rate and the cycle service level increases. Therefore using the cycle service level as a service level metric makes less sense. As you can see in Figure 7.7, the cycle service level can be around 60–70% for long cycles despite a fill rate of around 95%.

> **Important Point**
>
> Don't assume that you get service level for free—you do not: the average cycle stock is increasing as the review period length increases. So you have inventory—a lot of it actually, and you pay for it!—but the model is smart enough not to add safety stock on top of it.

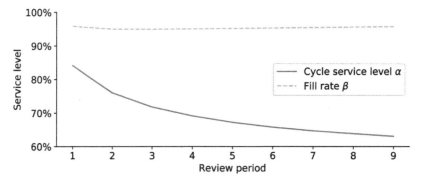

Figure 7.7: Service levels for $d \sim \mathcal{N}\left(100, 25^2\right)$ with 50 pieces of safety stock.

7.4.2 (s, Q) Policy

A similar effect arises with production batches. In an (s, Q) policy, if the production batch Q increases, the amount of safety stock can be decreased to achieve a similar fill rate.

7.4.3 Mathematical Analysis

Now that we understand the business intuition behind the fill rate and its relation to cycle stocks, we can look at the mathematics involved. Let's imagine that we have a fixed amount of safety stock S_s. These are the service level metrics to expect:

$$\alpha = \Phi^{-1}\left(\frac{S_s}{\sigma_x}\right) \qquad \beta = 1 - \frac{\sigma_x}{d_c}\mathcal{L}_N^{-1}\left(\frac{S_s}{\sigma_x}\right)$$

(R, S) Policy
We have

$$d_c = d \cdot R \qquad \sigma_x = \sqrt{(R + L)\sigma_d^2 + d^2\sigma_L^2}$$

If we increase R,
- α will decrease as σ_x increases and S_s stays constant.
- β will change, but the direction is not straightforward:
  1. $\frac{\sigma_x}{d_c}$ should decrease (approximately) proportionally to $\sqrt{R}$ as
     σ_x will increase at worst by $\sqrt{R}$ (if L is deterministic).
     d_c will increase proportionally to R.
  2. $\mathcal{L}_N^{-1}(S_s/\sigma_x)$ will increase as S_s is constant and σ_x increases.

This means that the relationship between the fill rate β and R can't be easily computed and can go in both directions; on the other hand, an increase in R can only result in a decrease of α.

(s, Q) Policy

We have

$$d_c = Q \qquad \sigma_x = \sqrt{L\sigma_d^2 + d^2\sigma_L^2}$$

If we increase Q,

- α is not impacted.
- β **increases** as the expected lost sales per cycle stays constant but the cycle gets longer.

Increasing the order quantity (or the batch size) will result in a higher fill rate. Again, this extra service level doesn't come for free: you also get a higher amount of cycle stock as $C_s = Q/2$.

Example

Let's go back to our bakery shop example. We defined a good inventory policy for the flour and now we want to look at sugar. It does not deteriorate over time, so we can easily buy it in bulk. Let's compare two policies: either buying enough sugar each week for the week to come, or buying it per month.

The weekly sugar consumption is around 25 kg with a deviation of 5 kg and can be assumed to be normal. You want to have a fill rate of 99%. Let's assume that there is no supply lead time (you can buy the sugar over the weekend).

With a **weekly** replenishment, you have:

$$d_c = d \cdot R = 25 \qquad \sigma_x = 5$$

Let's start from the β definition.

$$\beta = 1 - \frac{\sigma_x}{d_c} \mathcal{L}_N\left(\frac{S_s}{\sigma_x}\right)$$

We then have,

$$S_s = \sigma_x \mathcal{L}_N^{-1}\left(\frac{d_c(1 - \beta)}{\sigma_x}\right) = 5 \cdot \mathcal{L}_N^{-1}\left(\frac{25(1 - 0.99)}{5}\right) = 5 \cdot \mathcal{L}_N^{-1}(0.05)$$

We compute $\mathcal{L}_N^{-1}(0.05)$ easily in Python:

```
inverse_standard_loss(0.05)
>> 1.256
```

We obtain a safety stock of around 6.28 kg (= 1.256 · 5), so that our policy could be set as $(R = 1, S = 31.28)$ where $S = S_s + d_R$.

Let's imagine now a policy where we buy our sugar **once every 4 weeks** (more or less once per month). We now have:

$$d_c = d \cdot R = 100 \qquad \sigma_x = 5\sqrt{R} = 10$$

Therefore,

$$S_s = \sigma_x \mathcal{L}_N^{-1}\left(\frac{d_c(1 - \beta)}{\sigma_x}\right) = 10 \cdot \mathcal{L}_N^{-1}\left(\frac{100(1 - 0.99)}{10}\right) = 10 \cdot \mathcal{L}_N^{-1}(0.1)$$

Again we evaluate this in Python:

```
inverse_standard_loss(0.1)
>> 0.90
```

So that $S_s = 10 \cdot 0.9 = 9$ kg. We then have an (R, S) policy with $R = 4$ and $S = S_s + d_R = 109$.

7.5 Simulation

As shown in Table 7.2, our model works remarkably well for policies with a demand coefficient of variation $(CV_d = \sigma_d/\mu_d)$ below 50%.

Table 7.2: Simulated cycle service level (%) over 1,000,000 periods for an (R, S) policy with $R = 4$.

	L	CV_d	CV_x	Theoretical fill rate (%)				
				70	80	90	95	99
	1	.25	.11	69.9	80.0	90.0	95.0	99.0
$d \sim \mathcal{N}(100, 25^2)$	4	.25	.09	69.9	79.9	90.0	95.0	99.0
	10	.25	.07	70.0	80.0	90.0	95.0	99.0
	1	.50	.22	69.9	79.9	90.0	95.0	99.0
$d \sim \mathcal{N}(100, 50^2)$	4	.50	.18	69.7	79.8	89.9	95.0	99.0
	10	.50	.13	69.7	79.7	89.8	94.9	99.0
	1	1.0	.45	69.0	79.4	89.9	95.0	99.0
$d \sim \mathcal{N}(100, 100^2)$	4	1.0	.35	67.6	78.2	89.0	94.6	99.0
	10	1.0	.27	66.2	76.8	88.0	94.0	98.8

Negative Demand

As CV_d grows, so does the spread between the theoretical model and the simulation. This is due to the fact that our simulation forbids negative demand (as discussed in Section 5.3.2, "Negative Demand?"). We will solve this limitation by using a strictly positive demand distribution in Chapter 9, "Beyond Normality."

7.5.1 Random Lead Times

As we saw in Section 6.4, random lead times resulted in rather different actual cycle service levels compared to our theoretical expectations. This is actually not surprising because the length of an order cycle depends on the lead time (see Section 4.1). As you can see in Table 7.3, the simulated fill rates are much closer to the theoretical targets. This is reassuring because it means that our stochastic lead time model from Chapter 6 gives usable results and can therefore be used.

Table 7.3: Simulated cycle service level (%) over 1,000,000 periods for an (R, S) policy with $R = 4$.

	μ_L	σ_L	CV_d	CV_x	Theoretical fill rate (%)				
					70	80	90	95	99
	4	1	.25	.15	69.4	79.2	89.1	94.1	98.4
	4	2	.25	.27	67.5	77.5	87.7	92.9	97.7
$d \sim \mathcal{N}(100, 25^2)$	10	1	.25	.10	69.3	79.0	89.1	94.2	98.5
	10	2	.25	.16	67.9	77.6	87.7	93.0	97.8
	10	5	.25	.36	81.0	88.5	95.4	98.0	99.7
	4	1	.50	.22	69.5	79.1	89.1	94.1	98.4
	4	2	.50	.31	67.9	77.5	87.4	92.7	97.7
$d \sim \mathcal{N}(100, 50^2)$	10	1	.50	.15	69.9	79.4	89.2	94.3	98.6
	10	2	.50	.20	68.6	77.9	87.7	93.1	97.9
	10	5	.50	.38	79.8	87.4	94.5	97.6	99.6
	4	1	1	.38	67.8	77.7	88.2	93.7	98.5
	4	2	1	.43	66.2	75.6	86.2	92.0	97.5
$d \sim \mathcal{N}(100, 100^2)$	10	1	1	.28	66.6	76.6	87.6	93.4	98.5
	10	2	1	.30	65.5	75.0	85.7	92.0	97.6
	10	5	1	.45	74.4	82.4	91.1	95.4	98.9

DIY

We will use the same simulation loop as in Chapter 5 (see specifically Section 5.3.2). We use the function `inverse_standard_loss(target)` as defined in Section 7.3.2 to compute z.

```
beta = 0.95
d_c = d_mu * R
```

```
target = d_c*(1-beta)/x_std
z = inverse_standard_loss(target)
alpha = norm.cdf(z)
```

In order to record the fill rate, we will have to count the number of units short per period. We will record them in the array unit_shorts[t] (remember, time is the number of timesteps in our simulation).

```
unit_shorts = np.zeros(time,dtype=int)
```

We need, at each period, to compute the available stock. Remember, hand can be negative (it is then a backlog) and the transit inventory transit first serves the backlog before being available for new sales. We then have,

$$\text{available stock} = \max (0, \text{on hand} + \text{received orders (from supplier)})$$
$$= \max(0,\text{hand[t-1]} + \text{transit[t-1,0]})$$

To compute the period backorder unit_shorts[t] we need to compare the available stock to the period demand d[t].

$$\text{units short} = \max (0, \text{demand} - \text{available stock})$$

We then have this simulation loop:

```
for t in range(1,time):
    if transit[t-1,0]>0:
        stockout_cycle.append(stockout_period[t-1])
        unit_shorts[t] = max(0,d[t] - max(0,hand[t-1] + transit[t
            -1,0]))
    hand[t] = hand[t-1] - d[t] + transit[t-1,0]
    stockout_period[t] = hand[t] < 0
    transit[t,:-1] = transit[t-1,1:]
    if t%R==0:
        actual_L = int(round(max(np.random.normal(L,L_std),0),0))
        net = hand[t] + transit[t].sum()
        transit[t,actual_L] = S - net
```

We can then compute the fill rate:

```
fill_rate = 1-unit_shorts.sum()/sum(d)
print('Fill Rate:',round(fill_rate*100,1))
```

7.6 Recap

The fill rate service level is defined as the expected amount of demand that will be served from the on-hand inventory directly. The fill rate is impacted by the cycle stock as well as by the safety stock; whereas the cycle service level was only impacted by the safety stock.

We have developed mathematical tools to compute how much safety stock we need in order to achieve a certain fill rate, therefore we can update our policies:

	Reorder point (s, Q)	Review Period (R, S)
How much?	Order Quantity $\quad Q = \sqrt{\frac{2kD}{h}}$	Up-to level $\quad S = d_L + d_R + S_s$
When?	Reorder point $\quad s = d_L + S_s$	Review period $\quad R = 2^k T_B$
Cycle demand	$d_c = Q$	$d_c = d_R$
Cycle stock	$C_s = \frac{d_c}{2}$	
In-transit stock	$I_s = d_L$	
Risk-period	$\sigma_x = \sqrt{L\sigma_d^2 + \mu_d^2\sigma_L^2}$ $\quad\quad \mu_x = dL$	$\sigma_x = \sqrt{(R+L)\sigma_d^2 + \mu_d^2\sigma_L^2}$ $\quad\quad \mu_x = d(R+L)$
Safety stock	$S_s = z\sigma_x$	
Units short	$U_s = (1 - \beta)d_c = \mathcal{L}_{\mathcal{N}}(1; \mu_x, \sigma_x) = \sigma_x \mathcal{L}_N(S_s/\sigma_x) = \sigma_x \mathcal{L}_N(z)$	
Service level factor	$z_\alpha = \Phi^{-1}(\alpha)$ $z_\beta = \mathcal{L}_N^{-1}\left(\dfrac{d_c(1-\beta)}{\sigma_x}\right)$	
Service level	$\alpha = \Phi(z) = \Phi\left(\dfrac{S_s}{\sigma_x}\right)$ $\beta = 1 - \dfrac{\mathcal{L}_{\mathcal{N}}(1; \mu_x, \sigma_x)}{d_c} = 1 - \dfrac{\sigma_x}{d_c}\mathcal{L}_N\left(\dfrac{S_s}{\sigma_x}\right) = 1 - \dfrac{\sigma_x}{d_c}\mathcal{L}_N(z)$	

8 Cost and Service Level Optimization

Pecunia Nervus Belli – Money is the soul of war.

Ancient Roman quote

We discussed how much stock we need to achieve a desired service level in Chapter 4 through 7. We implicitly assumed that we had a good reason to desire this specific service level. Supply chain managers often will aim for a 95% or 99% "service level" (it is not always clear if they mean cycle service level or fill rate). But are these values optimal? Should we aim for 80% or for 99.5%? In order to answer this question, we will have to look at the total cost of our inventory policies... and minimize it.

Service level is merely used as a **mean** to reach the real **goal: profit**.

8.1 Profits and Losses

Let's start our profit maximization (or cost minimization[1]) journey with a general expression of the profits as below:

Profits = Sales − Purchasing costs − Holding costs − Transactions costs

− Backorders costs

Our profits are basically our sales incomes minus the purchasing,[2] holding, transaction and backorder costs. So that, over a period (a week, month, year, review period...), we have:

$$\text{Profits} = (p-c)\cdot\text{Demand} - h\cdot(\text{On-hand}+\text{In-transit}) - k\cdot\text{Transactions} - b\cdot\text{Backorders}$$

where,
p is the selling price per unit
c is the purchasing (or production) cost per unit
h is the holding cost per period per unit
k is the fixed cost of a single transaction
b is the cost of backlogging a unit

---

1 Technically, profit maximization and cost minimization are equivalent *only if* the opportunity costs are included in the cost minimization model. The intuition is the following: you could easily achieve 0 costs by having no inventory at all, but you would miss all the potential profits. For the sake of simplicity, we will often go from profit maximization to cost minimization.
2 Accountants often report the purchasing costs under the acronym COGS (cost of goods sold).

https://doi.org/10.1515/9783110673944-008

Let's review this expression in detail:

Demand We assume that all the excess demand is backlogged (i. e., excess demand does not result in lost sales but in backorders) so that the sales over a period are equal to the demand over this period. The profits resulting from the sales are then simply the period demand d multiplied by the margin $p - c$ (selling price p minus the purchasing cost c).

On-hand inventory We assume the (expected) average stock on-hand during a period to be the safety stock S_s plus the cycle stock C_s (see Table 8.1 for a recap, or Chapter 5, "Inventory Policies," for a detailed discussion about S_s and C_s).

In-transit inventory On top of this, the in-transit inventory I_s is also sometimes incurring holding costs (see Section 3.1 for more details). This is the case when, for example, the supply source is internal rather than an external supplier. Remember, the inventory in-transit is the amount of inventory that is shipped by the supplier but not yet received, and $I_s = dL$ (see eq. 3.4 in Section 3.2).

Transactions The average transaction costs per period are equal to k (the cost of one transaction) times the number of transactions during the period.

Backorders The expected costs due to backorders are the unit backorder cost b times the expected number of units short over the period.

Remember, the unit backorder cost b represents all the costs related to putting one item in the backlog. These costs can be penalties or loss of goodwill (see Section 2.1.3).

> **Going Further**
>
> A subtle assumption here is that b is the cost to *incur one backorder*. This is slightly different than the cost to *carry one unit of backorder over one period*. We assume here that we "pay" a penalty only once per backorder, no matter how long it stays in the backlog.
>
> See Axsäter (2015) for a cost per backorder per unit of time for an (s, Q) policy.

Table 8.1: Stock levels.

		(s, Q)		(R, S)
Safety stock	S_s		$z\,\sigma_x$	
Cycle stock	C_s	$Q/2$		$dR/2$
In-transit stock	I_s		dL	
Backorders	U_s		$\sigma_x \mathcal{L}_N(z)$	
demand deviation over the Risk-period	σ_x	$\sqrt{L\sigma_d^2 + \mu_d^2\sigma_L^2}$		$\sqrt{(R+L)\sigma_d^2 + \mu_d^2\sigma_L^2}$

For the sake of simplicity, we will look at the (inventory) costs rather than the profits (leaving aside sales and purchasing costs), and we will leave the in-transit inventory aside (assuming we do not incur holding costs for it). As shown in Figure 8.1, we then have:[3]

$$\textbf{Costs} = h \cdot \textbf{On-hand} + k \cdot \textbf{Transactions} + b \cdot \textbf{Backorders} \tag{8.1}$$

We will also focus on normally distributed demand in this chapter (you can find a general proof in Appendix B.4).

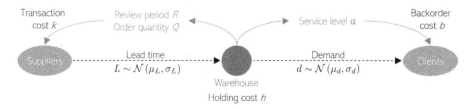

Figure 8.1: Supply chain model.

Let's now minimize the inventory costs for both the (R, S) and the (s, Q) policies.

8.2 (R, S) Policy

8.2.1 Expected On-Hand Inventory

A major contributor to our inventory costs are the holding costs. In order to compute these we have to know how much on-hand inventory we expect to have in stock. With high service levels ($\beta > 0.95\%$), we can easily stick to the assumption we made in Section 5.2 about expected on-hand inventory. Remember, as shown in Figure 8.2, we assumed that the stock on-hand varies (linearly) between:
- $d_c + S_s$ when we just received an order. That is, the safety stock S_s plus the expected demand over the order cycle $d_c = dR$.
- S_s when we are just about to receive an order (we only have the safety stock S_s left).

Our on-hand inventory varies then between $d_c + S_s$ and S_s so that the expected **average** on-hand inventory is (see Section 5.2.1 for a refresher about on-hand inventory):

$$\text{(average) On-hand} = C_s + S_s = \frac{d_c}{2} + S_s = \frac{dR}{2} + S_s$$

---

3 We don't need to include any opportunity cost here because we assume that all excess demand will result in backorders (and not in lost sales).

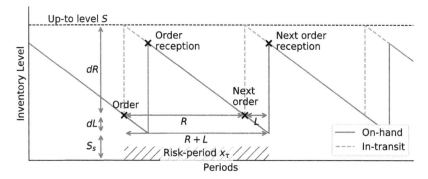

Figure 8.2: Stock level for an (R, S) policy.

> **Going Further**
>
> Our assumption about on-hand inventory level does not assume that we can have negative stock levels (shortages) from time to time. A more precise model of the expected on-hand inventory level should then be:
>
> $$\text{(average) On-hand} = C_S + S_S + B_S$$
>
> where B_S is the expected average backlog per period (which is not the same as the expected units short per cycle). Unfortunately, as B_S is complex to compute, we have to stick to the assumption that $B_S = 0$. You will see in the simulations that, when β decreases, the stock on-hand is (slightly) higher than the model prediction (see Section 8.4.1).
>
> See Axsäter (2015) for a detailed estimation of the expected average backlog in (s, Q) policies.

Cost Expression

Since we know the expected on-hand inventory level, we can express the total cost per review period R as:

$$C_{\text{per review period}} = hR(C_S + S_S) + k + b\,U_S$$

where hR is the holding cost of keeping one unit in stock during **a review period R**; and, because we do a transaction at each review period, the transaction cost per period review period is k.

We can also compute the (average) cost per period (noted simply C) as:

$$C_{\text{per period}} = C = \frac{C_{\text{review period}}}{R} = h(C_S + S_S) + \frac{k}{R} + \frac{b\,U_S}{R}$$

We also know that:

$$S_s = z\,\sigma_x$$
$$C_s = \frac{dR}{2}$$
$$U_s = \sigma_x \mathcal{L}(z)$$

So that we can express the average costs per period as:

$$C = h(dR/2 + z\,\sigma_x) + \frac{k}{R} + \frac{b\,\sigma_x \mathcal{L}_N(z)}{R} \tag{8.2}$$

Intuition

As shown in Figure 8.3, we understand that the more safety stock you have (which is to say, the higher z) the lower the backorder costs are ($b\,\sigma_x \mathcal{L}_N(z)$ is low) but the higher the holding costs are ($h\,z\,\sigma_x$ is high). In Chapter 2, we optimized the order quantity Q^* and saw that the holding costs were balancing the transaction costs (see Section 2.2.2). Now, with our stochastic model, the relationship is a bit more complex: holding costs increase when the backorders costs decrease (more safety stock results in fewer back-orders). The holding costs will also increase when the transaction costs decrease (i. e., if R is high, we make fewer orders but have a higher amount of cycle stock).

We will see in the following pages first how to optimize the required amount of safety stock, and then how to optimize the review period.

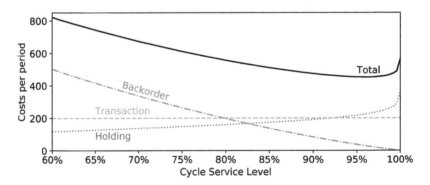

Figure 8.3: Cycle service level impact on transaction, holding and backorder costs. Example with $h = 2$, $k = 200$, $b = 50$, $L = 1$, $R = 1$ and $d \sim \mathcal{N}\left(100, 25^2\right)$.

You are responsible for the inventory policy of the best-selling product of your company. By default, you decided to order it every week—it is, after all, your best-selling product—and aim for a service level of 95%. You want to estimate what the costs related to this policy are.

Here is the information you could gather:

- the holding costs per period are 1.25€ per unit,
- the cost of backordering a unit is 50€,
- the transaction cost is 1000€,
- the review period and the lead time are both 1 period,
- the average demand per period is 100 pieces with a deviation of 25 pieces.

$$\sigma_x = \sqrt{R + L}\, \sigma_d$$

$$\sigma_x = \sqrt{1 + 1} \cdot 25 = 35.36$$

$$C(z) = h(dR/2 + z\,\sigma_x) + \frac{k}{R} + \frac{b\,\sigma_x \mathcal{L}_N(z)}{R}$$

$$= 1.25\left(100 \cdot 1/2 + (25 \cdot \sqrt{1+1})z\right) + \frac{1000}{1} + \frac{50 \cdot 25 \cdot \sqrt{1+1} \cdot \mathcal{L}_N(z)}{1}$$

$$= 1.25\left(50 + 35.36\,z\right) + 1000 + 1767.77 \cdot \mathcal{L}_N(z)$$

As $\alpha = 95\%$, we have $z = \Phi^{-1}(0.95) = 1.645$,

$$C(z) = 1.25(50 + 35.36 \cdot 1.645) + 1000 + 1767.77 \cdot \mathcal{L}_N(1.645)$$

We know that $\mathcal{L}_N(z) = \varphi(z) - z(1 - \Phi(z))$ (see Section 7.2.2). So that we can compute $\mathcal{L}_N(1.645)$ as:

$$\varphi(1.645) - 1.645(1 - \Phi(1.645)) = 0.0209$$

which can be obtained in Excel with

```
=NORM.S.DIST(1.645,FALSE)-1.645*(1-NORM.S.DIST(1.645,TRUE))
```

We then have:

$$C(z) = 1.25(50 + 35.36 \cdot 1.645) + 1000 + 1767.77 \cdot 0.0209 = 1172.12$$

This means that we have a cost of 1172.12€ per period. 1000 are due to the transaction costs, 135.20 due to the holding costs and 36.92 due to the backorders.

In Python, you can define a cost function (as below), and use it to compute the expected costs.

```
def normal_loss_standard(x):
    return norm.pdf(x) - x*(1-norm.cdf(x))

def cost(h,d_mu,R,z,x_std,k,b):
    return h*(d_mu*R/2+x_std*z)+k/R+b*x_std*normal_loss_standard(
        z)/R
```

We now have a good cost expression (see eq. 8.2 in Section 8.2.1). What can we do, as supply chain managers, to reduce these costs? We can easily tweak the service level factor z or change the review period R. We will do both in the following pages.

Cost Optimization: Service Level Factor z

Let's first optimize the cost function with regard to z. The question we ask ourselves is *"What is the optimal service level we should target in order to minimize our costs?"*

$$C(z) = h(dR/2 + z\,\sigma_x) + \frac{k}{R} + \frac{b\,\sigma_x \mathcal{L}_N(z)}{R}$$

Remember, the cycle service level is computed as:

$$\alpha = \Phi(z)$$

In order to find the optimal z^*, we can simply take the derivate of the cost function based on z and set it to zero.

$$z = z^* \Rightarrow \frac{\partial C(z)}{\partial z} = 0$$

$$\frac{\partial C(z)}{\partial z} = h\sigma_x \frac{\partial z}{\partial z} + \frac{b\,\sigma_x}{R}\frac{\partial \mathcal{L}_N(z)}{\partial z} = 0$$

$$hR\sigma_x + b\,\sigma_x(\Phi(z) - 1) = 0$$

$$hR + b\,(\Phi(z) - 1) = 0$$

$$\frac{hR}{b} + \Phi(z) - 1 = 0$$

$$\Phi(z) = 1 - \frac{hR}{b}$$

The demonstration proving $\frac{\partial \mathcal{L}_N(z)}{\partial z} = \Phi(z) - 1$ is given in Appendix B.3.

So that we have:

$$z^* = \Phi^{-1}\left(1 - \frac{hR}{b}\right) \Leftrightarrow \alpha^* = 1 - \frac{hR}{b} \tag{8.3}$$

This is a very important result because it shows that the **optimal cycle service level** (i. e., the one resulting in the lowest total cost) **is $1 - hR/b$**. Moreover, **this result holds for any demand distribution** (as proven in Appendix B.4).

Should You Keep Inventory?

This model shows that you should keep inventory when the backorder cost is higher than the holding cost over the review period. If not—since *keeping a unit in stock is more expensive than missing one item in stock*—you should use a make-to-order policy (i. e., produce only when a client makes an order) rather than a make-to-stock policy (produce and store goods in advance).

It's Your Turn Now!

If you are managing inventory policies, this simple equation $\alpha^* = 1 - hR/b$ should help you to easily reduce your total cost by optimizing the service levels. Go for it!

Example

In our last example, we had a holding cost per week per unit of 1.25€ and a review period of 1 week. Therefore the holding cost per unit over the review period is simply $1 \cdot 1.25€ = 1.25€$. This cost is balanced by a backorder cost per unit of 50€ (this includes customer goodwill).

The optimal cycle service level should then be:

$$\alpha^* = 1 - \frac{hR}{b} = 1 - \frac{1.25 \cdot 1}{50} = 97.5\%$$

Which means that the optimal service level factor is:

$$z^* = \Phi^{-1}(97.5\%) = 1.960$$

We compute the average cost per period as:

$$C(z) = h(dR/2 + z\,\sigma_x) + \frac{k}{R} + \frac{b\,\sigma_x \mathcal{L}_N(z)}{R}$$

where:
$$\sigma_x = \sqrt{R + L}\,\sigma_d = \sqrt{1 + 1} \cdot 25 = 35.36$$
$$\mathcal{L}_N(1.960) = 0.0094$$

So that the cost per week is now:

$$C(1.960) = 1.25(100 \cdot (1/2) + 35.36 \cdot 1.960) + 1000 + 35.36 \cdot 50 \cdot 0.0094$$
$$= 1165.82$$

We conclude that the optimal cycle service level is 97.5%, resulting in a cost per week of 1165.82€. This is 6.3€ less per week than with the initial cycle service level of 95%.

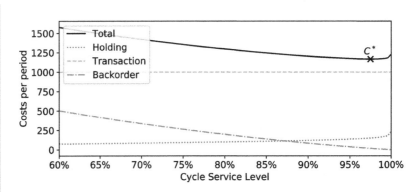

Figure 8.4: Example of cost optimization with $h = 1.25$, $k = 1000$, $b = 50$, $L = 1$, $R = 1$ and $d \sim \mathcal{N}\left(100, 25^2\right)$.

As shown in Figure 8.4, the transaction costs are still (much) higher than the backorder and holding costs. There must be room for further improvement.

DIY

We can easily create a Python function `cost_optimal(b,h,R)` to compute and return the optimal cycle service level:

```python
def CSL_optimal(b,h,R):
    return 1-(h*R)/b
```

We can use it together with the `cost(h,d_mu,R,z,x_std,k,b)` function previously defined.

```python
alpha = CSL_optimal(b,h,R)
z = norm.ppf(alpha)
print(cost(h,d_mu,R,z,x_std,k,b))
```

Cost Optimization: Review Period R

Now that we have an expression to find the best cycle service level α (eq. 8.3 see Section 8.2.1) based on a given review period R, we should optimize R.

This can be done either via the power-of-2 policy (see Section 3.2.1), or simply by looking at various possible values of R and picking the one resulting in the lowest cost. This is often a simple routine computation as, in real life, only a few values of R are possible.

Important Point

The optimal cycle service level depends on the review period. It means that when you test various possible review periods, the optimal cycle service level will be different for each review period. Keep in mind that a cycle service level of 90% for a review period of 4 will not result in the same fill rate as for a review period of 1.

DIY

Assuming we have defined in our code the various parameters h,d_mu,d_std, R,k,b we can easily compute the minimal inventory cost for each possible review period based on a simple loop. We will store each result (and the corresponding review period) in a DataFrame df.

```
def normal_loss_standard(x):
    return norm.pdf(x) - x*(1-norm.cdf(x))

def cost(h,d_mu,R,z,x_std,k,b):
    return h*(d_mu*R/2+x_std*z)+k/R+b*x_std*normal_loss_standard(
        z)/R

def CSL_optimal(b,h,R):
    return 1-(h*R)/b

df = pd.DataFrame(columns=['Review Period', 'Inventory Cost',
'Cycle Service Level', 'Fill Rate'])
for R in [1,2,3,4,5,6,7]:
    x_std = 25*np.sqrt(R+L)
    alpha = CSL_optimal(b,h,R)
    z = norm.ppf(alpha)
    beta = 1 - x_std*normal_loss_standard(z)/R/d_mu
    df = df.append({'Cycle Service Level':alpha, 'Fill Rate':beta
        , 'Inventory Cost':cost(h,d_mu,R,z,x_std,k,b), 'Review
        Period':R},ignore_index=True)
```

You can then print or plot the DataFrame (you will get something similar to Figure 8.5).

```
print(df)
df.plot(y=['Inventory Cost','Cycle Service Level','Fill Rate'],x
    ='Review Period',secondary_y=['Cycle Service Level','Fill
    Rate'],figsize=(8,4))
```

Example

We want to optimize our inventory policy further. We computed earlier that the optimal cost for a review period of one week is 1165.82€ (with a cycle service level of 97.5%). In Figure 8.4 we saw that the transaction costs were much higher than the backorder and holding costs.

We can now compute the optimal inventory cost for various possible review periods (from 1 to 7 weeks[a]) and pick the optimal one. We will use the loop defined above in the DIY section and define the parameters as below:

```
h = 1.25
d_mu = 100
d_std = 25
k = 1000
b = 50
```

We obtain the results shown in Figure 8.5.

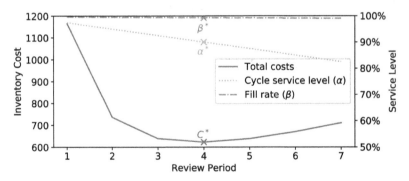

Figure 8.5: Review period optimization.

The optimal review period is $R = 4$ with an inventory cost per period of 622.63€ and a cycle service level of 90%. This is an impressive cost reduction of approximately 550€ per week (a reduction of 47%) compared to our initial policy ($R = 1$, $\alpha = 95\%$). Note that the fill rate is around 99.3% at the optimum.

It is important to understand that despite the fact that the cycle service level decreases when the review period increases, the fill rate remains more or less constant (as we discussed in Chapter 7, see Section 7.4).

---

a We know this is a reasonable range because, based on the deterministic EOQ model, $T^* = \sqrt{2k/hD} = \sqrt{(2 \cdot 1000)/(1.25 \cdot 100)} = 4$ (see eq. 3.5 in Section 3.2). Actually, for this example, choosing the review period is straightforward.

8.3 (s, Q) Policy

For the continuous (s, Q) policy—in which we order Q pieces when we reach a net inventory level of s—we will look at the cost per year, rather than the cost per period as we did for (R, S).

8.3.1 Cost Expression

We go back to the cost expression 8.1 (Section 8.1) and adapt it to the (s, Q) policy.

$$\text{Costs} = h \cdot \text{On-hand} + k \cdot \text{Transactions} + b \cdot \text{Backorders}$$

$$C = h(C_s + S_s) + k\frac{D}{Q} + b\,U_s\frac{D}{Q}$$

where:

h is the cost to keep one unit in stock for **a year**
D/Q is the number of transactions per year
C_s is the average amount of cycle stock ($C_s = Q/2$)
$S_s = z\,\sigma_x$
$U_s = \sigma_x \mathcal{L}_N(z)$

As we did for the (R, S) policy, we will see two ways to reduce the costs: optimize z and Q.

Cost Optimization: Service Level Factor z

We can then express the costs C based on z:

$$C(z) = h(Q/2 + z\,\sigma_x) + k\frac{D}{Q} + b\,\sigma_x \mathcal{L}_N(z)\frac{D}{Q}$$

Once again, to find the optimal z^* factor, we can simply take the derivative of the cost function with regard to z and set it to zero:

$$z = z^* \Rightarrow \frac{\partial C(z)}{\partial z} = 0$$

$$h\left(\sigma_x \frac{\partial z}{\partial z}\right) + b\frac{D}{Q}\sigma_x \frac{\partial \mathcal{L}_N(z)}{\partial z} = 0$$

$$h\sigma_x + b\,\sigma_x \frac{D}{Q}(\Phi(z) - 1) = 0$$

$$hQ + b\,D\,(\Phi(z) - 1) = 0$$

$$\Phi(z) = 1 - \frac{hQ}{bD}$$

This is a very important result, since we can now *easily* compute the optimal cycle service level for an (s, Q) policy as:

$$z^* = \Phi^{-1}\left(1 - \frac{hQ}{bD}\right) \Leftrightarrow \alpha^* = 1 - \frac{hQ}{bD} \tag{8.4}$$

Note, in this equation h is expressed as the holding cost of keeping one unit in stock for **a whole year** (and not just over a review period as we did for the (R, S) policy).

Similarly, as for the (R, S) model (see eq. 8.3 in Section 8.2.1), the optimal service level found with eq. 8.4 **can be used for any demand distribution** (as proven in Appendix B.4). Actually, the solution for the (s, Q) policy is the same as that for the (R, S) (see eq. 8.3) if we replace R with Q/D.

Cost Optimization: Order Quantity Q

In Chapter 2 (see eq. 2.2 in Section 2.2.2), we computed the optimal order quantity Q as

$$Q^* = \sqrt{\frac{2kD}{h}}$$

This works for a deterministic demand, but what about a stochastic one? Let's go back to the cost expression:

$$C(Q) = h(Q/2 + z\,\sigma_x) + k\frac{D}{Q} + b\,\sigma_x \mathcal{L}_N(z)\frac{D}{Q}$$

Just as we did for z^*, in order to find the optimal Q^*, we have to take the derivative of the cost function with regard to Q and set it to zero:

$$Q = Q^* \Rightarrow \frac{\partial C(Q)}{\partial Q} = 0$$

$$h\frac{1}{2}\frac{\partial Q}{\partial Q} + (k + b\,\sigma_x \mathcal{L}_N(z))\frac{\partial}{\partial Q}\left(\frac{1}{Q}\right) = 0$$

$$\frac{h}{2} + (k + b\,\sigma_x \mathcal{L}_N(z))\frac{-1}{Q^2} = 0$$

$$-Q^2\frac{h}{2} + (k + b\,\sigma_x \mathcal{L}_N(z)) = 0$$

$$Q^2 = \frac{2}{h}(k + b\,\sigma_x\mathcal{L}_N(z))$$

$$Q^* = \sqrt{\frac{2(k + b\,\sigma_x\mathcal{L}_N(z))D}{h}} \tag{8.5}$$

Equation 8.5 is specific to the normal distribution. More generally, we have:

$$Q^* = \sqrt{\frac{2(k + b\,U_s)D}{h}}$$

Intuition

You can understand intuitively that this equation is similar to the EOQ equation: $Q = \sqrt{2kD/h}$ (see eq. 2.2 in Section 2.2.2) with $k' = k + b\,\sigma_x\mathcal{L}_N(z)$. $b\,\sigma_x\mathcal{L}_N(z) = b\,U_s$ are the expected backorder costs over a demand cycle, which is seen by our model as a fixed transaction cost. In other words, the model sees the backorder costs per cycle as an extra transaction cost.

	Deterministic	Stochastic
Q^*	$\sqrt{\dfrac{2kD}{h}}$	$\sqrt{\dfrac{2(k + b\,U_s)D}{h}}$

Cost Optimization: Q and z

A simple way to optimize our costs is to iteratively use equations 8.4 and 8.5 until both Q and z are reasonably stable. We say that the algorithm *converges* (i. e., it has found a solution). The convergence will happen rather quickly if we force Q to take integer values.

1. Initialize Q as $\sqrt{2kD/h}$ (based on the EOQ model)
2. Set z as $\Phi^{-1}\left(1 - \frac{hQ}{bD}\right)$
3. Update Q as $\sqrt{2(k + b\,\sigma_x\mathcal{L}_N(z))D/h}$
4. Repeat steps 2 and 3 until both z and Q are reasonably stable.

$$Q = \sqrt{\frac{2kD}{h}}$$

$$z = \Phi^{-1}\left(1 - \frac{hQ}{bD}\right)$$

$$Q = \sqrt{\frac{2(k + b\mathcal{L}_N(z))D}{h}}$$

DIY

In order to compute the optimal order quantity Q^* and the optimal cycle service level α^*, we first have to define 4 functions to perform all the needed computations:

```
def normal_loss_standard(x):
    return norm.pdf(x) - x*(1-norm.cdf(x))

def EOQ(k,D,h):
    return np.sqrt(2*k*D/h)

def CSL_optimal(h,Q,D,b):
    return 1-(h*Q)/(D*b)

def Q_optimal(k,D,h,b,z,x_std):
    return np.sqrt(2*(k+b*x_std*normal_loss_standard(z))*D/h)
```

We can now create a new function sQ_optimal(k,D,h,b,z,x_std) that will return the optimal service level factor z and the order quantity Q. We can start our loop to compute the optimal Q^* and α^*. We initialize Q based on the EOQ formula. Then we update it in a while *loop*[a] until its value is stable (i. e., Q_old is the same as Q).

```
def sQ_optimal(k,D,h,b,x_std):
    Q = EOQ(k,D,h)
    Q_old = 0
    while Q_old != Q:
        Q_old = Q
        z = norm.ppf(CSL_optimal(h,Q,D,b))
        Q = round(Q_optimal(k,D,h,b,z,x_std))
    return z,Q
```

---

a A while loop will perform its operations over and over as long as its condition is met.

Example

We can use our new sQ_optimal(k,D,h,b,z,x_std) function to compute the optimal service level factor and order quantity for our example.

Let's define the various parameters:

```
k = 1000 #Fixed cost of a transaction
D = 100*52 #Yearly demand
h = 1.25*52 #Yearly holding cost of keeping one unit
b = 50 #Cost of backordering one unit
x_std = 25 #Demand deviation over the risk-period
```

We can then call our function

```
print(sQ_optimal(k,D,h,b,x_std))
>> (1.265, 412.0)
```

After only two iterations, we obtain $Q^* = 412$ and $z = 1.265 \Leftrightarrow \alpha^* = 89.7\%$. Which is aligned with what we had for the (R, S) policy where R^* was 4 weeks, corresponding to a demand of 400 units.

8.4 Simulation

In this section we will run our simulations in order to answer these two questions:
1. Is the simulated on-hand inventory level aligned with the model?
   This is crucial because the on-hand inventory level is driving the holding costs. Therefore a correct estimation of this inventory level is required to get the total costs right.
2. Is the model giving us an overall correct cost estimation, despite the assumption we made?

8.4.1 On-Hand Inventory Level

In order to properly simulate the holding costs of our policy, we need to measure the average on-hand inventory level (the inventory physically available for clients to buy).
   Remember, so far, this is our simulation loop (see Section 7.5.1):

```
for t in range(1,time):
    if transit[t-1,0]>0:
        stockout_cycle.append(stockout_period[t-1])
    unit_shorts[t] = max(0,d[t] - max(0,hand[t-1] + transit[t-1,0]))
    hand[t] = hand[t-1] - d[t] + transit[t-1,0]
    stockout_period[t] = hand[t] < 0
    transit[t,:-1] = transit[t-1,1:]
```

```
if t%R==0:
    actual_L = int(round(max(np.random.normal(L,L_std),0),0))
    net = hand[t] + transit[t].sum()
    transit[t,actual_L] = S - net
```

with hand[t] being the on-hand inventory level at the **end** of the timestep t. Actually, hand[t] is not exactly the on-hand inventory as we defined it in Section 1.1: *the inventory physically available for our clients to buy*. The difference is that hand[t] will be negative when we have backorders. We did this for the sake of simplicity, in order to avoid a more complex simulation loop. We then have to create another variable p[t] to keep track of the physically available inventory. p[t] will be strictly positive (p[t]>=0).

How Do We Measure the Average Physical Inventory Level During a Period?

We will review three methods, each more correct than the previous. Let's review them one by one.

First Method

One way to track the average physical inventory level through a period is to compute it as:

```
p[t] = max(hand[t],0)
```

Remember, hand[t] is negative when we have a backlog, therefore we have to use max(hand[t],0) to track the physical inventory.

Unfortunately, this method is *too simple*.

As shown in Figure 8.6, the issue is that hand[t] is the stock level at the **end** of a period, i. e., after the period demand d[t] is consumed and before the next replenishment transit[t,0] arrives (if any). In other words, hand[t] is the **lowest** inventory point during the period. So if we define p[t] as max(hand[t],0) we will undershoot the actual physical inventory.

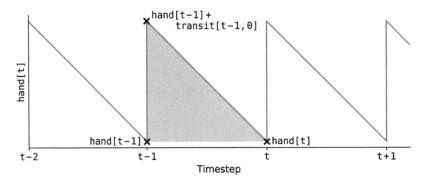

Figure 8.6: Average physical inventory through a period.

Second Method

A second way to compute the average physical inventory is to take the average of the highest and lowest inventory levels of each period. As shown in Figure 8.6, the highest inventory level is reached at the beginning of the period—just after we received a delivery if any (max(hand[t-1]+transit[t-1,0],0))—and the lowest is reached at the end of the period (max(hand[t],0)).

The average physical inventory level during the period can then be expressed as:

```
p[t] = (max(hand[t-1] + transit[t-1,0],0)+max(hand[t],0))/2
```

Third Method

We can refine the computation of the physical inventory even further. The second method is actually only correct when both the starting and ending inventory positions of a period are positive. But, in the cases where the physical inventory is depleted by the end of the period (hand[t]<0), we can expect that the inventory went to zero **before** the end of the period.

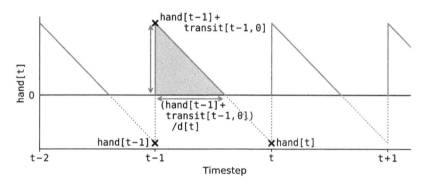

Figure 8.7: Average physical inventory through a period when hand[t]<0.

The average physical inventory level during a period is the grey area in Figure 8.7. As any triangle, this area can be computed as its height (hand[t-1] + transit[t-1,0]) multiplied by its base ((hand[t-1] + transit[t-1,0])/max(d[t],1)) divided by 2: (hand[t-1] + transit[t-1,0])**2/max(d[t],1)/2. Note that we take max(d[t],1) instead of d[t] in order to avoid division by zero in the exceptional case of d[t]==0. We then have:

```
if hand[t] > 0: #there is enough stock by the end of the period
    p[t] = (hand[t-1] + transit[t-1,0] + hand[t])/2
else: #there is not
    p[t] = max(hand[t-1] + transit[t-1,0],0)**2/max(d[t],1)/2
```

Obviously we assume a linear demand consumption through each period.

Simulation vs. Model

We see in Figure 8.8 that the model and the simulation give very close results if the demand deviation per period stays relatively low. But, as shown in Figure 8.9, if the demand coefficient of variation becomes too high ($CV_d \geq 100\%$) we start to have an offset between the model and the simulation. Remember, as we discussed in previous chapters, when CV_d increases the simulated demand is higher than the theoretical demand, due to the fact that we don't allow negative demand in the simulation.[4]

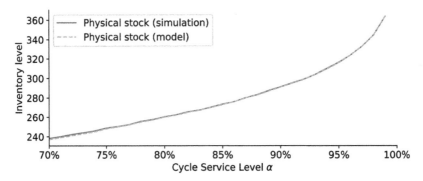

Figure 8.8: Average physical inventory level per period with a low CV_d with $d \sim \mathcal{N}(100, 25^2)$, $R = 4$ and $L = 4$ over 1 million timesteps.

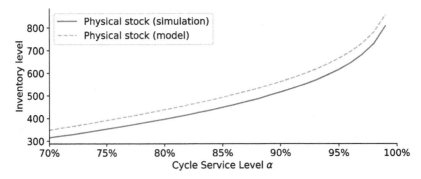

Figure 8.9: Average physical inventory level per period with a high CV_d with $d \sim \mathcal{N}(100, 100^2)$, $R = 4$ and $L = 4$ over 1 million timesteps.

We also observe that as the service level gets lower, the spread between the model and the simulation grows (slightly). As noted in Section 8.2.1, the model does not take into account, in its on-hand inventory level, the expected backlog per period. Nevertheless,

---

4 We will discuss in Chapter 9, "Beyond Normality," the gamma distribution—which is strictly positive.

as we observe for these cases, this spread is virtually zero even for relatively low cycle service levels.

8.4.2 Cost Estimations

Now that we understand how to compute the physical inventory level, we can work on the cost simulations.

> **DIY**
>
> Let's first store the fixed cost per transaction in the variable k, the holding cost per unit per period in h and the backorder cost per unit in b.
>
> ```
> k = 1000 #Fixed cost per transaction
> h = 1.25 #Holding cost per unit per period
> b = 50 #Backorder cost per unit
> ```
>
> We also use p as the physical inventory per period. We initialize it as S - d[0]/2, which is the average physical inventory during the first timestep (assuming the initial inventory level is enough to cover the demand during this timestep).
>
> ```
> p = np.zeros(time)
> p[0] = S - d[0]/2
> ```
>
> We will use throughout our simulations three variables c_k, c_h and c_b to store the transaction, holding and backorder costs (see Chapter 2, "How Much Should I Order?" for a refresher about the transaction and holding costs). We will increment these at each timestep, so that at the end of the simulation we will have to divide these three variables by time (the number of timesteps) in order to get the average cost per period.
>
> ```
> c_k = k #Transaction costs
> c_h = h*p[0] #Holding costs
> c_b = 0 #Backorder costs assuming no backorders during the first
>        period
> ```
>
> We initialize c_k as k since we assume that we make an order on the first timestep.
>
> We can now run our simulation. The changes compared to previous chapters are highlighted below in grey.

```
for t in range(1,time):
    if transit[t-1,0]>0:
        stockout_cycle.append(stockout_period[t-1])
    unit_shorts[t] = max(0,d[t] - max(0,hand[t-1] + transit[t
        -1,0]))
    hand[t] = hand[t-1] - d[t] + transit[t-1,0]
    stockout_period[t] = hand[t] < 0
    transit[t,:-1] = transit[t-1,1:]
    if t%R==0:
        actual_L = int(round(max(np.random.normal(L,L_std),0),0))
        net = hand[t] + transit[t].sum()
        transit[t,actual_L] = S - net
        c_k += k
    if hand[t] > 0: #there is enough stock by the end of the
        period
        p[t] = (hand[t-1] + transit[t-1,0] + hand[t])/2
    else: #there is not
        p[t] = max(hand[t-1] + transit[t-1,0],0)**2/max(d[t],1)/2
    c_h += h*p[t]
    c_b += b*unit_shorts[t]
```

Let's look in detail at how we update our costs variables:

c_k is incremented by k at each review period. This could be refined further by incrementing c_k only when an order is actually made.

c_h is incremented by multiplying the holding cost per period per unit by the physical inventory of each period.

c_b is simply incremented by b times the number of units short at the end of each timestep.

At the end of our simulation we can show the cost per period and compare it to our theoretical model.

```
def cost(h,d_mu,R,z,x_std,k,b):
    return h*(d_mu*R/2+x_std*z)+k/R+b*x_std*normal_loss_standard(
        z)/R
print('Model:\t\t',round(cost(h,d_mu,R,z,x_std,k,b),1))
print('Simulation:\t',round((c_h+c_b+c_k)/time,1))
```

> **Important Point**
>
> We assumed here that the in-transit inventory does not result in holding costs
> for our supply chain. If so, you need to add it to the model and the simulation.

Simulation vs. Model

As for the physical inventory simulation, we can confirm, thanks to our simulations,
that for a low demand coefficient of variation ($CV_d \sim 25\%$), the model and the simulation are virtually alike (see Figure 8.10). Again, a difference arises when the demand
coefficient of variation is high ($CV_d \geq 100\%$) as shown in Figure 8.11.

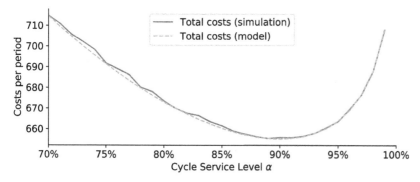

Figure 8.10: Cost simulation for low demand variation with $d \sim \mathcal{N}(100, 25^2)$, $k = 1000$, $h = 1.25$,
$b = 50$, $R = 4$ and $L = 4$ over 1 million timesteps.

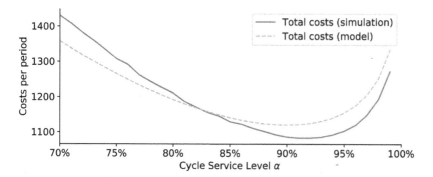

Figure 8.11: Cost simulation for high demand variation with $d \sim \mathcal{N}(100, 100^2)$, $k = 1000$, $h = 1.25$,
$b = 50$, $R = 4$ and $L = 4$ over 1 million timesteps.

8.5 Recap

In this chapter we answered the (tremendously important) question: *"What is the optimal service level?"* We obtained simple expressions for both periodic and continuous review policies as shown in Table 8.2.

Table 8.2: Optimal cycle service levels for each inventory policy.

Policy		(s, Q)	(R, S)
Cycle service level	α^*	$1 - \dfrac{hD}{bQ}$	$1 - \dfrac{hR}{b}$
Order quantity	Q^*	$\sqrt{\dfrac{2(k + b\,U_s)D}{h}}$	

where
  R is the review period
  Q is the order quantity
  b is the cost of backordering an item
  k is the fixed cost per transaction
  h is the holding cost per unit per period (for the (R, S) policy), or per year (for the (s, Q) policy)
  U_s is the expected backlog by the end of the risk-period
  D is the yearly demand

In the case of a periodic review policy, the optimal review period can be obtained either via the power-of-2 policy (see Section 3.2.1) or by testing a set of possible review periods (see Section 8.2.1).

In order to optimize both the cycle service level α and the order quantity Q of a continuous review policy (s, Q), you can simply loop through both equations given in Table 8.2 until both Q and α converge (see Section 8.3.1).

9 Beyond Normality

Important Point

This chapter is a bonus chapter for those who want to improve their inventory policies further with more advanced tools than the usual normal distribution. This chapter is therefore more technical. Despite the amount of math involved, all the models shown here can be *easily* implemented in Excel and Python.

The rest of the book is independent to this chapter.

9.1 When Normality Fails

Through Part II we added variation to our model by describing the demand as following a normal probability distribution (see Chapter 4). In Chapter 6, we did the same for the lead time. Actually, if you open any academic book about inventory optimization—or supply chain in general—you will see this same normality assumption over and over.

Does this normality assumption really make sense?

Or are we oversimplifying a complex world?

Many items in a supply chain fluctuate around a regular demand with a few high-volume exceptions. Just think about a common product that you sell a certain number of pieces of each day. From time to time you will face an exceptionally high demand. This can be due to many factors: maybe there is a promotion running; or an unusually big group of customers wants to buy it; or the weather was exceptional; maybe your competitor was out-of-stock, etc. These small variations explain why we often observe items with a "usual" low demand have a few "unusual" high sales.

Let's look at an example. We show in Figure 9.1 the sales of Ford cars in Norway from 2007 to 2017.[1] Usually the sales are around 700–800 units per month with a few high exceptions.

---

[1] The dataset is published by the Opplysningsrådet for Veitrafikken (OFV) a Norwegian organization in the automotive industry. It was initially retrieved by Dmytro Perepølkin and published on Kaggle. You can download the dataset on supchains.com/download.

https://doi.org/10.1515/9783110673944-009

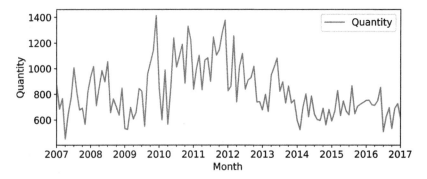

Figure 9.1: Ford car sales in Norway.

DIY

You can reproduce this graph by downloading the dataset available on supchains.com/download. We will make a function get_data(car_maker) to get the dataset we need (the function is only about data gathering and cleaning). For this function to work as-is you will need to store your Python script and the file on the same folder.

```
def get_data(car_maker):
    df = pd.read_csv('norway_new_car_sales_by_make.csv')
    df['Date'] = pd.to_datetime(df['Year'].astype(str)+df['Month'
        ].astype(str),format='%Y%m')
    df = (df.loc[df['Make'] == car_maker,['Date','Quantity']]
        .rename(columns={'Quantity':'Sales'}).set_index('Date'))
    return df
```

We can then use it to extract the Ford sales and plot them.

```
df = get_data('Ford')
df.plot(figsize=(8,4))
```

We will use this dataframe df throughout this chapter in our examples.

9.1.1 Density Histogram

Let's plot a histogram of the density of these monthly sales as well as their mode, median and mean (respectively, 732, 772 and 824).

Mode, Median and Mean

Mode is the most common value in a dataset.

Median is the value that cuts a dataset in half: half of the values are above the median, and half below.

Mean is the sum of the values in a dataset divided by the number of observations. In other words, this is the middle value in a dataset.

The mode is normally the most common value in a dataset. However, computing the mode of a highly scattered distribution—as we face here—can be tricky and meaningless. In order to overcome this, we grouped the sales in bins and defined the mode as the bin with the highest number of occurrences (as shown in Figure 9.2). In other words, we made a histogram and selected the highest bar as the mode.

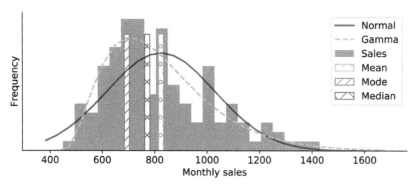

Figure 9.2: Monthly Ford car sales in Norway.

A density histogram is a good empirical estimation of the actual probability distribution function (PDF) of our demand distribution. We will discuss PDF estimation further in Chapter 12, "Discrete Probabilistic Demand." The trick here is to select the right number of bins as well as the proper minimum and maximum limits. As a rule of thumb we will use a number of bins equal to around a third of the available data points; and force the histogram range to go 20% beyond the dataset min and max. On top of this histogram we will add a normal curve fitted to the sales mean and variance $\mathcal{N}(824, 207^2)$. As you can see, a normal distribution fits this demand dataset poorly.

DIY

Let's use df as extracted above and make a density histogram from the sales. We can use the function np.histogram(data,bins,density=True)

```
y_actuals, edges = np.histogram(df, bins=30, density=True)
```

Note that y_actuals won't be normalized to 1, despite the fact that we use density=True. We have to normalize it ourselves by dividing it by its sum.

```
print(y_actuals.sum())
>> 0.031
y_actuals = y_actuals/sum(y_actuals)
print(y_actuals.sum())
>> 1.000
```

You can also define a custom range for the bins using the parameter range.

```
hist_range = (df.Sales.min()*0.8,df.Sales.max()*1.2)
y_actuals, edges = np.histogram(df, bins=30, density=True, range
    =hist_range)
y_actuals = y_actuals/sum(y_actuals)
```

np.histogram returns the bin **edges**, not their centers. So that edges contains one more element than y_actuals. In order to get the center of each bin you should use:

```
centers = (edges + np.roll(edges, -1))[:-1] / 2
```

You can also easily plot a histogram using pandas or matplotlib.

```
#With matplotlib
import matplotlib.pyplot as plt
plt.hist(df.Sales.values,bins=30,density=True,label='Sales',
    range=hist_range)
plt.show()

#With pandas
df.plot(kind='hist',density=True,bins=30,range=hist_range)
```

9.1.2 Why Does Normality Fail?

Let's take a moment to discuss why normal distributions often fail to properly describe a *real* supply chain demand dataset (or lead time fluctuations). Normal distributions have two main characteristics that make them a poor fit:

1. **Normal distributions contain negative values.** Only returns could (potentially) justify having negative demand in some specific cases. Arguably, often in a supply

chain, a return can't compensate a sale from the on-hand inventory. So, if you face returns, you might want to consider forecasting and managing them apart from the normal demand.

Negative lead times are just nonsense.

2. **Normal distributions are symmetric.** In a normal distribution, the mode, the median and the mean are the same value and the distribution is **symmetrically** distributed around it. That's the theory. In real supply chains, as shown in Figure 9.3, the demand—and the lead time—often fluctuate around a mode with a few exceptional (positive) values. *Real* supply chain demand is therefore not symmetrical around the mean; it is often skewed to the right. This means that we have more high exceptions than a normal distribution would usually predict (and fewer low exceptions).

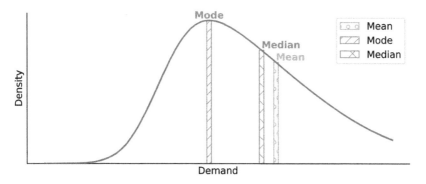

Figure 9.3: Mode, mean and median for a typical demand distribution.

9.2 Skewness

In statistics, the **skewness** is a measure of a distribution asymmetry. It is noted y_1 and is expressed as a number—just as the mean or the standard deviation. A positive number means a right-tail skew, and a negative one means a left-tail skew as you can see in Figure 9.4.

Just as for the mean or the standard deviation, you can compute the skewness of a dataset based on the formula:

$$y_1 = \frac{1}{n} \sum_{i=1}^{n} \left(\frac{x_i - \mu_x}{\sigma_x} \right)^3 \tag{9.1}$$

Usually (but not always) $-1 < y_1 < 1$ so that a skewness close to -1 or 1 is rather high. A skewness of 0 represents a distribution that is perfectly symmetrical around its mean (e. g., the normal distribution).

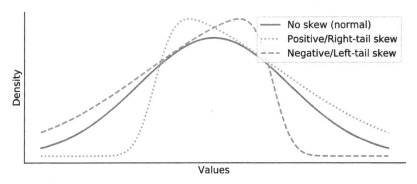

Figure 9.4: Examples of skewness.

Right-skewed distributions always have a mean higher than the median, and they usually are both higher than the mode (as shown in Figure 9.3). This assertion is often correct when describing a supply chain demand. Remember that for a normal distribution—as assumed in our safety stock model so far—the mode, the mean and the median are equal.

DIY

Excel In Excel you can use the formula =SKEW(range) to compute the skewness of a range of cells.

Python You can easily compute the skewness of a dataset in Python with the library SciPy.

```
from scipy import stats
data = np.array([2, 8, 0, 4, 1, 9, 9, 0])
print(stats.skew(data))
>> 0.265
```

You can of course compute it yourself as well:

```
m = np.mean(data)
s = np.std(data)
sum(((data - m)/s)**3)/len(data)
>> 0.265
```

9.3 Gamma Distribution

We understand now why a normal distribution is not always suited to approximate a supply chain demand pattern. Because of this, we need to replace this distribution with a more appropriate one that is right-skewed. Statisticians have many potential distributions that match this description and inventory academics usually work with either triangular, gamma or log-normal distributions.[2]

We will focus on the gamma distribution and leave the triangular and log-normal ones aside. Log-normal and gamma distributions are very much alike, but we will favor the latter since it is mathematically easier to deal with. Triangular distributions can also be used for inventory optimization, especially for (new) products with few (or no) data available.[3]

It seems that using gamma distributions for inventory optimization was analyzed at least since the late 1960s when T. A. Burgin—an English practitioner working for the tire manufacturer Dunlop—published his first articles.[4] He was soon followed by others.[5]

Unfortunately, gamma distributions never got the fame that normal distributions have in the inventory world. Today, most academics, software and consultants still rely on normal assumptions, even when a gamma distribution might be more appropriate. The few practitioners using non-normal distributions are often seen as using some sort of advanced magic to optimize inventory models.

Let's see how we can use gamma distributions to improve our inventory models, while keeping the mathematical complexity within reasonable levels.

9.3.1 Mathematical Definition

A **gamma distribution** $\Gamma(k, \theta)$ (Γ is the capital greek letter gamma) is defined by two parameters: its **shape** k and its **scale** θ (theta). Both parameters can be estimated based on a dataset mean and standard deviation:

$$k = \frac{\mu^2}{\sigma^2} \qquad \theta = \frac{\sigma^2}{\mu}$$

So that,

$$\Gamma(k, \theta) = \Gamma\left(\frac{\mu^2}{\sigma^2}, \frac{\sigma^2}{\mu}\right)$$

Note that both k and θ are strictly positive.

As you can see in Figure 9.5, when the standard deviation of a dataset increases, the gamma distribution is more skewed resulting in a longer tail and a lower mode.

---

2 As extra resources about non-normal demand distributions, you can check Strijbosch and Moors (1999), Cobb et al. (2013) for detailed models.

3 See Wanke et al. (2016) for more details.

4 Burgin and Wild (1967), Burgin (1972, 1975).

5 Murphy (1975), Snyder (1984).

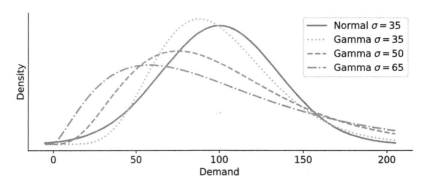

Figure 9.5: Gamma and normal distributions with $\mu = 100$.

On the other hand, as the standard deviation of a dataset decreases, the gamma distribution gets closer and closer to a normal distribution.

Another important property of the gamma distribution is that it is a strictly positive distribution. Yet, as you can see in Figure 9.5, its PDF around 0 is usually very low (i. e., there is a low probability for a gamma distribution to get a value close to 0).

DIY

Excel   You can compute the PDF of a gamma distribution evaluated at x with the formula =GAMMA.DIST(x,k,θ,FALSE). You can use the same function to get the CDF (see Section 4.2.1 for a refresher about the cumulative density function) by changing the last parameter: =GAMMA.DIST(x,k,θ,TRUE).

Python   You can use the function gamma.pdf(x,shape,scale=scale) and gamma.ppf(alpha,shape,scale=scale) from scipy.stats in order to compute the PDF and CDF of a gamma distribution. Remember that shape is k and scale is θ.

Let's try an example and plot a gamma density function fitted to our example dataset:

```
std = df.Sales.std()
mu = df.Sales.mean()
shape = mu**2/std**2 #k
scale = std**2/mu #theta
```

You need to compute a set of x values for the graph. Rather than simply using some arbitrary limits for this set, we will define these as the values that correspond to a cumulative probability of 1% and 99%–just as we did for the normal distribution. We can easily compute these values for the gamma distribution with the gamma.ppf() function from scipy.stats.

```
from scipy.stats import gamma
x_min = gamma.ppf(0.01, shape, scale=scale)
x_max = gamma.ppf(0.99, shape, scale=scale)
```

Now that we have our limits for the x-axes, we can distribute an arbitrary number of points on it by using np.linspace(min,max,n), which distributes n points between min and max. Then we compute the corresponding PDF for each of them (using stats.gamma.pdf()).

```
x = np.linspace(x_min, x_max, 200)
y = gamma.pdf(x, shape, scale=scale)
```

We can then plot our density function which should be similar to Figure 9.6.

```
plt.plot(x,y)
```

Skewness

The skewness of a gamma distribution can be computed as such:

$$\gamma_1 = \frac{2}{\sqrt{k}}$$

If we replace k in the above definition with μ^2/σ^2, we obtain:

$$\gamma_1 = \frac{2\sigma}{\mu}$$

This matches what we saw in Figure 9.5: skewness is proportionally related to σ.

9.3.2 Fitting Gamma

Thanks to these straightforward relationships between k, θ, μ and σ, we can easily fit a gamma distribution to any demand dataset because we can compute μ_d and σ_d and therefore derive k_d and θ_d. Then we would simply have:

$$k_d = \frac{\mu_d^2}{\sigma_d^2} \qquad \theta_d = \frac{\sigma_d^2}{\mu_d} \qquad d \sim \Gamma(k_d, \theta_d) = \Gamma\left(\frac{\mu_d^2}{\sigma_d^2}, \frac{\sigma_d^2}{\mu_d}\right)$$

Demand Offset

Gamma distributions always allocate some (low) probability for values close to 0, so that the fitting shown above works well if the **minimum demand value d_{min}** is close to 0. But this is not always the case. For example, if we look at the monthly sales of Ford cars in Norway (Figure 9.6), the minimum monthly sales ever observed is around 400. In order to fix this and to improve gamma fitting to our sales, we should offset the gamma distribution by d_{min} as summarized in Table 9.1 (so the distribution will then start at our demand minimum value).

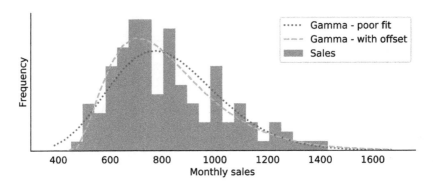

Figure 9.6: Fitting gamma distributions to Ford car sales with and without offset parameters.

Table 9.1: Gamma-distributed period demand based on μ_d, σ_d and d_{min}.

Period demand	Parameters		
$d \sim \Gamma(k_d, \theta_d)$	$k_d = \frac{\mu_d^2}{\sigma_d^2}$	$\theta_d = \frac{\sigma_d^2}{\mu_d}$	
$d \sim \Gamma(k_d', \theta_d') + d_{min}$	$k_d' = \frac{\mu_d'^2}{\sigma_d^2}$	$\theta_d' = \frac{\sigma_d^2}{\mu_d'}$	$\mu_d' = \mu_d - d_{min}$

Let's note k', θ' and μ_d' the offset parameters.

$$\mu_d' = \mu_d - d_{min} \qquad \sigma_d' = \sigma_d \qquad k_d' = \frac{\mu_d'^2}{\sigma_d^2} \qquad \theta_d' = \frac{\sigma_d^2}{\mu_d'}$$

$$d \sim \Gamma(k_d', \theta_d') + d_{min} = \Gamma\left(\frac{\mu_d'^2}{\sigma_d^2}, \frac{\sigma_d^2}{\mu_d'}\right) + d_{min}$$

Note that we do not use σ_d' in our equations, because offsetting the demand by d_{min} does not impact σ_d.

Optimal Value for d_{min}

As discussed, gamma distributions start with a PDF of zero at their minimum (i.e., $f_\Gamma(0; k, \theta) = 0$, as shown in Figure 9.5). Therefore, you might want to define d_{min} slightly below the *actual* minimum observed demand. In practice, the impact of this approximation is (very) low.

> **DIY**
>
> **Python**   We will use the parameter `loc` from `gamma.pdf` in order to *move* the distribution to the demand minimum. Let's create a short code to plot the new PDF. You should then obtain a curve better fitted to the sales as in Figure 9.6.
>
> ```
> std = df.Sales.std() #std = std'
> d_min = df.Sales.min()
> mu = df.Sales.mean()
> mu_p = mu - d_min #mu'
> shape_p = mu_p**2/std**2 #k'
> scale_p = std**2/mu_p #theta'
>
> x_min = gamma.ppf(0.01, shape_p, loc=d_min, scale=scale_p)
> x_max = gamma.ppf(0.99, shape_p, loc=d_min, scale=scale_p)
> x = np.linspace(x_min,x_max, 200)
> y = gamma.pdf(x, shape_p, loc=d_min,scale=scale_p)
> plt.plot(x,y)
> ```
>
> You can also directly use the `gamma.fit(dataset)` method from `scipy.stats`. It will return the shape, minimum, and scale of the fitted gamma distribution.
>
> ```
> shape_auto, min_auto, scale_auto = gamma.fit(df.Sales)
> ```

9.4 Distribution Selection

Now that we can properly fit a gamma distribution to a demand dataset, we need to find a proper way to estimate if a distribution is more gamma than normal. Let's discuss two rules of thumb.[6]

9.4.1 Method #1 – Skewness

The first technique is to compare the *actual* (i. e., observed) demand skewness y_1 to those of fitted normal and gamma distributions. Remember, we saw in eq. 9.1 that you

---

6 See chi-square, Kolmogorov-Smirnov or Anderson–Darling tests for more rigorous goodness-of-fit tests.

can compute the actual skewness γ_1 of the observed demand as:

$$\gamma_1 = \frac{1}{n}\sum_{i=1}^{n}\left(\frac{d_i - \mu_d}{\sigma_d}\right)^3$$

We know that if the demand is close to a normal distribution its skewness should be close to 0; and if the demand is close to a gamma distribution its skewness should be close to $2\sigma_d/\mu_d$.

$$d \sim \mathcal{N}(\mu_d, \sigma_d^2) \Rightarrow \gamma_1 = 0 \qquad d \sim \Gamma(k_d, \theta_d) \Rightarrow \gamma_1 = \frac{2\sigma_d}{\mu_d}$$

Thereby we can use the actual demand skewness to assess if it is closer to a normal or a gamma distribution:

$$d \sim \begin{cases} \mathcal{N}(\mu_d, \sigma_d^2) & \text{if } \gamma_1 < \dfrac{\sigma_d}{\mu_d} \\[2ex] \Gamma(k_d, \theta_d) & \text{if } \gamma_1 > \dfrac{\sigma_d}{\mu_d} \end{cases}$$

One of the great merits of this technique is that it is straightforward to implement. Even in Excel. As soon as you can compute the demand mean, deviation and skewness, you can assess if it is more normal or more gamma. This should allow you to massively segregate demand signals between normal and gamma distributions.

Demand Offset
If there is a minimal demand observed in the dataset, you can also try to fit the demand as $d \sim \Gamma(k_d', \theta_d') + d_{min}$ and see if the skewness obtained $(2\sigma_d/(\mu_d - d_{min}))$ is closer to the actual one.

If the actual skewness is still (much) higher than $2\sigma_d/\mu_d$, you might want to look at custom distributions (as we will discuss in Chapter 12, "Discrete Probabilistic Demand").

Limitation
The limitation of assuming the demand to be normal or gamma based on its skewness is that, since we focus only on matching the skewness of the demand dataset against our fitted distribution, we do not care if the fitted distribution *looks* like the actual demand distribution. In other words, your demand can be skewed like a gamma distribution but not distributed like one.

> ### Example
>
> In our example of Ford car sales in Norway, we obtain the skewness below based on the assumed distributions:
>
> | Distribution | Skewness γ_1 | Computation |
> |---|---|---|
> | Actual | 0.76 | $= \frac{1}{n} \sum_{i=1}^{n} \left(\frac{d_i - \mu_d}{\sigma_d} \right)^3$ |
> | Normal | 0.00 | $= 0$ |
> | Gamma | 0.50 | $= 2\sigma_d / \mu_d = 2 \cdot 207/824$ |
> | Gamma and d_{min} | 0.98 | $= 2\sigma_d / (\mu_d - d_{min}) = 2 \cdot 207/(824 - 400)$ |
>
> We see that the assumption $d \sim \Gamma(k'_d, \theta'_d) + d_{min}$ obtains the closest skewness.
>   You can get the same results in Python with:
>
> ```
> std = df.Sales.std()
> mu = df.Sales.mean()
> skew_actual = df.Sales.skew()
> skew_gamma = 2*std/mu #Gamma
> d_min = 400
> skew_gamma_p = 2*std/(mu-d_min) #Gamma and d_min
> ```

9.4.2 Method #2 – Root Mean Square Error

Another (less straightforward) way to test the goodness-of-fit of a fitted distribution compared to the actual demand distribution is to compute the difference between the two distributions. One way to do this is to compute the **Root Mean Square Error (RMSE)** between the actual and the fitted PDF.
   We define the RMSE as

$$RMSE = \sqrt{\frac{1}{n} \sum \left(f_d(x) - f(x) \right)^2}$$

where $f_d(x)$ is the actual demand PDF estimated at x and $f(x)$ is the PDF of either a gamma or a normal distribution (evaluated at x).

Limitations

–   There is no such thing as a perfect representation of the PDF of our actual demand. We can only *estimate* it based on a density histogram of the demand, which comes with some arbitrary choices that we will discuss in detail in Chapter 12, "Discrete Probabilistic Demand."

- The RMSE test proposed here allocates as much importance to the left-tail as to the right-tail of the demand distribution. The left-tail is less interesting to us since we often aim for high service levels. We want to know the 90th or 99th percentile of the demand over the risk-period, not the 10th. Therefore, we might want to allocate more importance to the right-tail of the distribution because we are interested in extreme demand cases.[7]

DIY

Python First, we define a function rmse(a,b) that returns the *RMSE* between two datasets a and b.

```
def rmse_percent(a,b):
    rmse = np.sqrt(sum((a-b)**2)/len(a))/np.mean(b)
    return round(rmse*100,1)
```

Then, we create a histogram of the actuals (as discussed in Section 9.1.1).

```
hist_range = (df.Sales.min()*0.8,df.Sales.max()*1.2)
y_actuals, edges = np.histogram(df, bins=30, density=True, range
    =hist_range)
x = (edges + np.roll(edges, -1))[:-1] / 2.0
```

We can now create the PDF of three potential distributions (normal, gamma, fitted gamma) and fit each of them to the actuals.

```
#Normal fit
mu = df.Sales.mean()
std = df.Sales.std()
y_normal = norm.pdf(x, mu, std)

#Gamma fit
shape = mu**2/std**2 #k
scale = std**2/mu #theta
y_gamma = gamma.pdf(x, shape, loc=0, scale=scale)

#Gamma fit with minimum demand
mini = df.Sales.min() #d_{min}
```

---

7 Turrini and Meissner (2019) discusses a goodness-of-fit test that allocates more importance to the right end of the distribution.

```
mu_p = mu - mini #mu'
shape_p = mu_p**2/std**2 #k'
scale_p = std**2/mu_p #theta'
y_gamma_p = gamma.pdf(x, shape_p, loc=mini, scale=scale_p)
```

As usual, we then have to scale each PDF vector.

```
y_actuals /= y_actuals.sum()
y_normal /= y_normal.sum()
y_gamma /= y_gamma.sum()
y_gamma_p /= y_gamma_p.sum()
```

We can then compute their respective root mean square error compared to the actual histogram.

```
rmse_normal = rmse_percent(y_actuals,y_normal)
rmse_gamma = rmse_percent(y_actuals,y_gamma)
rmse_gamma_p = rmse_percent(y_actuals,y_gamma_p)
```

We obtain, respectively, 58.7% (normal), 50.2% (gamma) and 43.5% (gamma fitted). These results show that the effort we took to properly fit the gamma distribution is worth it because the *fitted* gamma distribution adds as much extra precision compared to the regular gamma distribution as the normal gamma distribution adds compared to the normal one.

9.5 Impact on Inventory Policies

Now that we have learned what a gamma distribution is and how to fit it to our (period) demand distribution, we can use it to improve our inventory policies. We will now model the supply chain as shown in Figure 9.7.

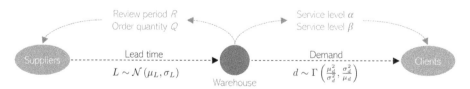

Figure 9.7: Supply chain model.

> **Important Point**
>
> This section is one of the most mathematically intensive in this book. We will see in the following pages how to use gamma distributions in inventory policies. The extra effort required to use gamma distributions is often worth it as, in practice, many demand patterns are more gamma than normal. This section is full of examples and DIY sections to allow you to use this distribution right away in your inventory policies. Note also that, despite the mathematical complexity, gamma policies can easily be implemented even with Excel. A recap is also presented in Section 9.7.

9.5.1 Gamma Demand over the Risk-Period

We have analyzed the gamma distribution over one period, we now have to analyze the gamma demand distribution over the *risk-period* (i. e., lead time and review period).[8]

Fixed Lead Time

If the demand follows a gamma distribution $d \sim \Gamma(k_d, \theta_d)$ over one period, we can compute its distribution over τ periods.[9] To do this, we first have to compute the expected demand mean and standard deviation over τ periods.

$$\mu_\tau = \tau \mu_d \qquad \sigma_\tau = \sqrt{\tau} \sigma_d$$

So that,

$$k_\tau = \frac{\mu_\tau^2}{\sigma_\tau^2} = \frac{\tau^2 \mu_d^2}{\tau \sigma_d^2} = \tau k_d$$

$$\theta_\tau = \frac{\sigma_\tau^2}{\mu_\tau} = \frac{\tau \sigma_d^2}{\tau \mu_d} = \theta_d$$

Let's note d_τ **the demand over τ periods.** We can express it based on either k_τ and θ_τ; or k_d and θ_d; or μ_τ and σ_τ; or even on μ_d and σ_d.

$$d_\tau \sim \Gamma(k_\tau, \theta_\tau) = \Gamma(\tau k_d, \theta_d) = \Gamma\left(\frac{\mu_\tau^2}{\sigma_\tau^2}, \frac{\sigma_\tau^2}{\mu_\tau}\right) = \Gamma\left(\tau \frac{\mu_d^2}{\sigma_d^2}, \frac{\sigma_d^2}{\mu_d}\right)$$

---

8 Risk-period (x_τ): maximum amount of time you need to wait to receive an order (from your supplier). During this period your inventory is at risk of being depleted. $x_\tau = R + L$ in an (R, S) policy and $x_\tau = L$ in an (s, Q) policy. See Section 5.1.1.

9 Assuming that the demand is independent from one period to another. Keep in mind that this is still a strong assumption as discussed in Section 4.3.3.

Table 9.2: Gamma-distributed risk-period demand based on μ_d, σ_d and d_{min}.

Policy	Risk-period Length	Demand	Parameters		
(R,S)	$x_\tau = R+L$	$d \sim \Gamma(k_x, \theta_x)$	$k_x = x_\tau \frac{\mu_d^2}{\sigma_d^2}$	$\theta_x = \frac{\sigma_d^2}{\mu_d}$	
(s,Q)	$x_\tau = L$				
(R,S)	$x_\tau = R+L$	$d \sim \Gamma(k_x', \theta_x') + x_{min}$	$k_x' = x_\tau \frac{\mu_d'^2}{\sigma_d^2}$	$\theta_x' = \frac{\sigma_d^2}{\mu_d'}$	$\mu_d' = \mu_d - d_{min}$
(s,Q)	$x_\tau = L$				

As shown in Table 9.2, we can express the demand over the risk-period by replacing τ by either $R+L$ for an (R,S) policy or by L for an (s,Q) policy. Remember, we note x_τ the length of the risk-period, so that we have either $x_\tau = R+L$ or $x_\tau = L$.

Note that, as the number of periods τ increases (in other words, as the risk-period gets longer), the coefficient of variation of the distribution gets smaller so that the gamma distribution is less and less skewed and looks more and more like a normal distribution. In other words, the more you look into the demand distribution over a long period, the more it will follow a normal distribution.[10]

Demand Offset
If we offset the gamma distribution by a minimum (as discussed in Section 9.3.2), we simply use $\mu_d' = \mu_d - d_{min}$ to compute k_d' and θ_d' (with x_{min} being the demand offset over the risk-period $x_{min} = x_\tau d_{min}$).

Stochastic Lead Time
What if we have a random lead time and a gamma demand? As we discussed in Section 6.3.1, we already know a couple of parameters of the expected demand over the risk-period:

$$\mu_x = (\mu_L + R)\mu_d \qquad \sigma_x = \sqrt{(\mu_L + R)\sigma_d^2 + \sigma_L^2 \mu_d^2}$$

Even though we can estimate the demand deviation and mean over the risk-period, we do not know what its *distribution* looks like. Will we get the same distribution if the lead time is normal than if it is gamma-distributed? What about a gamma lead time and a normal demand?

The exact mathematics to answer these questions are not always controllable.[11] Moreover, working with such mathematics might only slightly improve our inventory policies whereas the extra complexity will make the maintenance of the model, at

---

10 This is called the central limit theorem.
11 See Burgin (1972) for an approximation of a normal demand over a gamma lead time; and Murphy (1975) for a gamma demand over a gamma lead time.

best, very difficult. We have two solutions: using more simplifying assumptions or using simulations to optimize the policy.

As an extra simplifying assumption, we could approximate the demand over the (stochastic) lead time as gamma. Using μ_x and σ_x, as defined above, we can compute k_x and θ_x, so that:

$$d_x \sim \Gamma(k_x, \theta_x) = \Gamma\left(\frac{\mu_x^2}{\sigma_x^2}, \frac{\sigma_x^2}{\mu_x}\right) = \Gamma\left(\frac{((\mu_L + R)\mu_d)^2}{(\mu_L + R)\sigma_d^2 + \sigma_L^2\mu_d^2}, \frac{(\mu_L + R)\sigma_d^2 + \sigma_L^2\mu_d^2}{(\mu_L + R)\mu_d}\right)$$

As discussed in Chapter 6, "Stochastic Lead Times," the *normal* stochastic lead time model only worked well when $R \gg L \gg \sigma_L$. We now have a second layer of approximations because we assume that the demand over the lead time follows a gamma distribution. This means that we should use this model with caution (e. g., test it with a simulation before using it). As we will see with our later simulations (in Section 9.6.2), if the lead time variability is rather low, simulations will be relatively aligned with the theoretical model.

In conclusion, if you face gamma demand and stochastic lead time, it is advised not to use a mathematical model to optimize your inventory policy but to use simulations instead as we will do in Chapter 13.

9.5.2 Safety Stocks

Let's note ι the inventory level at the beginning of the risk-period. In other words,

$$\iota = \begin{cases} s & \text{if } (s,Q) \\ S & \text{if } (R,S) \end{cases} \qquad \text{Risk-period} = \begin{cases} L & \text{if } (s,Q) \\ R+L & \text{if } (R,S) \end{cases}$$

We can compute ι (i. e., s or S) easily as:

$$\iota = F_\Gamma^{-1}(\alpha; k_x, \theta_x)$$

where $F_\Gamma^{-1}(\alpha; k_x, \theta_x)$ is the inverse of the gamma distribution $\Gamma(k_x, \theta_x)$ evaluated at service level α.

The various possible expressions of ι are shown in Table 9.3. The safety stock level can then be easily computed as:

$$S_s = \iota - \mu_x$$

Table 9.3: Expression of ι depending on the inventory policy and the assumed demand distribution.

Policy	Period demand	General expressions	Explicit expressions
(R,S) (s,Q)	$d \sim \Gamma(k_d, \theta_d)$	$\iota = F_\Gamma^{-1}(\alpha; k_x, \theta_x)$	$S = F_\Gamma^{-1}(\alpha; (R+L)k_d, \theta_d)$ $s = F_\Gamma^{-1}(\alpha; L\,k_d, \theta_d)$
(R,S) (s,Q)	$d \sim \Gamma(k_d', \theta_d') + d_{min}$	$\iota = F_\Gamma^{-1}(\alpha; k_x', \theta_x') + x_{min}$	$S = F_\Gamma^{-1}(\alpha; (R+L)k_d', \theta_d') + (R+L)d_{min}$ $s = F_\Gamma^{-1}(\alpha; L\,k_d', \theta_d') + L\,d_{min}$

Demand Offset

In the case of a demand offset ($d \sim \Gamma(k_d, \theta_d) + d_{min}$), we have:

$$\iota = F_{\Gamma}^{-1}\left(\alpha; k_x', \theta_x'\right) + x_{min}$$

where k_x' and θ_x' are computed based on $\mu_x' = \mu_x - x_{min}$. We still have $S_s = \iota - \mu_x$

You are the inventory planner responsible for a product with a skewed demand. Your company sells around 800 of this product per week, with a deviation of 200 pieces. You estimate that this demand is highly skewed so that you assume it follows a gamma distribution. The demand never got below 400 units per week. You want to secure a cycle service level of 95% with a weekly review period. The supplier takes 4 weeks to replenish your inventory.

Let's note the data at hand and compute the various gamma parameters.

$$\mu_d = 800 \qquad d_{min} = 400 \qquad \sigma_d = 200 \qquad R = 1 \qquad L = 4$$

$$\mu_d' = \mu_d - d_{min} = 400 \qquad k_d' = \frac{\mu_d'^2}{\sigma_d^2} = \frac{400^2}{200^2} = 4 \qquad \theta_d' = \frac{\sigma_d^2}{\mu_d'} = \frac{200^2}{400} = 100$$

We can now compute the up-to level S and the required safety stock S_s to reach the 95% service level.

$$\iota = S = F^{-1}\left(\alpha; (R+L)k_d', \theta_d'\right) + (R+L)d_{min}$$

$$S = F^{-1}(0.95; 5 \cdot 4, 100) + 5 \cdot 400$$

$$S = F^{-1}(0.95; 20, 100) + 2000$$

In Excel we obtain 4787.92=GAMMA.INV(0,95;20;100)+2000, so that our up-to level is 4788 units. We compute the safety stock as

$$S_s = \iota - \mu_x = S - (R+L)\mu_d = 4788 - (1+4) \cdot 800 = 788$$

We can also get the same results in Python (using the general expression of S):

```
d_mu, d_std, d_min = 800, 200, 400
alpha, L, R = 0.95, 4, 1
x_min = (R+L)*d_min
x_mu = (R+L)*d_mu
x_mu_p = x_mu - x_min #mu_x'
x_std = np.sqrt(R+L)*d_std #std_x = std_x'
x_shape_p = x_mu_p**2/x_std**2 #k_x'
x_scale_p = x_std**2/x_mu_p #theta_x'
```

```
S = round(gamma.ppf(alpha,x_shape_p,scale=x_scale_p),0) + x_min
Ss = S - x_mu
```

9.5.3 Unit Shorts

If we want to get serious about using a gamma distribution for an inventory model, we also need to compute the expected units short U_s per order cycle, in order to know the expected fill rate β.

By definition, the expected units short for an initial inventory position ι over an order cycle where $d \sim \Gamma(k, \theta)$ is:

$$U_s = \mathcal{L}_\Gamma(\iota; k, \theta) = \int_\iota^\infty (d - \iota) f_\Gamma(d; k, \theta) dd$$

As a reminder, we note $f_\Gamma(d; k, \theta)$ the probability density function (PDF) of the gamma distribution $\Gamma(k, \theta)$ evaluated at demand d. We solve $\mathcal{L}_\Gamma(\iota; k, \theta)$ as:[12]

$$\mathcal{L}_\Gamma(\iota; k, \theta) = k\theta(1 - F_\Gamma(\iota; k + 1, \theta)) - \iota(1 - F_\Gamma(\iota; k, \theta)) \tag{9.2}$$

Unit Shorts over the Risk-Period
Obviously we are interested in the expected units short U_s over the risk-period of our inventory policy:

$$U_s = \mathcal{L}_\Gamma(\iota; k_x, \theta_x) = k_x \theta_x (1 - F_\Gamma(\iota; k_x + 1, \theta_x)) - \iota(1 - F_\Gamma(\iota; k_x, \theta_x))$$

Remember, ι is the inventory at the beginning of the risk-period: $\iota = S$ for an (R, S) policy, $\iota = s$ for an (s, Q) policy.

Demand Offset
If we define the demand as $d \sim \Gamma(k'_d, \theta'_d) + d_{min}$, we have:

$$U_s = \mathcal{L}_\Gamma(\iota'; k'_x, \theta'_x) = k'_x \theta'_x (1 - F_\Gamma(\iota'; k'_x + 1, \theta'_x)) - \iota'(1 - F_\Gamma(\iota'; k'_x, \theta'_x))$$

where:

$$k'_x = \frac{\mu_x'^2}{\sigma_x'^2} \qquad \theta'_x = \frac{\sigma_x'^2}{\mu'_x} \qquad \iota' = \iota - x_{min}$$

We summarize in Table 9.4 the expression of the expected units short based on x_τ (the risk-period length), μ_d, θ_d, d_{min}.

---
12 See Silver et al. (2016) for a proof.

Table 9.4: Units short expression based on x_τ, k_d, k_d and d_{min}.

Policy	Risk-period Length	Demand	Units short U_s
(R,S) (s,Q)	$x_\tau = R+L$ $x_\tau = L$	$x \sim \Gamma(x_\tau k_d, \theta_d)$	$x_\tau k_d \theta_d \left(1 - F_\Gamma\left(\iota; x_\tau k_d + 1, \theta_d\right)\right)$ $-\iota\left(1 - F_\Gamma\left(\iota; x_\tau k_d, \theta_d\right)\right)$
(R,S) (s,Q)	$x_\tau = R+L$ $x_\tau = L$	$x \sim \Gamma(x_\tau k_d', \theta_d') + x_\tau d_{min}$	$x_\tau k_d' \theta_d' \left(1 - F_\Gamma\left(\iota'; x_\tau k_d' + 1, \theta_d'\right)\right)$ $-\iota'\left(1 - F_\Gamma\left(\iota'; x_\tau k_d', \theta_d'\right)\right)$

DIY

Excel You can use the following formula in order to compute the expected units short over an order cycle where $d \sim \Gamma(k, \theta)$ and inv is the initial inventory level:

```
=k*θ*(1-GAMMA.DIST(inv;k+1;θ;TRUE))-inv*(1-GAMMA.DIST(inv;k;θ;TRUE))
```

If the demand follows $\Gamma((R+L)k, \theta)$, we have

```
=(R+L)*k*θ*(1-GAMMA.DIST(inv;(R+L)*k+1;θ;TRUE))
        -inv*(1-GAMMA.DIST(inv;(R+L)*k;θ;TRUE))
```

For more information and examples of gamma distributions in Excel, see Tyworth et al. (1996).

Python Let's first define a function `gamma_loss(inv,mu,std)` that returns the expected loss based on `inv`, `mu` and `std`. This function is similar to `normal_loss(inv,mu,std)` that we defined in Section 7.2.1. Remember that in SciPy k is shape and θ is scale.

```
def gamma_loss(inv,mu,std):
    shape = mu**2/std**2 #k
    scale = std**2/mu #theta
    loss = shape*scale*(1-gamma.cdf(inv, shape+1, scale=scale)) -
        inv*(1-gamma.cdf(inv,shape,scale=scale))
    return loss
```

We can now use this and compare the results to a normal function.

```
inv, mu, std = 120, 100, 50
gamma_loss(inv,mu,std)
>> 12.32
normal_loss(inv,mu,std)
>> 11.52
```

As we will discuss in Section 9.5.4, in this case, the expected lost sales are higher with a gamma distribution. Note that, if you try a lower inventory value (for example inv=90), the gamma distribution will give you a lower value of expected lost sales than a normal distribution.

Example

In our previous example (with a gamma demand with a mean of 800, a minimum demand of 400 and a deviation of 200), we are interested in the expected units short per order cycle. Let's first describe the demand distribution over the risk-period:

$$\mu_x = (R + L)\mu_d = 5 \cdot 800 = 4000 \qquad \sigma_x = \sqrt{R + L}\,\sigma_d = \sqrt{5} \cdot 200 = 447.21$$
$$\mu'_x = \mu_x - (R + L)d_{min} = 4000 - 5 \cdot 400 = 2000$$
$$k'_x = \frac{\mu'^2_x}{\sigma^2_x} = \frac{2000^2}{447.21^2} = 20 \qquad \theta'_x = \frac{\sigma^2_x}{\mu'_x} = \frac{447.21^2}{2000} = 100$$

We can then plug these numbers into the loss gamma function.

$$U_s = \mathcal{L}_\Gamma(\iota'; k'_x, \theta'_x) = k'_x \theta'_x \left(1 - F_\Gamma\left(\iota'; k'_x + 1, \theta'_x\right)\right) - \iota'\left(1 - F_\Gamma\left(\iota'; k'_x, \theta'_x\right)\right)$$

Remember that $\iota' = S - (R + L)d_{min} = 2788$.

$$\mathcal{L}_\Gamma(2788; 20, 100) = 20 \cdot 100\left(1 - F_\Gamma\left(2788; 21, 100\right)\right)$$
$$- 2788\left(1 - F_\Gamma\left(2788; 20, 100\right)\right)$$

We can compute this in Excel:

```
=20*100*(1-GAMMA.DIST(2788,21,100,TRUE))
-2788*(1-GAMMA.DIST(2788,20,100,TRUE))
```

And we get 12.21 units short. This is a fill rate of

$$\beta = 1 - \frac{U_s}{d_R} = 1 - \frac{12.21}{1 \cdot 800} = 98.5\%$$

For a cycle service level of 95%.

You can obtain the same result in Python with the code below.

```
d_mu, d_std, d_min = 800, 200, 400
alpha, L, R = 0.95, 4, 1
```

```
x_mu_p = (R+L)*(d_mu - d_min) #mu_x'
x_std = np.sqrt(R+L)*d_std #std_x = std_x'
x_shape_p = x_mu_p**2/x_std**2 #k_x'
x_scale_p = x_std**2/x_mu_p #theta_x'
S_p = round(gamma.ppf(alpha,x_shape_p,scale=x_scale_p),0) #S'
S = S_p + (R+L)*d_min
unit_shorts = gamma_loss(S-d_min*(R+L),x_mu_p,x_std)
beta = 1-unit_shorts/(d_mu*R)
```

Gamma Inverse Loss Function

Just as for the normal distribution, there is no tractable equation to express the inverse of the gamma loss function. We will again have to use a solver to compute it. This is what we are looking for:

$$U_s = \begin{cases} d_c(1-\beta) \\ \mathcal{L}_\Gamma(\iota; k_x, \theta_x) \end{cases} \Rightarrow \beta = 1 - \frac{U_s}{d_c} = 1 - \frac{\mathcal{L}_\Gamma(\iota; k_x, \theta_x)}{d_c}$$

Where ι is either s or S depending on the policy, and

$$\mathcal{L}_\Gamma(\iota; k_x, \theta_x) = k_x \theta_x (1 - F_\Gamma(\iota; k_x + 1, \theta_x)) - \iota(1 - F_\Gamma(\iota; k_x, \theta_x))$$

The objective of our solver will be to minimize the difference between:

$$d_c(1-\beta) \quad \text{and} \quad \mathcal{L}_\Gamma(\iota; k_x, \theta_x)$$

by changing ι. We formalize this mathematically as

$$\iota = \arg\min_\iota \left[\left| \mathcal{L}_\Gamma(\iota; k_x, \theta_x) - d_c(\beta - 1) \right| \right]$$

which means that ι is the value that minimizes the absolute difference between $\mathcal{L}_\Gamma(\iota; k_x, \theta_x)$ and $d_c(1-\beta)/\sigma_x$.

DIY

Python We will create a function gamma_loss_inverse(x_mu, x_std, d_c, beta) that will return the inventory level (S or s depending on the policy) required to reach a fill rate beta, with a cycle demand d_c, and a demand over the risk-period as x_mu and x_std.

The function will use the solver minimize_scalar(f) from scipy.optimize (as used in Section 7.3.2).

```
def gamma_loss_inverse(x_mu, x_std, d_c, beta):
    target = d_c*(1-beta)
    shape = x_mu**2/x_std**2
    scale = x_std**2/x_mu

    def unit_shorts(inv):
        return shape*scale*(1-gamma.cdf(inv, shape+1, scale=scale
            )) - inv*(1-gamma.cdf(inv, shape, scale=scale))

    def f(inv):
        return abs(unit_shorts(inv) - target)

    result = optimize.minimize_scalar(f)
    return result.x
```

We can now test our function against the function gamma_loss(inv,mu,theta) that we defined earlier in Section 9.5.3.

```
beta = 0.95
R, L = 1, 4
d_mu, d_std = 800, 200

d_c = R*d_mu
x_mu = (R+L)*d_mu
x_std = np.sqrt(R+L)*d_std

S = round(gamma_loss_inverse(x_mu, x_std, d_c, beta))
fill_rate = 1-gamma_loss(S, x_mu, x_std)/d_c
print('S:',int(S),'\tFill Rate:',round(fill_rate,3)*100)
>> S: 4454 Fill Rate: 95.0
```

This confirms that the fill_rate computed via the gamma_loss(inv,mu,theta) function gives us the same results as the initial target beta.

If we want to define the demand with a minimum, we have these changes:

```
x_mu_p = (R+L)*(d_mu - d_min)
S_p = round(gamma_loss_inverse(x_mu_p, x_std, d_c, beta))
fill_rate = 1-gamma_loss(S_p, x_mu_p, x_std)/d_c
S = S_p+ d_min*(R+L)
```

Note that, in some cases, the solver will get lost or stuck. To avoid these issues, you can provide it with arbitrary bounds:

```
optimize.minimize_scalar(f,bounds=(x_mu, x_mu+x_std*5), method=
    'bounded')
```

Note that, with small fill rates (< 80%) you might want your solver to look for values below μ_x (i. e., negative safety stock).

9.5.4 Gamma vs. Normal

Now that we have created a gamma model, we can analyze the differences with the normal model we created in Part II, "Stochastic Supply Chains." To do this, we show in Table 9.5 and Figure 9.8 the various fill rates and cycle service levels achieved for different values of ι (the stock level at the beginning of the risk-period) based on a risk-period demand $\mu_x = 100$, $\sigma_x = 50$.

Table 9.5: Expected cycle service level α and fill rate β based on ι with $\mu_x = 100$ and $\sigma_x = 50$.

Service level	Risk-period demand	ι 80	100	120	140	160	180	200
α	$x \sim \Gamma(k_x, \theta_x)$	39.7	56.7	70.6	80.9	88.1	92.8	95.8
	$x \sim \mathcal{N}(\mu_x, \sigma_x^2)$	34.5	50.0	65.5	78.8	88.5	94.5	97.7
β	$x \sim \Gamma(k_x, \theta_x)$	70.1	80.5	87.7	92.5	95.5	97.4	98.5
	$x \sim \mathcal{N}(\mu_x, \sigma_x^2)$	68.5	80.1	88.5	94.0	97.2	98.8	99.6

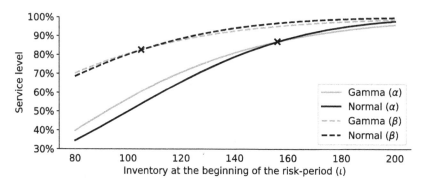

Figure 9.8: Expected cycle service level α and fill rate β based on ι with $\mu_x = 100$ and $\sigma_x = 50$.

We see two cross-over points when the normal model predicts higher service levels than the gamma model (both for the cycle service level and fill rate).

Low service levels It is usually easier to obtain a low service level with a gamma demand than with a normal one. In other words, a small amount of inventory will result in a higher service level when the demand over the risk-period follows a gamma distribution rather than a normal one. This makes sense as the gamma distribution is right-skewed resulting in a high probability for the demand not to be too far away from the mode (which is lower than the average demand).

High service levels On the other hand, targeting a high service level is more difficult if the demand is gamma-distributed due to its long right-tail (as there is always a small probability that the demand will be *really* high).

9.6 Simulation

9.6.1 Fixed Lead Time

Let's start our simulations by assuming the lead time is fixed.

As shown in Tables 9.6 and 9.7, the gamma model works well even for high levels of demand variation over the risk-period ($CV_d > 0.5$). Remember, for the normal model (analyzed in Table 5.3) we had a misalignment between the simulation and the theory $CV_d > 0.25$.

Table 9.6: Simulated cycle service level (%) over 1,000,000 periods for an (R, S) policy with $R = 4$ and $\mu_d = 100$.

σ_d	L	CV_d	CV_x	Theoretical cycle service level (%)				
				70	80	90	95	99
	1	.25	.11	70.4	80.1	90.1	95.0	99.0
25	4	.25	.09	70.7	80.4	90.2	95.1	99.0
	10	.25	.07	70.3	80.4	90.2	95.1	99.0
	1	1.0	.45	70.1	80.0	90.0	95.0	99.0
100	4	1.0	.35	70.3	80.1	90.1	95.1	99.0
	10	1.0	.27	70.3	79.9	90.0	94.9	99.0
	1	2.0	.89	74.5	82.9	91.4	95.6	99.1
200	4	2.0	.71	74.9	83.2	91.4	95.8	99.2
	10	2.0	.53	75.2	83.5	91.7	95.8	99.1

We see that the simulated service level (fill rate or cycle service level) tends to be higher than the theoretical prediction from our model. This is especially true when the lead time is long compared to the review period and the service level target is low.

Table 9.7: Simulated fill rate (%) over 1,000,000 periods for an (R, S) policy with $R = 4$ and $\mu_d = 100$.

σ_d	L	CV_d	CV_x	Theoretical fill rate (%)				
				70	80	90	95	99
	1	.25	.11	70.0	80.1	90.0	95.0	99.0
25	4	.25	.09	70.0	80.0	90.0	95.0	99.0
	10	.25	.07	69.9	79.8	90.1	95.0	99.0
	1	1.0	.45	70.3	80.2	90.0	95.0	99.0
100	4	1.0	.35	71.8	80.8	90.3	95.1	99.0
	10	1.0	.27	74.0	82.2	90.8	95.3	99.1
	1	2.0	.89	72.2	81.3	90.7	95.3	99.1
200	4	2.0	.71	76.3	83.7	91.8	95.7	99.1
	10	2.0	.53	80.1	86.4	92.8	96.2	99.3

Going Further

de Kok (1991) proposed a correction to the usual (R, S) inventory model (the intuition and details are out-of-scope of this book). He argued that we should add the terms in brackets to the computation of β.

$$\beta = 1 - \frac{\mathcal{L}_\Gamma(\iota, k_x, \theta_x)}{d_c} \left[+ \frac{\mathcal{L}_\Gamma(\iota, k_{xL}, \theta_{xL})}{d_c} \right]$$

where k_{xL} and θ_{xL} are, respectively, the demand scale and shape over the lead time ($k_{xL} = Lk$ and $\theta_{xL} = \theta_d$).

Or more generally (not restricted to the gamma distribution),

$$\beta = 1 - \frac{\mathcal{L}_x(\iota)}{d_c} + \frac{\mathcal{L}_{xL}(\iota)}{d_c}$$

where $\mathcal{L}_x(\iota)$ is the loss function of the distribution x (which can be gamma, normal, or any other) evaluated at ι.

With this correction the simulation and the model will be virtually perfectly aligned. The impact is meaningful when L is big ($L > R$), β is small and the demand deviation is high (as observed in Table 9.7).

9.6.2 Random Lead Times

Let's now simulate our model with random lead times. As discussed in Section 6.4, random lead times come with a lot of questions that theoretical models (and simulations alike) often ignore:

-   Is there a correlation between the lead times of different orders?

- Is the lead time independent to the demand, or seasonal?
- How do we model discrete lead time?

We see in Tables 9.8 and 9.9 that our model is giving appropriate results for both normal and gamma-distributed lead times when the lead time variation is limited. Nevertheless, for high lead time variation, the model seems to give stock targets that are too high, resulting in higher than targeted service levels.

Table 9.8: Simulated fill rate (%) over 1,000,000 periods for an (R, S) policy with $R = 4$ and $\mu_d = 100$, $\sigma_d = 100$. **Lead time distributed as $L \sim \mathcal{N}(\mu_L, \sigma_L^2)$.**

μ_L	σ_L	CV_x	Theoretical fill rate (%)				
			70	80	90	95	99
	0.5	.36	71.8	80.8	90.2	95.0	99.0
4	1.0	.38	71.7	80.7	90.1	95.0	99.0
	1.5	.40	70.8	79.8	89.4	94.6	98.8
	1.0	.28	74.0	82.1	90.7	95.2	99.0
10	2.5	.32	73.8	82.0	90.6	95.2	99.0
	5.0	.45	81.5	88.7	95.6	98.4	99.9

Table 9.9: Simulated fill rate (%) over 1,000,000 periods for an (R, S) policy with $R = 4$ and $\mu_d = 100$, $\sigma_d = 100$. **Lead time distributed as $L \sim \Gamma(k_L, \theta_L)$.**

μ_L	σ_L	CV_x	Theoretical fill rate (%)				
			70	80	90	95	99
	0.5	0.36	71.7	80.8	90.3	95.2	99.0
4	1.0	0.38	71.8	80.7	90.1	94.9	98.9
	1.5	0.40	71.2	80.1	89.7	94.6	98.8
	1.0	0.28	74.1	82.0	90.6	95.1	99.0
10	2.5	0.32	74.0	82.1	90.6	95.3	99.0
	5.0	0.45	82.2	89.2	95.5	98.3	99.8

DIY

We will initialize the simulation with a gamma-distributed demand.

```
d_mu, d_std, d_min = 100, 25, 0
d_mu_p = d_mu - d_min #d_mu'
d_shape_p = d_mu_p**2/d_std**2 #k_d'
d_scale_p = d_std**2/d_mu_p #theta_d'
```

```
d = np.maximum(np.random.gamma(d_shape_p,d_scale_p,time).round
    (0).astype(int)+d_min,0)
```

For the simulation, we will use a fixed lead time so that the various parameters can be computed as such.

```
L, R = 1, 4
d_c = R*d_mu
x_std = np.sqrt((R+L)*d_std**2) #x_std' = x_std
x_mu_p = (R+L)*(d_mu-d_min) #x_mu'
x_shape_p = x_mu_p**2/x_std**2 #k_x'
x_scale_p = x_std**2/x_mu_p #theta_x'
```

If you want to set a cycle service level target, you can initialize your simulation as:

```
alpha = 0.95
S_p = round(gamma.ppf(alpha,x_shape_p,scale=x_scale_p),0)
beta = 1-gamma_loss(S_p,x_mu_p,x_std)/d_c
S = S_p + (R+L)*d_min
```

Or if you want to set a fill rate target:

```
beta = 0.99
S_p = round(gamma_loss_inverse(x_mu_p, x_std, d_c, beta))
alpha = gamma.cdf(S_p,x_shape_p,scale=x_scale_p)
S = S_p + (R+L)*d_min
```

We can also compute the expected stock levels (safety, cycle and in-transit). Note that, with low fill rates (< 80%) the safety stock can become negative. In other words, you will order less than the expected cycle demand.

```
Cs = 1/2 * d_mu * R
Is = d_mu * L
Ss = S - 2*Cs - Is
```

From here, you simply use the simulation as shown in Section 5.3.2.

Stochastic Lead Times You can simulate gamma-distributed lead times by using the command (normally distributed lead times are commented):

```
if t%R==0:
    #actual_L = int(round(max(np.random.normal(L,L_std),0),0))
    actual_L = int(round(np.random.gamma(L_shape,L_scale),0))
    net = hand[t] + transit[t].sum()
    transit[t,actual_L] = S - net
```

L_shape and L_scale are computed (during the initialization phase) as

```
L_shape = L**2/L_std**2 #k_L'
L_scale = L_std**2/L #theta_L'
```

9.7 Recap

Policy	Reorder point (s, Q)	$\iota = s$	$x_\tau = L$	$d_c = Q$
	Review Period (R, S)	$\iota = S$	$x_\tau = R + L$	$d_c = d_R$
Risk-period	$\sigma_x = \sqrt{x_\tau}\sigma_d$	$\mu_x = x_\tau \mu_d$		
Demand distribution	$d \sim \Gamma(k_d, \theta_d)$	$d_x \sim \Gamma(k_x, \theta_x) = \Gamma(x_\tau k_d, \theta_d)$		
	$k = \dfrac{\mu^2}{\sigma^2} \qquad \theta = \dfrac{\sigma^2}{\mu}$			
Cycle service level	$\alpha = F_\Gamma(\iota; k_x, \theta_x)$			
	$\iota = F_\Gamma^{-1}(\alpha; k_x, \theta_x)$			
Fill rate	$\beta = 1 - \dfrac{\mathcal{L}_\Gamma(\iota; k_x, \theta_x)}{d_c}$			
	$\iota = \arg\min_\iota \left[\left\| \mathcal{L}_\Gamma(\iota; k_x, \theta_x) - d_c(\beta - 1) \right\| \right]$			
	$\mathcal{L}_\Gamma(\iota; k_x, \theta_x) = k_x\theta_x\,(1 - F_\Gamma(\iota; k_x + 1, \theta_x)) - \iota\,(1 - F_\Gamma(\iota; k_x, \theta_x))$			
Safety stock	$S_s = \iota - \mu_x$			

Solver

If you want to compute the required stock level ι (at the beginning of the risk-period) to reach a fill rate β, you need to use a solver that will look for the ι that minimizes the difference between $d_c(1 - \beta)$ and $\mathcal{L}_\Gamma(\iota; k_x, \theta_x)$.

Demand Offset

If the period demand is distributed as $d \sim \Gamma(k_d, \theta_d) + d_{min}$, the computations can be done as above by replacing μ_x and ι by:

$$\mu'_x = \mu_x - x_{min}$$
$$\iota' = \iota + x_{min}$$

where $x_{min} = x_\tau d_{min}$.

10 Multi-Echelon Inventory Optimization

Per ardua ad astra – Through adversity to the stars.

Royal Air Force motto

So far, we have discussed models that described supply chains with only one stocking point and one item. Real-world supply chains are often made up of multiple stocking points, each one usually stocking several different items. In this chapter we will broaden our model by optimizing inventories across multiple stocking points. Ton de Kok—professor at the Eindhoven University of Technology—argued, *"There is no hope to find optimal control policies for real-world multi-item multi-echelon systems."*[1] Nevertheless, as you will see, we can *easily* come up with good (enough) policies—thanks to specific assumptions.

10.1 Supply Chain Network Topology

As shown in Figure 10.1, we will represent a supply chain as a network of **nodes** and **edges**. Each node is a (possible) stocking point and each edge symbolizes the customer-supplier relationship between two nodes.

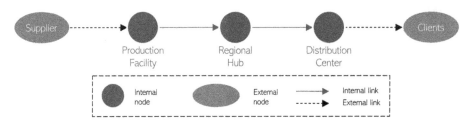

Figure 10.1: Supply chain represented as a network with nodes and edges.

Internal vs. External Nodes

We can differentiate two types of nodes: internal and external. You could say that an external node is a stocking point that is not *owned* by a company. But actually, a company can have visibility and control beyond its own warehouses. Therefore "internal" nodes could include stocking points that are not fully owned by a company. This is typically the case in supply chains that use **vendor managed inventory (VMI)**.

---

1 See de Kok (2018).

https://doi.org/10.1515/9783110673944-010

> ### Vendor Managed Inventory (VMI)
>
> Vendor Managed Inventory (VMI) is a business model where the supplier of a product takes ownership of the stock its client holds. In practice, it means that the supplier is managing (and responsible for) its client inventory policy. In some cases the supplier can also own the inventory held at its client premises; it is then called **consignment**. VMI will realize its full potential if a supply chain is able to deploy a proper multi-echelon inventory optimization.

We will call each layer of a supply chain network an **echelon** (think tier or stage).[2] A supply chain with only one echelon is called a single-echelon supply chain; a supply chain with more than one echelon is called a **multi-echelon supply chain**. As shown in Figure 10.2, the first echelon of a supply chain (that is in contact with an external supplier if any) is the **supply echelon**; the last one (directly facing the customer demand) is called the **demand echelon**.

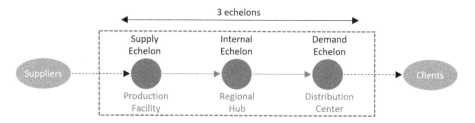

Figure 10.2: Multi-echelon supply chain.

10.1.1 Types of Multi-Echelon Supply Chains

As shown in Figure 10.3, we can classify multi-echelon supply chains in 4 main types of networks: serial, assembly, distribution and general.

Serial This is the simplest supply chain network where each node (i. e., possible stocking point) only has one downstream node (its client-node) and one upstream node (its supplier-node).

Assembly Each node has only one downstream node (except for the demand nodes obviously) and possibly multiple upstream nodes. We call this "assembly" as we need multiple suppliers to supply a single node. This is a situation similar to an assembly production unit where multiple items are assembled into a final prod-

---

2 An echelon is a layer of a supply chain, whereas a node is just a stocking point.

uct. We will discuss the parallel between multi-echelon inventory optimization and production processes in Section 10.2.2.

Distribution This is the opposite of an assembly supply chain. In a distribution system, each node has (possibly) multiple downstream nodes but only one upstream node. This is often the case for distributors that have one central warehouse distributing goods in multiple shops.

General This is the general case where one node can have multiple upstream and downstream nodes. These general networks are often segmented further into **cyclic** and **acyclic** supply chains. Acyclic means that there can be no cycle between various nodes, whereas cyclic supply chains describe potential return flows.

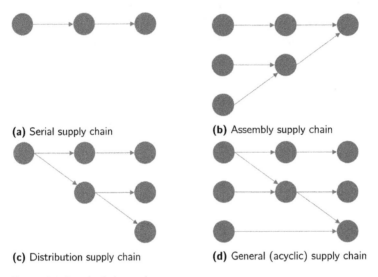

(a) Serial supply chain

(b) Assembly supply chain

(c) Distribution supply chain

(d) General (acyclic) supply chain

Figure 10.3: Supply chain topology.

10.2 Local vs. Global Inventory Optimization

In many supply chains, each echelon is still managed separately—often based on simple rules of thumb. **Multi-echelon inventory optimization (MEIO)** should then bring added value by performing a global rather than local optimization. Let's first discuss the issues of pursuing a siloed local optimization before discussing the benefits of MEIO.

10.2.1 Local Inventory Optimization

In a supply chain that is **locally optimized**, each node (in Figure 10.4, the production facility, the regional hub and the distribution center) can choose (*optimize*) its own inventory policy—without any alignment with the other echelons. It means that each node can pick their own safety stock levels, optimal order quantity, review periods and so on. They could even change their inventory policies without letting the others know. You can easily imagine that, with such a siloed myopic organization, the slightest change in the external demand might drastically impact the supply chain. Different nodes can even start to pursue rogue behaviors to secure some (profitable) stock, to the detriment of the supply chain as a whole.

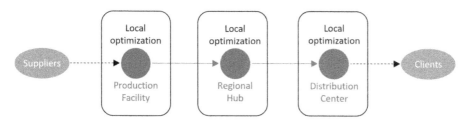

Figure 10.4: Locally optimized supply chain.

Bullwhip Effect
In many cases, supply chains that are stuck in local inventory optimization face a bigger issue than simple misalignment. They face the risk of a massive **bullwhip effect**.

As shown in Figure 10.5, the bullwhip effect describes a situation where the more upstream an echelon is, the more demand variation it faces, despite the fact that the final demand is rather steady. The more upstream a node is, the more pronounced the effect. The name "bullwhip" comes from the fact that a small deviation of the final

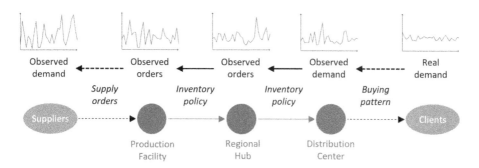

Figure 10.5: Bullwhip effect.

customer demand will produce a large variability at the manufacturer end. Just like cracking a whip by a fast flick of the wrist.

A Brief History of the Bullwhip Effect

The bullwhip effect was initially theorized in the 1960s by Jay Forrester (professor at MIT). It got more attention in the late 1990s, when the name "bullwhip" was bestowed by Procter & Gamble (P&G) management team. P&G observed that, despite the fact that the final demand for Pampers was stable (babies consumed a steady flow), the orders at the manufacturing sites were highly variable.

As identified by Lee et al. (1997), there are 4 main causes to the bullwhip effect:
1. Order forecasting
2. Order batching
3. Price fluctuation and promotions
4. Shortage gaming

Let's investigate them one by one.

1. Order forecasting If each node in the supply chain forecasts its demand based on the direct orders coming from its downstream nodes—rather than on the final client demand—the supply chain faces an issue. Each node will create a new forecast that will tend to distort its own demand signal and (very often) overreact to it. Then, based on the node inventory policy, this demand signal will be distorted further (as we will discuss later). These forecasts are not "demand forecasts" anymore but "order forecasts."

For example, let's imagine that you think that demand decreased by 10% per week. Your current up-to level target is around 4 weeks of inventory (because of lead time, review period and safety stock—see Chapter 5) so, you will then decrease it by 4 times the demand decrease you observed. In turn, the node directly upstream will see a massive order reduction from you (its client). This will result in an even steeper order decrease from this node to the node upstream. And so on. The smallest final client demand variation results in a massive variation at the manufacturer end.

The *beer game*[3]—a supply chain simulation game often played at universities—shows this effect to its players: everyone tends to overreact to the order patterns they observe.

Being able to forecast directly the final clients demand is particularly important when the supply chain includes multiple steps (and actors). Supply chains that are able to accurately react as they see the final client demand, will get a definitive

---

3 This game describes a 4-echelon beer supply chain where each player manages one node (without any information about the final demand). The game originates from the 1960s. It was initially developed by Jay Forrester (from MIT) and was codified later in its "modern" setup in Sterman (1992).

edge over their siloed competitors. This is particularly important when an external event results in massive demand shifts (as we saw with the coronavirus crisis).

2. **Order batching** Usually the more upstream a node is, the bigger its batch size (or the longer its review period). This means that as we move upstream in the supply chain we face fewer but bigger orders (resulting in a lumpier order signal). Policies such as discounts for full truckloads will push this effect further. As each node is batch ordering, the demand signal will get distorted along the supply chain.

3. **Price fluctuation and promotions** Price fluctuations (very) often create demand distortions resulting in a more variable demand (but not always higher overall). As we saw earlier, as we move upstream in the supply chain, small variations in final demand will result in a massive bullwhip effect. Often the various supply chain nodes are not aware that this demand variation is simply caused by pricing variations or promotions. Promotions for the final client can also force manufacturing to produce goods months in advance to compensate for lack of production flexibility and capacity. Order batching and order forecasting will only make the impact of price fluctuation worse.

4. **Shortage gaming** In some cases, when the supply chain is very siloed, each node might place oversized orders in a rogue move to protect itself against a speculative future supply shortage (this will often happen in time of supply crisis such as caused by the coronavirus). This will be done at the expense of other nodes who will suffer from the supply shortage (often resulting from a self-fulfilling prophecy). While the one node which ordered too much will suffer from excess inventory.

   I witnessed this specific issue in a distribution company that had one central warehouse and multiple (independent) shops. Each shop usually tried to "steal" inventory from the central warehouse to protect itself from future shortage. They obviously do this only for profitable products. Overall, this behavior increased stress and resentment among employees; and resulted overall in lower sales (as one shop had excess inventory while others suffered shortages).

   Shortage gaming can also happen at the very end of a supply chain when final customers fear that they will lack supply. We observed this effect during the coronavirus with toilet paper runs.

How Can We Fight the Bullwhip Effect?

The causes above can be fought one by one. Usually it requires a supply chain to:

1. Have a global view on demand and supply across each inventory node. This will reduce shortage games and order forecasting. Typically using vendor managed inventory (VMI) will allow a supplier to properly capture the final demand.

2. Have a central team responsible for setting inventory policies across the supply chain, and check that these policies are followed. This will remove the shortage gaming.

3. Use a fair-share allocation in case of shortage. And make sure everyone is playing by the rules.
4. Reduce review periods, lead times and order quantities. This will reduce the impact of order batching.
5. Orchestrate pricing, promotions and marketing based on supply and inventory availability. This is often done through *S&OP*.[4]

10.2.2 Global Inventory Optimization

Multi-echelon inventory optimization (MEIO) consists of optimizing inventory allocation across a supply chain in order to achieve a desired service level while minimizing the costs. We will first discuss what to expect from MEIO and what drives inventory allocation across a supply chain, before looking into MEIO models.

What to Expect from MEIO

Many software companies have been promoting multi-echelon inventory optimization advantages through the late 2000s and 2010s, advancing the idea that MEIO can save from 20% to 30% of inventory (compared to single-echelon inventory optimization). Many MEIO projects have been documented in academic papers as well as in business cases. Observed inventory reductions often vary from 10% to 35%. Let's mention a few cases:

- Graves and Willems (2000) described an MEIO project done for Kodak in the late 90s. After two years, they could reduce the inventory by one-third while improving the service level.
- Billington et al. (2004) reports saving $130 million for HewlettPackard. Their inventory level decreased by over 30 percent for the digital-camera business, resulting in a supply chain total cost reduction of more than 5% (while keeping similar service levels).
- In a blog post, Tayur (2007) reported that Deere & Company implemented an MEIO solution for one of their divisions (accounting for 300 products across more than 2500 stock locations). This resulted in an inventory reduction of $1 billion, while improving the service level.
- Thonemann (2011) describes a project undertaken by a big pharmaceutical company that reduced the working capital tied up in safety stocks by 19% (keeping similar service levels) for one of their best-selling drugs (in a global supply chain).

---

4 S&OP stands for Sales and Operations Planning. It is used to align sales, marketing and supply chain teams (production, logistics, inventory).

- In a survey, Aberdeen (2012) reported for MEIO users an average 3.1% service level increase along with a 15% reduction in cash-to-cash cycle.[5]
- I personally witnessed extreme cases where inventory reduction was up to 40% thanks to MEIO (and some warehouse-resizing adjustments).

Naturally, the magnitude of the results also depends on the supply chain initial maturity level. Depending on the supply chain management objectives, one could also decide not to reduce the total inventory level (or only partially), keeping it constant and increasing the service level instead (thanks to a better allocation of safety stocks). In such cases, MEIO projects won't deliver an inventory reduction but a better service level.

Inventory Position Drivers
Let's discuss three drivers that influence where the (safety) stock should be located in a supply chain (as shown in Figure 10.6):[6]
- Lead time pooling
- Demand pooling
- Value increase

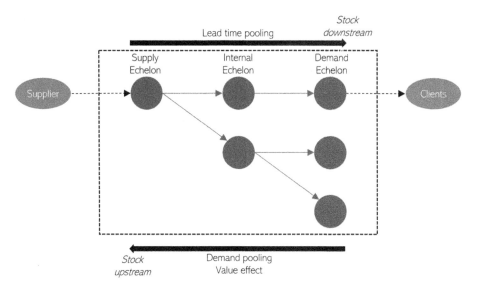

Figure 10.6: Stock allocation drivers for multi-echelon inventory optimization.

---

5 The cash-to-cash cycle is the time between when a business pays its suppliers and collects payments from its customers.
6 See Thonemann (2011).

Lead time pooling [pushing downstream] As we aggregate demand variation over a longer lead time (risk-period), we would need less safety stock to achieve the same service level (see Section 4.3). In other words, it requires less safety stock for one site to hold safety stock against a lead time of 10 weeks, rather than 10 consecutive sites to keep safety stocks against one week of lead time each. We would then prefer to locate our stock downstream in order to aggregate the demand over a longer lead time.

Demand pooling [pushing upstream] As we move upstream in the supply chain, various different demand signals are aggregated and therefore smoother—for example, the demand at a manufacturing site is more stable than the one that each shop faces. Since it is easier to use safety stocks to bridge a stable (big) demand flow than many small highly variable flows, you want to have the safety stocks upstream.

Value increase [pushing upstream] Stocking products upstream is often less expensive than downstream. This is the case for multiple reasons, for example:

- Manufacturing sites are often located in cheaper locations than the selling points (often in big cities), resulting in lower holding costs for upstream echelons.
- In a manufacturing process, raw materials are cheaper (and often easier to store) than finished products, so you would prefer keeping inventory at the early stages of the manufacturing process.

MEIO for Production Optimization

So far we discussed MEIO as a method to solve inventory localization in a supply chain network, but it can also be used to decide **where to keep inventory within a production process**.[7] A production process can be described as a network with various (possible) stocking points, lead times, varying holding costs and product values, and finally with different demand signals for each possible final product. Production processes often rely on **postponement** or **decoupling points**: you need to define which stage of the manufacturing process should hold inventory. These can be optimized via MEIO techniques.

10.3 Multi-Echelon Inventory Optimization

Now that we reviewed the pitfalls related to single-echelon optimization, and saw the benefits that await a properly optimized supply chain, we can now discuss multi-echelon models.

---

7 See for example Graves and Willems (2003).

10.3.1 Two Schools of Thoughts

During the second half of the 20th century, two different schools of thoughts emerged concerning the best way to optimize inventory policies across multi-echelon supply chains. Let's quickly describe the two different sets of assumptions on which they were based and the models that resulted.

Stochastic-service model (SSM) This model attempts to **model the multi-echelon network entirely, including all the possible variability.** It was initially described in 1960 by Clark and Scarf for a serial supply chain.[8] They already noticed, in their initial paper, that even though the "regular" lead time from an upstream node to a downstream node might be deterministic—the actual time it takes for a downstream node to be replenished by its upstream node depends on the supplier node's current inventory level.

For example, your supplier will deliver your orders in 2 weeks *when* it has some inventory, but in an unknown amount of time if it has no inventory left.

This means that the *actual* lead time between two nodes is (always) stochastic. The stochastic-service model becomes massively complex when one node faces multiple supplier-nodes with various internal service levels (resulting in various internal stochastic lead times).

Guaranteed-service model (GSM) This model was first described in 1958 by K. Simpson (an operation consultant at Arthur D. Little).[9] It is simpler than the SSM, thanks to a counter-intuitive (yet central) assumption: **the safety stock is only used to cover demand variation up to a threshold.**[10] The demand above this threshold (if any) will be served through **exceptional means** (e. g., the order can be delayed, extra hours can be worked, fast shipments can be made, the production can be externalized, etc.).[11] Thanks to this assumption, the model can elegantly (and relatively simply) optimally allocate safety stocks through a multi-echelon supply chain. Each node will quote (i. e., guarantee) a maximum replenishment lead time (the "guaranteed-service time") to its downstream nodes: if the demand over the lead time is lower than a bound (as assumed initially), it will consistently deliver its orders within this time. And if it isn't, the extra demand won't impact the inventory model, because it will be served through other means.

---

8 Clark and Scarf (1960).

9 See Simpson (1958) for the original paper. See Eruguz (2014), Li (2013) for a more complete literature review and an extensive GSM model explanation. Both theses are available online on tel.archives-ouvertes.fr

10 The idea of inventory optimization assuming bounded demand was initially developed in 1955 by Kimball (also a consultant at Arthur D. Little) in an unpublished article. It was reprinted later in Kimball (1988).

11 Guaranteed-service model takes the joke: "95% of the time, it works every time," literally.

Comparing both Models

The stochastic-service model (SSM) analyzes the stochastic time it takes from one node to replenish another (based on its inventory level). The **stochastic-service model is driven by internal service levels**; whereas the guaranteed-service (time) model[12] assumes that each node will always serve its clients within a fixed quoted time, assuming that the demand is bounded. The **guaranteed-service model is driven by internal guaranteed-service times** (in other words, how much risk-period each node should cover). In short, where the SSM uses safety stocks as buffer against the entire demand variability (resulting in random lead times), the GSM assumes that safety stocks will be used until a certain demand threshold.

Results

We already saw that the GSM is simpler than the SSM (it is also faster to optimize mathematically). But which one will deliver the best inventory policy? In order to see which model would result in the lowest cost, academics threw both models into competitions over simulated supply chains. Even though no definitive answer can be drawn on which one is best, De Smet et al. (2018) saw that in most cases GSM would result in lower costs than SSM (depending on parameters such as service level), with an overall cost reduction of 10%; whereas Klosterhalfen and Minner (2010) showed that the difference between the two models was around 4% maximum depending on the supply chain features.

Conclusion

We will focus on the GSM because it is—compared to the stochastic model—simpler to understand, faster to run, and equally performing (even slightly better).

10.4 Serial Supply Chains Using GSM

Let's start our journey with the guaranteed-service model by solving the simplest multi-echelon supply chain: a serial network. Rather than first theorize about the model and then use it, we will get an intuition on how it works (and its limitations) by solving it for a simple network—*Vires acquirit eundo*, we gather strength as we go.

The question we ask ourselves is: *"How much safety stock should each node keep?"*

---

[12] Academics often use "guaranteed-service model" (GSM). We can also call it "guaranteed-service time model" and therefore use both terms interchangeably.

10.4.1 Case Description

For this example that we will use throughout this section, we will examine a supply chain with 3 echelons (a production facility, a regional hub and a distribution center) as shown in Figure 10.7. Each node has its own incoming natural lead time (L_1 = 4, L_2 = 3, L_3 = 2) and its own holding costs (h_1 = 1, h_2 = 2, h_3 = 4). Remember that it is usual for downstream nodes to be more expensive (see Section 10.2.2).

Review period = 1 week

$h_1 = 1$ $h_2 = 2$ $h_3 = 4$ $d \sim \mathcal{N}(100, 25^2)$

Supplier   4 weeks $L_1 = 4$ 3 weeks $L_2 = 3$ 2 weeks $L_3 = 2$ Clients

Production Facility   Regional Hub   Distribution Center

Figure 10.7: Example of a serial supply chain.

Review Policy
This supply chain also follows a periodic review policy, with a periodic review of 1 week. More importantly, we assume that each stocking point is following the *same* review period, so that the 3 nodes review their stock at the same moment in time. We also assume that each stocking point has a full view of the current inventory position of all the other stocking points.

Goods Flow
We assume that an order received by the end of a period in a node is directly available for shipment at the beginning of the next period. In other words, in our example with a supply chain with a weekly review period, it means that even an order received on Friday evening in the production facility will be shipped on Monday morning to the regional hub.

10.4.2 Theory: Guaranteed-Service Model

The guaranteed-service time model is based on the **allocation of guaranteed-service times to each node** and the fact that the **demand is bounded**. We will review these two concepts in detail, before moving to an original **risk-period framework** that is more intuitive to use (and aligned with the previous chapters). If you are not interested in the theory of the GSM (or its academic description), feel free to go to the paragraph Risk-Period Framework later in this section.

Guaranteed-Service Times

In the guaranteed-service time model, the question of inventory allocation is solved thanks to the **guaranteed-service time** that each node quotes to its downstream direct clients.

Guaranteed-service time (gs_τ)

The guaranteed-service time is the maximum amount of time, quoted from a supplier-node to its client, that the supplier-node will take to deliver any of its client orders. This maximum guaranteed-service time can only be quoted if the orders from the client stay below a maximum demand (in other words, the demand is bounded).

Our initial question of optimal safety stock allocation is answered with another question: *"how much guaranteed-service time should each node quote?"*

Naturally, the allocation of guaranteed-service times needs to respect some requirements:

1. Service times cannot be negative (you cannot quote a service time of minus one week).
2. The demand nodes (those facing final clients) need to quote a guaranteed-service time of 0 (except if clients accept otherwise).

Example

Continuing with our simple network, Figure 10.8 shows one way to solve our serial supply chain:

- The production facility (site 1) promises a guaranteed-service time of 0 ($gs_\tau^1 = 0$), this means that this site will deliver any order it receives as soon as it receives it. The production facility therefore needs to be protected against the risk over its supplier lead time. We note x_τ^i the risk-period covered by node i, so that we have $x_\tau^1 = 4$.
- The regional hub (site 2) promises a guaranteed-service time of 3 weeks ($gs_\tau^2 = 3$) to site 3, this means that this node will order from its own supplier-node any order it receives. It won't keep any safety stocks ($x_\tau^2 = 0$) as its guaranteed-service time is equal to its incoming lead time; this is a transparent node.
- The distribution center promises to the final clients a guaranteed-service time of 0 weeks ($gs_\tau^3 = 0$), this is normal: we don't want our clients to wait. This site will then need to keep enough safety stock to cover a risk-period of 6 weeks ($x_\tau^3 = 6$) made up of:
  - Its immediate lead time from the regional hub (2 weeks),

- Plus the guaranteed-service time from the regional hub (3 weeks),
- Plus for the review period (1 week).

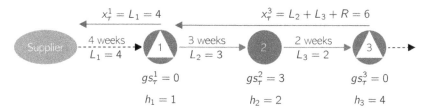

Figure 10.8: Example of guaranteed-service times allocation ($gs_\tau^i = [0,3,0]$). A node with a white triangle means that it holds enough safety stock to cover its incoming risk-period.

We will discuss later in Section 10.4.3 other possible stock allocations across this simple supply chain.

Bounded Demand

A supplier-node can only guarantee a maximum service time to its clients if the client demands are bounded. For example, you can only promise your clients to deliver all their orders within 3 weeks if they agree never to order more than 1000 pieces over 3 weeks. In practice, no supply chain will forbid demand to be too high. Instead, the demand will be managed via safety stocks up to a certain threshold (as shown in Figure 10.9). Thereafter, it will be served via **exceptional** means.

Typically, we say that the demand over τ periods, noted $d(\tau)$, is bounded by the **demand bound** $\hat{d}(\tau)$. We can set this bound similarly to the one for the cycle ser-

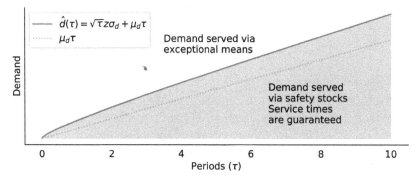

Figure 10.9: Bounded demand over τ periods.

vice level:[13]

$$d(\tau) \leq \hat{d}(\tau) = z \, \sigma_d \, \sqrt{\tau} + \mu_d \, \tau$$

Based on factor z (see Section 4.2.4 for a refresher), we know the probability for the demand during τ periods to be within the bound.

Note, the GSM assumes that the demand is bounded by $\hat{d}(\tau)$ for **each** τ within the total risk-period of the supply chain. For example, if the total risk-period is 10 (as in our example), we expect that:

$$d(\tau) \leq \hat{d}(\tau)$$

for **any** $\tau \leq 10$.

In other words, as long as the clients buy less than $\hat{d}(\tau)$ over τ periods, it will be served fully on time.

Example

Let's imagine an example where the demand per period follows $d \sim \mathcal{N}(100, 25^2)$. We will set the demand bound at 95% probability (as shown in Figure 10.10). You can compute easily in Excel and Python that $\Phi(0.95) \Rightarrow z = 1.645$. So as long as the final client respects:

$$\hat{d}(\tau) \leq 1.645 \cdot 25 \cdot \sqrt{\tau} + 100 \cdot \tau$$

for any $\tau \leq 10$ (as $x_\tau = 10$ over the total supply chain), you should be able to deliver all the products on time.

Figure 10.10: Serial supply chain with bounded demand $\hat{d}(\tau)$.

Risk-Period Framework

The traditional approach to GSM is done based on the guaranteed-service times quoted by each supplying-node to its client-nodes and under the restrictive assumption of bounded demand. We prefer here an original (simplified) approach based on

---

[13] We assume that the demand is independent from one period to another, see Section 4.3 for a discussion about demand temporal aggregation and independence.

risk-periods.[14] The question we ask is, *"Over which risk-period should each node protect itself?"* We have a few (obvious) constraints to respect:

- **The total risk-period of the supply chain needs to be covered.**
  In our previous example, the total risk-period was 10 weeks ($L_1 + L_2 + L_3 + R = 4 + 3 + 2 + 1$) so that the 3 nodes should cover, in total, 10 weeks of risk.
- **Each node can only have protection over the maximum risk-period they face.**
  In other words, if the total incoming lead time of a node is 4 weeks, this node cannot cover more than 4 weeks of risk-period.
- **The demand-nodes will support the review period.**

As we will see in the simulations (Section 10.5), as long as the targeted service level is rather high, we shouldn't worry too much about the bounded demand assumption. The risk-period framework will therefore allow us to easily allocate safety stocks in a multi-echelon supply chain.

10.4.3 How to Allocate Safety Stock in a Serial Supply Chain

As already shown by Simpson in 1958, the optimal safety stock allocation in a serial supply chain follows an **all-or-nothing** policy (if we assume deterministic lead times). It means that **a stocking point will either keep enough safety stock to cover all the *reasonable* demand (i. e., until $\hat{d}$) over its (incoming) risk-period, or no safety stock at all**. This will greatly help us to solve our serial supply chain since we don't have to compute many combinations. For our serial supply chain, we know that there are only 4 potential cases that can be optimal (as shown in Figure 10.11). More generally, the number of cases to test is $2^{\text{nodes}-1}$.[15] That is $2^{3-1} = 4$ in our example.

You can see in Figure 10.11 the 4 resulting possible (optimal) cases (where x_τ^i is the length of the incoming risk-period of the stocking point i). A node with a white triangle means that it holds enough safety stock to cover its incoming risk-period.

In order to see what is the optimal safety stock allocation, we need to compute the total safety stock requirement for each case. This is done by summing the safety stock required at each stocking point S_s^i (computed based on eq. 4.3 in Section 4.3.2).

$$S_s^i = z\,\sigma_d\,\sqrt{x_\tau^i} \tag{10.1}$$

---

14 Risk-period: maximum amount of time you need to wait to receive an order (from your supplier). During this period your inventory is at risk of being depleted.
15 We take 2 to the power of "nodes - 1" as the demand nodes always need to have enough safety stock in order to guarantee no waiting time to the final client.

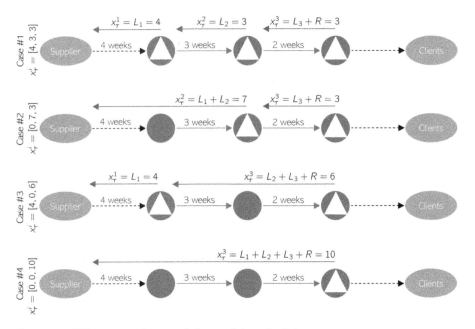

Figure 10.11: Different scenarios to optimize a serial supply chain.

Cost Optimization

Actually, we are more interested in the total cost of each case. Minimizing safety stocks is not our objective, minimizing costs is. The total costs C_h can be computed simply by multiplying the safety stock in each site by its holding costs.

$$C_h = \sum_i C_h^i = \sum_i S_s^i \, h^i = \sum_i z \, \sigma_d \, \sqrt{x_\tau^i} \, h^i$$

We leave the cycle stocks aside from this cost equation as cycle stocks are expected to flow through the supply chain (we assume that there is no minimum order quantity and the review periods are aligned across the supply chain).

Example

Let's continue our last example where the period demand follows $d \sim \mathcal{N}(100, 25^2)$. You can see in Table 10.1 the overall results based on:

$$S_s^i = z \, \sigma_d \, \sqrt{x_\tau^i} = 1.645 \cdot 25 \cdot \sqrt{x_\tau^i} \quad \text{(see eq. 10.1)}$$

Table 10.1: Safety stocks and holding costs per node per case.

| | Safety stocks | | | | Holding costs | | | |
| | Node | | | | Node | | | |
Case	$i = 1$	$i = 2$	$i = 3$	Total	$i = 1$	$i = 2$	$i = 3$	Total
#1	82	71	71	224	82	142	284	508
#2		109	71	180		218	284	502
#3	82		101	183	82		404	**486**
#4			130	**130**			520	520

We conclude that for this example:

- The case resulting in the lowest total safety stock is case #4. This is obvious: by grouping all the safety stock at the most downstream node we group all the lead times and benefit from the **lead time pooling effect** (that we already described in Section 10.2.2).
- The case resulting in the lowest holding cost is case #3. It is the best trade-off between the lead time pooling and the **value increase** effect (here represented by the fact that $h_1 < h_2 < h_3$).

Going Further

We looked at normal demand for this example, but we can also use different distributions.

Risk-Period Framework We can simply use the equations defined in Chapter 9, "Beyond Normality," if the demand is gamma-distributed.

Guaranteed-Service Model You can actually define the demand bound without the help of any specific distribution.
Equation 10.1 is then generalized to,

$$\text{Order up-to level of node } i = S^i = \hat{d}(x^i_\tau)$$
$$\text{Safety stock of node } i = S^i_s = S^i - \mu^i_x = \hat{d}(x^i_\tau) - \mu^i_x$$

where μ^i_x is the expected demand over the risk-period covered by node i and $\hat{d}(x^i_\tau)$ is the demand bound over the risk-period.

10.4.4 Multi-Echelon Inventory Policies

Local Inventory Policies

We just computed the optimal safety stock allocation for our serial supply chain. As we know, safety stocks are only a part of the inventory policy. Because we are following a periodic review policy (R, S), we still have to compute each node order up-to level S^i. As shown in Table 10.2, we have for each node, $S^i = \mu_x^i + S_S^i$ where μ_x^i is the expected demand over the risk-period of the stocking point i (see Chapter 5 for a recap about (R, S) policies).

Table 10.2: Order up-to level S^i for each node.

Case	Order up-to levels S^i		
	$i = 1$	$i = 2$	$i = 3$
#1	482	371	371
#2		809	371
#3	482		701
#4			1130

Global Inventory Policies

In order to manage the supply chain globally, we have to follow **global inventory policies** (also known as **echelon policies**). The policies we discussed so far are **local** policies: they deal with how much stock should be present at a certain stocking point. **An echelon inventory policy will deal with the stock present at an echelon and all those downstream.** The **echelon order up-to level of node** i, noted $\mathcal{S}^i$, is the sum of all the up-to levels of this node and its (direct and indirect) client-nodes. Formally we have,

$$\mathcal{S}^i = \sum_{j \le i} S^j$$

For example, as shown in Table 10.3, the echelon policy of the second node (the regional hub) is 1180 units in the second case ($\mathcal{S}^2 = S^2 + S^1 = 809 + 371$).

Table 10.3: Order up-to level S^i for each node.

Case	Order up-to levels S^i			Echelon up-to levels $\mathcal{S}^i$		
	$i = 1$	$i = 2$	$i = 3$	$i = 1$	$i = 2$	$i = 3$
#1	482	371	371	1224	742	371
#2		809	371	1180	1180	371
#3	482		701	1183	701	701
#4			1130	1130	1130	1130

In practice, when a node places its order, it will order based on the difference between its echelon (actual current) inventory (i. e., its inventory plus all its client-nodes inventories) and its echelon order up-to level.

> **Example**
>
> Let's imagine you have a supply chain policy setup as Case #1 described in Table 10.3. If you have currently the following inventory level in each node:
>
> $$I = [300, 250, 100]$$
>
> you have the following echelon inventory level:
>
> $$\mathcal{I} = [300 + 250 + 100, 250 + 100, 100]$$
> $$= [650, 350, 100]$$
>
> If you compare this echelon inventory level with the echelon order up-to levels ($\mathcal{S}$), you have the required orders:
>
> $$\text{Orders} = \mathcal{S} - \mathcal{I}$$
> $$= [1224, 742, 371] - [650, 350, 100]$$
> $$= 574, 392, 271]$$
>
> This means the first node should order 574 units from its external supplier (if any); the second node should order 392 units; and the final one (facing the final demand) should order 271 units.

10.5 Simulation

If we run simulations based on the cases described so far, as you can see in Table 10.4 and Figure 10.12, Cases #1 to #3 will result in a slightly less than expected cycle service level. Case #4 (where all the safety stocks are located downstream) will result in exactly the targeted service level. This makes sense, in Cases #1 to #3 the client-node is protected against its incoming risk-period but its upstream supply chain is still impacted by a possible lack of service level (in other words, Cases 1 and 2 will experience shortages since they don't assume a 100% service level). In case #4, the client-node is protected against the whole lead time and is therefore directly fulfilled by an external supplier (which we assume to be perfectly reliable with a 100% service level).

As you can see in Table 10.4, the results for cases #1 to #3 are close to the expected cycle service levels, which confirm that our model can be used to optimize a real-life supply chain.

Table 10.4: Simulation results for $\alpha = 95$ and $\alpha = 90$.

Cycle service level (target)	Case	Risk-period coverage	Safety stocks	Fill rate	Cycle service level
	#1	[4, 3, 3]	224	99.0	94.6
95	#2	[0, 7, 3]	180	98.9	94.4
	#3	[4, 0, 6]	183	98.7	94.9
	#4	[0, 0, 10]	130	98.4	95.1
	#1	[4, 3, 3]	174	97.3	88.4
90	#2	[0, 7, 3]	140	97.0	88.0
	#3	[4, 0, 6]	142	96.6	89.0
	#4	[0, 0, 10]	101	96.3	90.0

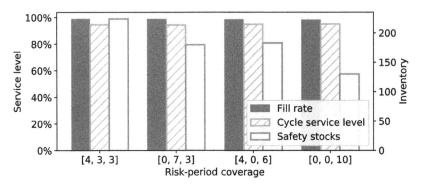

Figure 10.12: Simulation results for $\alpha = 95\%$.

We will discuss later, in Chapter 13, "Simulation Optimization," how to rely directly on simulations to optimize our supply chain.

DIY

We start our simulation by defining the number of sites (sites), their respective supply lead times (L) and the risk-period they will cover (x_tau). For the sake of simplicity, we will assume $R = 1$ throughout our simulation. We choose here Case #4 (you can choose any by uncommenting the appropriated row).

```
sites = 3
L = np.array([4,3,2])
#x_tau = np.array([4,3,3]) #if case 1
#x_tau = np.array([0,7,3]) #if case 2
#x_tau = np.array([4,0,6]) #if case 3
x_tau = np.array([0,0,10]) #if case 4
```

We can now define the safety stocks (Ss), order up-to levels (S) and echelon up-to levels (S_echelon) per node. Note that all these variables are now NumPy arrays rather than simple numbers (as in previous chapters).

```
x_std = np.sqrt(x_tau)*d_std
alpha = 0.95
z = norm.ppf(alpha)
Ss = np.round(x_std*z).astype(int)
S = Ss + x_tau*d_mu
S_echelon = (np.cumsum(S[::-1])[::-1]).astype(int)
```

Because we need to keep track of these inventory levels for each site, we define hand and transit as respectively 2 and 3 dimensional arrays.

```
hand = np.zeros([sites,time],dtype=int)
transit = np.zeros([sites,time,max(L)+1],dtype=int)
```

We initialize hand simply as the order up-to levels of each site. It is a more basic initialization than for the previous simulation models, so that the first timesteps of our simulation will not be representative of the *normal* supply chain regime.

```
hand[:,0] = S
```

We can now tackle the simulation loop. Its first part is relatively similar to those of the previous simulations we made (despite the fact that we update hand and transit for multiple sites at once). A second loop is performed through the sites to handle their respective orders. We assume in our supply chain that each node will send its delivery to its client-node directly (instantaneously) after receiving its own supply order. We will represent this by calculating the available stock at the upstream node (see the greyed line) including its incoming in-transit inventory which is supposed to arrive virtually at the same time as when the order is made. You can see in Figure 10.13 an example of the flow of one order through the simulation.

```
for t in range(1,time):
    hand[:,t] = hand[:,t-1] + transit[:,t-1,0]
    transit[:,t,:-1] = transit[:,t-1,1:]
    unit_shorts[t] = max(0,d[t] - max(0,hand[-1,t]))
    hand[-1,t] = hand[-1,t] - d[t]
    stockout_period[t] = hand[-1,t] < 0
```

```
for site in range(sites):
    net = hand[site:,t].sum() + transit[site:,t].sum()
    order = S_echelon[site] - net
    if site > 0: #all nodes but the supplier-node
        available = hand[site-1,t] + transit[site-1,t,0] #
            stock available at the supplier-node
        order = min(available, order) #constraint the order
        hand[site-1,t] -= order #consume the order at the
            supplier-node
        transit[site,t,L[site]-1] = order
    elif site == 0: #supplier-node
        transit[site,t,L[site]] = order
```

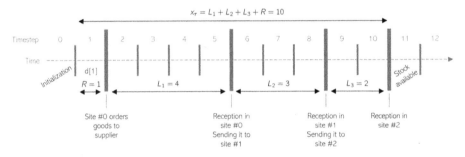

Figure 10.13: How goods are flowing in our serial supply chain.

10.6 Distribution Supply Chains Using GSM

Thirty-three years after Simpson published his paper about serial supply chains, in 1991, Inderfurth (Professor at the University of Bielefed, Germany) published an article that shows how to optimize a distribution supply chain according to the guaranteed-service model.[16]

Remember, as shown in Figure 10.14, a distribution supply chain is a supply chain where each node has a maximum of one supplier (upstream node), and possibly multiple clients (downstream nodes).

Inderfurth showed that optimizing a distribution supply chain (under the GSM framework) is similar to solving a serial supply chain. Each site should either cover all

---

16 See Inderfurth (1991).

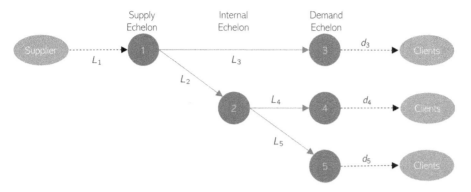

Figure 10.14: Distribution supply chain.

its in-coming risk-period (i. e., until the first upstream node that holds safety stocks) or none. This means that, even for very wide distribution supply chains (tens or hundreds of sales points), **only a few cases are worth being checked** in order to find the optimal case. As shown in Figure 10.15, in a distribution supply chain with 3 echelons, only 4 cases need to be checked.

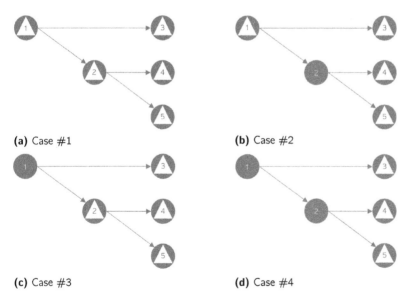

(a) Case #1

(b) Case #2

(c) Case #3

(d) Case #4

Figure 10.15: Different scenarios to optimize distribution supply chains.

The resulting risk-periods against which each node should be protected are shown for each case in Table 10.5.

Table 10.5: Risk-period x_t^j for each node in each case.

Case	Node				
	1	2	3	4	5
#1	L_1	L_2	$L_3 + R$	$L_4 + R$	$L_5 + R$
#2	L_1	–	$L_3 + R$	$L_2 + L_4 + R$	$L_2 + L_5 + R$
#3	–	$L_1 + L_2$	$L_1 + L_3 + R$	$L_4 + R$	$L_5 + R$
#4	–	–	$L_1 + L_3 + R$	$L_1 + L_2 + L_4 + R$	$L_1 + L_2 + L_5 + R$

10.6.1 Demand Pooling

In a distribution supply chain, some nodes are aggregating the demand of multiple end-clients. In our example, this is the case of node 1, that deals with d_3, d_4, d_5 and node 2 that deals with d_4, d_5. This is serious business because the optimization of a distribution supply chain depends on these specific nodes. We have two ways to deal with these:

1. Simply assume that all the final demands are independent (not correlated).

    For normally distributed demand, we have these relationships (in our example):

    $$d_1 = d_3 + d_4 + d_5 \sim \mathcal{N}\left(\mu_{d3} + \mu_{d4} + \mu_{d5}, \sigma_{d4}^3 + \sigma_{d5}^4 + \sigma_{d5}^2\right)$$
    $$d_2 = d_4 + d_5 \sim \mathcal{N}\left(\mu_{d4} + \mu_{d5}, \sigma_{d4}^2 + \sigma_{d5}^2\right)$$

    But these relationships will only hold if all the final demands are normally and independently distributed (see Section 4.3.3 for a discussion about demand independence).

    What if d_3 is gamma-distributed? What if they are not independently distributed?

2. We can also estimate the demand at each node directly by studying the demand flowing through this node. In our example it means that we would directly estimate d_1 by summing the observations of d_3, d_4, d_5 and assessing the resulting μ_{d1}, σ_{d1}, and the distribution (normal, gamma...) as we discussed in Section 9.4. This second approach will usually be more accurate but will require more data processing.

Going Further

Solving assembly or acyclic inventory networks will require dynamic programming or a solver with a set of constraints. See Moncayo-Martínez and Ramirez (2016) for a tutorial on how to use dynamic programming for solving MEIO with GSM.[a] See Graves and Willems (2000) for more details about the guaranteed-service model. Two theses (Li (2013) and Eruguz (2014)) are also freely available on tel.archives-ouvertes.fr.

[a] It is available on www.researchgate.net/publication/308015442_A_tutorial_to_set_safety_stock_under_guaranteed-service_time_by_dynamic_programming

10.7 A Brief History of the Guaranteed-Service Model

Even though the very first MEIO models were published in 1958 and 1960 (for the guaranteed-service and stochastic-service models respectively), the application of MEIO is rather recent for multiple reasons:

1. The first papers were limited to very specific and serial supply chain networks. We had to wait until the end of the 20th century for new, more general and applicable models to be published by academics.
2. MEIO requires information systems able to centrally manage wide supply chain networks (including inventory, supply and demand visibility across multiple countries and business units).
3. MEIO requires more computation power and is more complex than single-echelon inventory optimization (SEIO).

The guaranteed-service time model was initially proposed in 1955 by Kimball. This framework was used by Simpson (both consultants for A. D. Little) in 1958 to solve a serial supply chain.[17] After the initial papers in the late 50s, it took 30 years to see more advanced models thanks to a renewed interest from the academic world that started in the 90s (as shown in Figure 10.16). Inderfurth was the first to show how to solve a distribution network in 1991.[18] In the following decade, more advanced models were proposed.[19] Most notably, Graves and Willems (2000) had a profound impact on GSM: they showed how to solve a general (acyclic) supply chain thanks to dynamic pro-

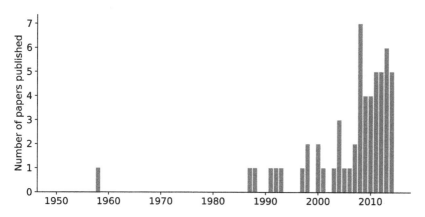

Figure 10.16: Papers published on GSM per year. Source: Eruguz et al. (2016).

---

17 See Kimball (1988), Simpson (1958).
18 See Inderfurth (1991).
19 See Thonemann (2011) for a in-depth (business) review or Eruguz et al. (2016) for an academic review.

gramming.[20] Since this article was published, many academics published new models (removing some of the initial assumptions)... And software developers implemented them as they developed tight relationships with academics.

MEIO has been seen as the new frontier for supply chain optimization software as of the mid 2000s to mid 2010s—and it is now being replaced by the rise of artificial intelligence.

---

20 See Moncayo-Martínez and Ramirez (2016) for an implementation.

10.8 Recap

Siloed supply chains face many risks (too much inventory, fights over shortages, bull-whip effect) that can be overcome with a proper global inventory policy. In order to do it, we need:
- Visibility and control over the inventory levels in the supply chain
- Multi-Echelon Inventory Optimization (MEIO) models

We saw in Sections 10.4 and 10.6 how to optimize serial and distribution supply chains thanks to the risk-period framework: a simplification of the guaranteed-service time model. It is based on three rules:
- The total risk-period of the supply chain to be covered
- Each node can only take protection over the maximum risk-period they directly face
- The nodes facing the final clients will support the review period

For more complex networks (assembly and acyclic general) you can use the guaranteed-service time model. See Graves and Willems (2000), Moncayo-Martínez and Ramirez (2016) for its implementation.

Part IV: **Discrete Inventory Optimization**

11 Newsvendor

In this chapter, we will discuss the *newsvendor model*,[1] one of the most thoroughly studied inventory models among academics. We will first go through the model with an example of a small bakery shop. Then, we will discuss the theory behind this model in detail. As we discover the newsvendor model, we will take the opportunity to discuss discrete demand distributions for the first time. Remember, *discrete* demand distributions means that the demand can only take integer values. Whereas *continuous* demand distributions can take any value. In practice, it is often more accurate to assume that the demand can only take integer values as often a client can only buy a round number of products.

11.1 A Question of Chocolate Muffins

You open a small bakery shop. Every evening, you need to decide how many (delicious) chocolate muffins you want to bake for your clients to buy the following day. This is an important decision. Baking muffins takes hours, mostly due to the time it takes to cook them in the oven. This means that, if a client enters your shop during the day and wants to buy one of your delicious muffins, you can't take the time to bake a new one. You need to bake them in advance—through the night—for the next day.

Every evening you have to make a decision on how many muffins you should bake for the next day.

Through experience, you have analyzed how many muffins clients wanted to buy per day, as shown in Figure 11.1 and Table 11.1.

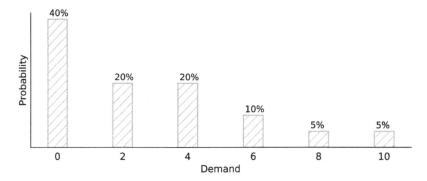

Figure 11.1: Muffin daily demand probability distribution.

---

1 The name "newsvendor" comes from the fact that this model is often used to describe the case of newsvendors that have to replenish their stock of newspapers every day. We will discuss this in detail in Section 11.2.

https://doi.org/10.1515/9783110673944-011

Table 11.1: Muffin demand PMF $p(d)$ and CDF $P(D \leq x)$.

x	0	2	4	6	8	10
$p(d)$	40%	20%	20%	10%	5%	5%
$P(D \leq x)$	40%	60%	80%	90%	95%	100%

We will note
- $p(d)$ the **demand probability mass function**. This is the probability for the demand to be d. In this chapter, for the sake of clarity, we abuse the notation a bit by using $p(d)$ instead of $p_D(d)$, as we implicitly assume that we are referring to the demand probability mass function.
- $P(D \leq x)$ the **probability for random discrete variable D to be smaller than or equal to x**. This is equivalent of $F_D(x)$ for a continuous distribution.

> **Probability mass function $(p_{\mathcal{X}}(x))$**
>
> The **probability mass function** is the probability that a **discrete** probability distribution $\mathcal{X}$ takes the integer x as a value. It is the discrete equivalent to the probability density function $f_{\mathcal{X}}(x)$ (see Section 4.2.1).

You took the time to analyze your costs. It costs 2€ to bake a muffin (mostly flour, sugar, chocolate, electricity and love) and you sell them at 6€ per piece. If at the end of the day you couldn't sell all of them, you reduce their price to 1€ and by doing so, they always get sold. We will call this the **salvage value**. You have to do this, because the muffins will lose their taste and texture throughout the night anyway.

> **Salvage value (s_v)**
>
> The discounted price at which a product is sold when the inventory needs to be cleared. It can also be the cost a company has to pay to clear its inventory (e. g., recycling, waste disposal).

So, how many muffins should you bake?

11.1.1 Do It Yourself

Excel
In order to see how the quantity we decide to bake impacts our expected profits, let's create a simple model in Excel (later in Python), rather than diving directly into a mathematical model.

◢	A	B	C	D	E	F	G	H	I	J
1					Quantity					
2	Prob	Demand	2	4	6	8	10		Price (p)	6
3	40%	0							Cost (c)	2
4	20%	2							Salvage (s$_v$)	1
5	20%	4								
6	10%	6								
7	5%	8								
8	5%	10								

Figure 11.2: Table setup.

Let's start by setting up a table as shown in Figure 11.2.
- The demand values and probabilities are on columns B and A respectively.
- The different possible order quantities (or in this case, the baked quantities) are spread across the second row (range C2:G2). Note that the choice is here arbitrary, you could create another table to test a quantity of 20 muffins.
- The different cost variables are on cells J2:J4.

Now, we have to compute the **profit** (or cost) for each combination of demand and quantity, we note it $P(Q, d)$ and compute it as below:

$$P(Q, d) = p \cdot \min(Q, d) + s_v \cdot \max(0, Q - d) - c \cdot Q$$

Where:
$p \cdot \min(Q, d)$ is the price per unit multiplied by the amount of sales.
$s_v \cdot \max(0, Q - d)$ is the salvage value multiplied by the excess units (if any).
$c \cdot Q$ is the cost per unit multiplied by the order quantity.

This formula is translated into Excel by typing this formula in cell C3.

        C3 = MIN($B3;C$2)*$J$2+MAX(0;C$2-$B3)*$J$4-C$2*$J$3

This formula can then be dragged onto the range C3:G8.

Finally we need to compute the expected profit for each quantity: we want to answer questions like *"What is the expected profit if I bake 4 muffins?"* We can answer this by using the formula below:

$$P(Q) = \sum_d P(Q, d) \cdot p(d)$$

where $p(d)$ is the demand probability mass function (the probability for the demand to be d). We can compute this easily in Excel by typing this formula in cell C10 and then copy and paste it in the range C10:G10.

        C10 = SUMPRODUCT(C3:C8,$A$3:$A$8)

You should then obtain a table as shown in Figure 11.3.

	A	B	C	D	E	F	G	H	I	J
1					Quantity					
2	Prob	Demand	2	4	6	8	10		Price (p)	6
3	40%	0	-2	-4	-6	-8	-10		Cost (c)	2
4	20%	2	8	6	4	2	0		Salvage (s_v)	1
5	20%	4	8	16	14	12	10			
6	10%	6	8	16	24	22	20			
7	5%	8	8	16	24	32	30			
8	5%	10	8	16	24	32	40			
9										
10			4	6	6	5	3,5			

Figure 11.3: Final table.

Therefore, we have the answer to our question *"How many muffins should I bake?"* We should bake between 4 and 6 muffins per day to maximize our profits.

Python
We can also solve this case easily with Python. Let's first define the demand values and probability mass function PMF and the possible order quantities as lists.

```
demand = [0,2,4,6,8,10]
pmf = [0.4,0.2,0.2,0.1,0.05,0.05]
quantity = [2,4,6,8,10]
p = 6; c = 2; s_v = 1
```

We will store the profits for each combination of demand and quantity in a NumPy array called results. In order to do so, we will iterate through demand and quantity and update results for each combination. Note that, instead of the usual method range(), we use the method enumerate() which returns at once an iterator and a counter.

```
results = np.empty(shape=(len(demand),len(quantity)))
for row, d in enumerate(demand):
    for column, q in enumerate(quantity):
        results[row,column] = min(q,d)*p - q*c + max(0,q-d)*s_v
```

You can then print results to confirm that it worked.

```
>> print(results)
[[ -2.   -4.   -6.   -8.  -10.]
 [  8.    6.    4.    2.    0.]
 [  8.   16.   14.   12.   10.]
 [  8.   16.   24.   22.   20.]
 [  8.   16.   24.   32.   30.]
 [  8.   16.   24.   32.   40.]]
```

Let's now compute the expected profit for each order quantity, we will store the results in profits.

```
profits = np.empty(shape=len(quantity))
for column in range(len(quantity)):
    profits[column] = sum(results[:,column] * pmf)
```

Again, we can print profits to confirm that our code worked.

```
>> print(profits)
[4. 6. 6. 5. 3.5]
```

Finally, we want to get the optimal order quantity (EOQ).

```
>> EOQ = quantity[np.argmax(profits)]
>> print('EOQ:',EOQ,'\nProfits:',max(profits))
EOQ: 4
Profits: 6.
```

We used here the escape character \n which prints a line break. We also used np.argmax() which returns the position of the highest element of a list or array-like.

11.2 Newsvendor Model

11.2.1 A Brief History of the Newsvendor Problem

A horse, a horse, my kingdom for a horse.

Richard III by Shakespeare (around 1593)

In 1888, an Anglo-Irish economist—Francis Edgeworth—made an analysis to compute how much cash a bank should hold to serve its clients,[2] by using the normal probability function which was discovered and analyzed 80 years earlier by Gauss and Laplace. This is usually referred to as the first newsvendor model.

Actually, the modern formulation of the newsvendor problem dates back to 1951 with the article "Optimal Inventory Policy" by K. Arrow, T. Harris and J. Marschak.[3] To illustrate the shortage cost, they quoted Richard III in the Shakespeare play about his horse. Where Richard III badly missed a horse to finish his battle. Traditionally, this model is explained as followed:

---

2 Edgeworth (1888).
3 Kenneth et al. (1951).

You sell newspapers. Every morning you have to decide how many you want to buy from your distributor. You can't buy new ones during the day and if you have remaining newspapers at the end of the day you won't be able to sell them. How many newspapers should you buy?

We can generalize this story (and the chocolate muffins one from above) as the case where, as you won't be able to replenish your stock through the sale cycle (or season), you have to decide how many products you want to source before the sales come in. In other words, this model is applied for products with a limited lifecycle that you need to produce or order in advance.

Let's define 4 conditions for an inventory problem to be defined as a newsvendor problem:

1. The order is placed before the season.
2. You cannot make an order through the season.
3. There is a cost for buying too much (i. e., excess cost).
4. There is a cost for buying too low (i. e., shortage cost).

Here are some examples:

Seasonal products Products that are purchased ahead of the season. This is typically the case for most of the fashion industry (especially when sourced overseas).

A typical historical example are calendars: these are seasonal products (with a very finite lifecycle) for which the production setup cost is high. It may then be cheaper to make one order for the whole year. Nowadays, thanks to digitization, the printing industry could reduce these setup costs.

Stock for a special event How much coffee—or champagne—to buy for a special event is a typical newsvendor problem: you can't buy more during the event, you face excess costs if there are any leftovers and shortage costs if you don't buy enough (attendees won't be happy!).

Safety stock The safety stock model (as created in Part II and III) is a newsvendor problem with the season being one order cycle: you have to decide before the cycle how much you want to source (until the next one).

Now that we understood what the newsvendor problem is about, let's solve it and determine what is the best order quantity. In order to do so, we will first **model the supply chain costs**, then **minimize them** and finally **find the optimal order quantity** as shown in Figure 11.4.

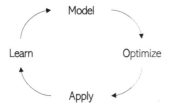

Figure 11.4: Inventory optimization journey.

11.2.2 Costs

As we did in Chapter 2 for the EOQ model, let's start this new model by discussing the costs and see how we can minimize them later.

We will be looking at two types of costs for the newsvendor model: the **overage costs** c_o and the **underage costs** c_u.

Overage Costs (c_o)

These are the costs the supply chain faces if a product is not sold at the end of a period (they would literally be over the saleable age). These costs are also sometimes called **excess costs** and actually have multiple components:

Purchase cost (c) If we assume that the products can't be sold anymore at the end of a period (in other words, they are considered to be lost), the main overage cost is then the product purchasing costs (including all transportation, packaging and other costs). Note that, in the newsvendor literature, the purchase cost is sometimes noted w, as the model often describes a retailer buying its products from a wholesaler.

Salvage value (s_v) The salvage value can either be an income (*salvage price*) or a cost (*salvage cost*).

  Income In some cases, you will be able to sell the remaining goods at the end of a period at a discounted price. This happens, for example, if your supplier will take back the goods or if you have a sales channel selling the remaining goods at a discounted price (think about the multiple yearly sales in the fashion industry). This salvage value reduces the overage costs, as part of the purchase cost will be recovered. When the salvage value is an extra income we call it the salvage *price*.

  Cost In other cases, a company faces extra costs to dispose of its excess inventory (e. g., waste disposal). In such a case, the salvage *cost* should then be added on top of the purchasing cost.

Holding costs (h) If you can sell your products over the next period, you don't lose the full purchase cost but simply the expense of the holding cost h (as defined in Section 2.1.1 for the EOQ model).

Let's recap the overage costs. If we assume that **we cannot sell the products in a later period**, we have:

$$\text{Overage Costs} = \text{Purchase cost} - \text{Salvage value}$$

$$c_o = c - s_v$$

Or, if **we can sell the products in another period**:

$$\text{Overage Costs} = \text{Holding cost}$$

$$c_o = h$$

Again, note that the salvage *costs* can be actually a salvage *revenue* in the case where the leftovers can still be sold for a profit. For example, that was the case in our muffin case where the salvage revenue was 1€ (i. e., you sold any remaining piece for 1€); so that the overall overage costs were actually 1€ (the muffins initial selling price was 2€). We could imagine another scenario where you have to pay a company to dispose of your leftovers (for example, in the case of hazardous goods).

Underage Costs (c_u)
These are the costs we face if we lose a sale due to a lack of inventory, they are sometimes called **shortage costs**.

Profit ($p - c$) If you lose a sale, you lose the opportunity to make a profit. The amount of unrealized profits are then more an opportunity cost rather than a real expense or loss. We simply define the profit as the price p minus the cost c.

The profits are included as an underage cost in the newsvendor model when it minimizes the costs (so that we want to minimize the *unrealized* profits); but are not included in the underage cost when the newsvendor model maximizes the overall profits (otherwise it would include an opportunity cost into an actual profits estimation).

Goodwill (g) This represents any extra cost associated with the risk of losing a client or—even worse—the damage to your reputation, which could affect other clients buying decision. As we already discussed in Section 2.1.3, this aspect is particularly difficult to estimate and might be left to gut feelings rather than academic research.

Penalty A penalty can be incurred for each lost sale or demand that cannot be delivered directly from the stock on-hand. For example, these penalties are often used for maintenance parts when the client values a high service level. When there are penalties between parties for a lack of service, they are usually defined in the service agreement between the supplier and the client.

As penalties have a similar effect as goodwill (i. e., an extra cost), we won't give it a special symbol in our model. We will group the penalties directly into the goodwill for the sake of simplicity.

We then have:

$$\text{Underage Costs} = \text{Price} - \text{Cost} + \text{Goodwill}$$

$$c_u = p - c + g$$

Note that, in case of potential confusion, we will call the cost of ordering 1 unit too much (respectively too low) the **unit** overage (underage) costs. Whereas we call the total expected overage (underage) costs the **total** overage (underage) costs.

Keep in mind that this underage cost—as it includes the opportunity cost of losing a sale—is for analysis purposes and not for accounting.

11.3 Newsvendor Model Optimization

Now that we have analyzed the various costs of our system, we can model the expected profits (or costs) based on the order quantity and the demand distribution. The demand in a newsvendor model can be modeled as a continuous probability function—such as normal or gamma—or as a discrete probability function (as we did for the muffin example). Remember, a discrete variable means that the function can only take integer values and is described by a **probability mass function**.

11.3.1 Expected Outcomes

As shown in Table 11.2, we can compute the expected sales, excess units and *units short*[4] for any given order quantity Q and demand d. Then, as we know the demand distribution (either discrete or continuous), we can compute the expected outcomes only based on Q.

Table 11.2: Expected outcomes based on d and Q.

	Expression (Q, d)	Discrete (Q)	Continuous (Q)
Sales	$\min(Q, d)$	$\sum_{d \leq Q} d\, p(d)$	$\int_{d=0}^{Q} d\, f(d)\, dd$
Excess units	$\max(0, Q - d)$	$\sum_{d < Q} (Q - d) p(d)$	$\int_{d=0}^{Q} (Q - d) f(d)\, dd$
Units short	$\max(0, d - Q)$	$\sum_{d > Q} (d - Q) p(d)$	$\int_{d=Q}^{\infty} (d - Q) f(d)\, dd$

You could see the "Expression (Q, d)" column as the formula you have to type in Excel to compute the actual expected values based on Q and d; the "Discrete (Q)" column are the formulas we will investigate in this chapter; finally the column "Continuous (Q)" contains the formula we discussed in Chapter 7.

Remember, $p(d)$ is the demand probability mass function PMF at the value d, that is the probability that the demand is d. This is the discrete equivalent to $f_D(d)$.

11.3.2 Expected Profit Based on Q and d

We can now express the total revenues, costs and profits of our model.

$$\text{Revenues} = p \cdot \text{Sales}$$
$$\text{Costs} = c_o \cdot \text{Excess units} + c_u \cdot \text{Units short} + c \cdot Q$$

---

4 Remember, units short can result in either backorders or lost sales, when excess demand is backordered or lost (respectively). We use then the concept of units short to be more general.

Profits = Revenues – Costs

$$= p \cdot \text{Sales} - c_o \cdot \text{Excess units} - c_u \cdot \text{Units short} - c \cdot Q$$

$$P(Q, d) = p \cdot \min(Q, d) - c_o \cdot \max(0, Q - d) - c_u \cdot \max(0, d - Q) - c \cdot Q$$

where p is the sales price, c_o the (unit) overage cost,[5] c_u the (unit) underage cost and c the purchasing cost. Note that, in this equation, the underage costs shouldn't include any opportunity cost (i. e., the unrealized profit) but only costs such as penalties or goodwill.

> **Example**
>
> We have to send a new order to our supplier for a seasonal item in a specific shop. Before that, we spoke with different teams and got these pieces of information:
> - The marketing team estimates that there is an underage cost of 350€ if we miss a sale.
> - The logistic team estimates that we face an overage cost of 200€ if we have excess inventory.
> - The demand planning team estimates that the probability for the demand to be 1 piece is 5% ($p(1) = 0.05$).
>
> If we order 10 pieces ($Q = 10$), and the demand d is 1, we will face an overage cost of 1800€ ($9 \times 200€$) and an underage cost of 0€ ($0 \times 350€$). This situation has a 5% chance to happen ($p(d) = 5\%$).

Of course, this example only showed us what would happen if the demand was 1 piece. What about all the other possibilities?

11.3.3 Expected Profit Based on Q

As we know the probability mass function of d, we can express the sales, excess units and units short solely based on Q.

$$\text{Sales}(Q) = \sum_{d \leq Q} p(d)d$$

$$\text{Excess units}(Q) = \sum_{d < Q} p(d)(Q - d)$$

---

5 We assume here that we express c_o and c_u as positive values if they describe a cost, and a negative value if they describe an extra revenue. In some cases, as we saw in the muffin example, it is possible that the overage costs are actually an extra income thanks to a positive salvage value.

$$\text{Units short } (Q) = \sum_{d>Q} p(d)(d-Q)$$

So that we can express the total expected profits $\mathcal{P}$ solely based on Q:

$$\text{Profits} = p \cdot \text{Sales} - c_o \cdot \text{Excess units} - c_u \cdot \text{Units short} - c \cdot Q$$

$$\mathcal{P}(Q) = p \sum_{d \leq Q} p(d)d - c_o \sum_{d<Q} p(d)(Q-d) - c_u \sum_{d>Q} p(d)(d-Q) - c \cdot Q \qquad (11.1)$$

What is particularly interesting about this profit expression is that it is universal regardless of the demand probability mass function. This was not the case with the continuous safety stock model from parts II & III, where a formula might change depending on the demand probability function. This means that we can use any discrete custom demand distribution we need.

Insights

As shown in Figure 11.5, the intuition here is as Q increases, so do the sales incomes (the higher Q is, the lower units short you face). The underage costs will also decrease as Q increases (again, as we face less units short). But, the overage costs and the purchasing costs will grow.

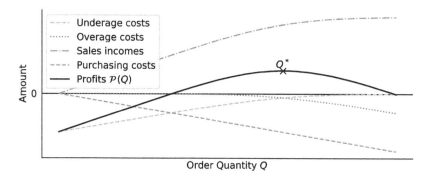

Figure 11.5: Optimal order quantity for the newsvendor model based on profits.

11.3.4 Expected Costs Based on Q

Instead of looking at the profits based on Q, we can simplify our model and only look at the costs $\mathcal{C}(Q)$. For both models to be equivalent, we have to include in the underage costs the unrealized profits per sale missed. We then have:

$$\text{Costs} = c_o \cdot \text{Excess units} + c_u \cdot \text{Units short}$$

$$C(Q) = c_o \sum_{d<Q} p(d)(Q - d) + c_u \sum_{d>Q} p(d)(d - Q) \qquad (11.2)$$

where c_u include the profit per item sold.

Insights

We already observe in Figures 11.6 and 11.7 that the minimal cost will be achieved when the underage costs and the overage costs will be equal.

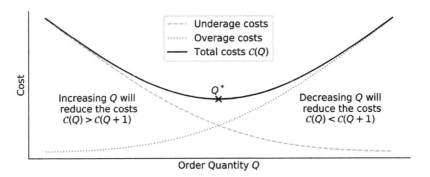

Figure 11.6: Optimal order quantity for the newsvendor model based on profits.

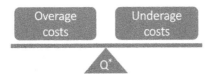

Figure 11.7: Optimal order quantity equilibrium for the newsvendor model.

11.3.5 Optimal Order Quantity

Now that we can express the expected costs based on the order quantity, we have to answer one last question: *"What is the optimal order quantity?"* We want to find the optimal order quantity Q which maximize our profits $P(Q)$ (eq. 11.1 in Section 11.3.3); or, as we did in Chapter 8, "Cost and Service Level Optimization," the quantity that minimizes the costs $C(Q)$ (eq. 11.2).

We start then from the following cost equation

$$C(Q) = c_o \sum_{d<Q} p(d)(Q - d) + c_u \sum_{d>Q} p(d)(d - Q)$$

Note that here the underage costs c_u include the unrealized profits per unit short.

Continuous Model

Economics teach us that the optimal order quantity of our model will be found when the marginal gain and loss of ordering an excess unit will be equal. In other words, we will reach the economical optimum when the marginal expected overage and underage costs of ordering an extra unit are equal. Let's compute these two marginal costs for the Qth unit ordered. As a reminder, we note $F_D(Q)$ the demand CDF at Q, that is the probability that the (continuous) demand is lower than Q.

Expected marginal overage costs: $c_o F_D(Q)$

This is the probability for the demand to be lower than the order quantity, multiplied by the unit overage cost.

Expected marginal underage costs: $c_u(1 - F_D(Q))$

This is the probability for the demand to be higher than the order quantity, multiplied by the unit underage cost. Note that, for this model, we will include the profit per unit in the expected marginal underage costs, in order to take into account the opportunity costs in the total costs.

We can find the **optimal order quantity Q^*** by equalizing the expected marginal overage and underage costs (as shown in Figure 11.8).[6]

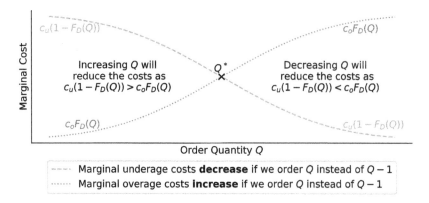

Figure 11.8: Optimal order quantity for the newsvendor model based on marginal costs.

Mathematically, we have:

$$c_o F_D(Q) = c_u (1 - F_D(Q))$$
$$(c_u + c_o)F_D(Q) = c_u$$
$$F_D(Q) = \frac{c_u}{c_u + c_o}$$

---

6 See Hill (2017) for more details.

This means that with the optimal order quantity Q^*, we have an optimal cycle service level α^* equal to the ratio $c_u/(c_u + c_o)$. This ratio is called the **critical ratio**.

$$\alpha^* = F_D(Q^*) = \frac{c_u}{c_u + c_o} \Leftrightarrow Q^* = F_D^{-1}\left(\frac{c_u}{c_u + c_o}\right) \tag{11.3}$$

In other words, if the demand is assumed to be continuous, the optimal cycle service level α^* should be equal to the critical ratio $c_u/(c_u + c_o)$.

Example

Next to your chocolate muffins, you decide to sell cookies in your bakery shop. You usually sell each cookie at 3€ and it costs 1€ to bake one. Just as for the muffins, you bake them in the morning to sell them during the day, so that you need to decide early in the morning how many you want to bake. The cookie demand varies around 15 per day with a deviation of 5 pieces. If you assume that the demand is normally distributed, how many cookies should you bake in the morning?

We know the optimal cycle service level is the critical ratio:

$$\text{Optimal cycle service level} = \frac{c_u}{c_u + c_o}$$

The underage cost c_u is 2€ (the selling price – the baking cost) and the overage cost is 1€ (the cost to bake one cookie). So that we have:

$$\text{Service Level} = \frac{c_u}{c_u + c_o} = \frac{p - c}{(p - c) + c} = \frac{3 - 1}{3 - 1 + 1} = 66.67\%$$

We can then compute the optimal order quantity Q^* using the formula $Q^* = F_D^{-1}(\alpha^*) = \mu_d + z_{\alpha} \cdot \sigma_d$ (see eq. 4.1)

$$Q^* = F_D^{-1}(0.67) = \mu_D + z_{.67} \cdot \sigma_D = 0.44 \cdot 5 + 15 = 17.2$$

You should bake 17 cookies per day, and therefore expect to run out of cookies 1 day out of 3 (service level is 66.67%).

Discrete Model

Optimizing the discrete newsvendor model is slightly more complex than the continuous one. In his book, Cachon proposes to tackle this problem by a similar approach (i. e., looking at marginal costs).[7] We want to increase our order quantity Q as long

---

7 Cachon (2018).

as the expected increase in overage costs is lower than the expected underage cost reduction of ordering an extra unit.

The (total) expected underage cost **reduction**, if we order $Q + 1$ instead of Q is:

$$c_u P(D > Q)$$

which is the probability that we sell more than Q, multiplied by the unit underage cost c_u.

The (total) expected overage cost **increase**, if we order $Q + 1$ instead of Q is:

$$c_o P(D \leq Q)$$

which is the probability that we sell Q or less units, multiplied by the unit overage cost c_o.

So, we want to order $Q+1$ instead of Q only if **the expected overage cost increase is lower than the expected underage cost reduction:**

$$c_o P(D \leq Q) \leq c_u P(D > Q)$$
$$c_o P(D \leq Q) \leq c_u (1 - P(D \leq Q))$$
$$c_o P(D \leq Q) \leq c_u - c_u P(D \leq Q)$$
$$c_u P(D \leq Q) + c_o P(D \leq Q) \leq c_u$$
$$P(D \leq Q)(c_u + c_o) \leq c_u$$
$$P(D \leq Q) \leq \frac{c_u}{c_u + c_o}$$

This means that, as long as we have,

$$P(D \leq Q) \leq \frac{c_u}{c_u + c_o}$$

we want to increase Q (i. e., it is simply more profitable to order more units). So that the optimal order quantity Q^* is the **lowest** order quantity Q that achieves

$$P(D \leq Q) \geq \frac{c_u}{c_u + c_o}$$

That is, the lowest value for which we do not want to order more.

Another demonstration, based on total costs, is available in Appendix B.5.

Example

Over time you realized that, when you are out of cookies, your clients usually simply buy another product instead (such as muffins). To reflect this, let's assume that you still get a profit of 1€ for each client that wanted to buy a cookie but had to choose another product.

You also took the time to refine the cookie demand distribution as shown below.

d	6	8	10	12	14	16	18	20	22
$p(d)$	0.05	0.10	0.10	0.15	0.20	0.15	0.10	0.10	0.05
$p(D \leq d)$	0.05	0.15	0.25	0.40	0.60	0.75	0.85	0.95	1.00

How many cookies should you bake now?

As the clients can buy another product if there are no cookies left, the unit underage cost is now lowered by 1€. In other words, you are now less afraid of running out of cookies. Let's see how this impacts Q^*:

$$\text{Cycle service level} = \frac{c_u}{c_u + c_o} = \frac{p - c - 1}{(p - c - 1) + c} = \frac{3 - 1 - 1}{(3 - 1 - 1) + 1} = 50\%$$

Based on the demand probabilities, $Q = 12$ would correspond to a service level of 40% and $Q = 14$ to a service level of 60%. Remember, we choose Q as the lowest integer that satisfies:

$$P(D \leq Q) \geq \frac{c_u}{c_u + c_o} = 50\%$$

which is 14 in our case. If we populate a table to show the profit based on Q and d, we obtain:

			Quantity				
$p(d)$	$P(D \leq d)$	d	10	12	14	16	18
5%	5%	6	8	6	4	2	0
10%	15%	8	14	12	10	8	6
10%	25%	10	20	18	16	14	12
15%	40%	12	22	24	22	20	18
20%	60%	14	24	26	28	26	24
15%	75%	16	26	28	30	32	30
10%	85%	18	28	30	32	34	36
10%	95%	20	30	32	34	36	38
5%	100%	22	32	34	36	38	40
		Profit	23.2	24.2	**24.6**	24.2	23.2

Where the profits are computed as such:

$$\text{Profits}(Q, d) = 3 \cdot \min(Q, d) + 1 \cdot \max(d - Q, 0) - 1 \cdot Q$$

We can then confirm that 14 pieces is now the best order quantity.

Going Further

If you are interested in learning more about the newsvendor problem, I would advise you to check the online resource "The Newsvendor Problem" written by Arthur Hill.[a] It contains both a good theoretical introduction to the subject and practical examples in Excel. The author also discusses the impact of human bias (i. e., loss aversion) on the stock targets.

See Silver et al. (2016) for a thorough review of various newsvendor extensions, and Qin et al. (2011) for a literature review as well as many recent extensions.

More recently, Oroojlooyjadid et al. (2020) used deep learning in order to optimize the order quantity in a Newsvendor model.

---

a Hill (2017).

11.4 Recap

The newsvendor model allows us to answer the question *"How much should I order before the season?"* for products that need to be ordered before the sales cycle. In order to do so, we have to compute two types of costs:

Overage costs (c_o) All the costs related to having too many products at the end of the season. This is typically the purchasing/production cost of the product.

Underage costs (c_u) All the costs related to having not enough products through the season. This is typically the expected profit of the lost sales.

We computed the optimal cycle service level α^* based on the critical ratio (see eq. 11.3 in Section 11.3.5):

$$\alpha^* = \frac{c_u}{c_u + c_o} \Leftrightarrow Q^* = F_D^{-1}\left(\frac{c_u}{c_u + c_o}\right)$$

We can compute the expected sales, extra units and units short (see Table 11.2) as:

	Expression (Q, d)	Discrete (Q)	Continuous (Q)
Sales	$\min(Q, d)$	$\sum_{d \leq Q} d\, p(d)$	$\int_{d=0}^{Q} df(d)\, dd$
Excess units	$\max(0, Q - d)$	$\sum_{d < Q}(Q - d)p(d)$	$\int_{d=0}^{Q}(Q - d)f(d)\, dd$
Units short	$\max(0, d - Q)$	$\sum_{d > Q}(d - Q)p(d)$	$\int_{d=Q}^{\infty}(d - Q)f(d)\, dd$

We have this general expression for the profits (see eq. 11.3.2 in Section 11.3.2):

$$\text{Revenues} = p \cdot \text{Sales}$$

$$\text{Costs} = c_o \cdot \text{Excess units} + c_u \cdot \text{Units short} + c \cdot Q$$

$$\text{Profits} = p \cdot \text{Sales} - c_o \cdot \text{Excess units} - c_u \cdot \text{Units short} - c \cdot Q$$

So that the total profits $\mathcal{P}$ can be expressed based on Q and d as:

$$\mathcal{P}(Q, d) = p \cdot \min(Q, d) - c_o \cdot \max(Q - d, 0) - c_u \cdot \max(d - Q, 0) - c \cdot Q$$

If the demand is discrete, we can then express the total profits based on Q solely as we know the demand probability mass function (see eq. 11.1 in Section 11.3.3):

$$\mathcal{P}(Q) = p \sum_{d \leq Q} p(d)d - c_o \sum_{d < Q} p(d)(Q - d) - c_u \sum_{d > Q} p(d)(d - Q) - c \cdot Q$$

12 Discrete Probabilistic Demand

In Part II, "Stochastic Supply Chains," we initially assumed our demand to be normally distributed. Later, in Chapter 9, "Beyond Normality," we analyzed gamma-distributed demand. We will discuss in this chapter multiple techniques to estimate a demand distribution (or density) via a **custom** probability mass distribution. In other words, we won't use a predefined continuous probability function to estimate our demand anymore, instead we will create a tailor-fitted discrete distribution for it instead. Next, in Chapter 13 "Simulation Optimization," we will discuss how to optimize a policy with a custom demand distribution.

12.1 Histograms

A first technique to estimate (discrete) demand density is to use histograms, as shown in Figure 12.1 (using Toyota sales in Norway with an arbitrary choice of 10 bins starting at 550 and ending at 2050).[1]

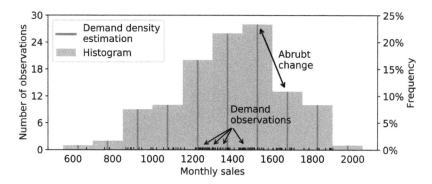

Figure 12.1: Demand density based on a histogram with 10 bins.

Creating a histogram is simple (see Section 9.1.1 for a DIY in Python), but it requires that you make **arbitrary** choices that come with issues. In order to understand the limitations, let's recap how a histogram is built.

How to Make a Histogram

The interval covered by data is first divided in sub-intervals, called **bins**. The frequency of each bin (its height on the figure) is the fraction of observations (i. e., data points) that fall into it. This frequency is then allocated to the **center** of each bin as shown in Table 12.1.

---

1 We use the same dataset as in Chapter 9, "Beyond Normality," with one exception: the sales of January 2007 are removed from the analysis (considered as an outlier). The dataset is available for download on supchains.com/download.

https://doi.org/10.1515/9783110673944-012

Table 12.1: Demand frequency based on a histogram with 10 bins.

Bins			# of	Frequency
left	center	right	observations	
550	625	700	1	0.8%
700	775	850	2	1.7%
850	925	1000	9	7.5%
1000	1075	1150	10	8.3%
1150	1225	1300	20	16.7%
1300	1375	1450	26	21.7%
1450	1525	1600	28	23.3%
1600	1675	1750	13	10.8%
1750	1825	1900	10	8.3%
1900	1975	2050	1	0.8%

12.1.1 Limitations

Using a histogram to estimate the demand distribution comes with 4 main issues:

1. A probability is only given to a few values: the values at the **center** of the bins. For example, in the resulting demand distribution from Table 12.1, there is 21.7% chance to have a demand of 1375 units, but 0% of having 1376.

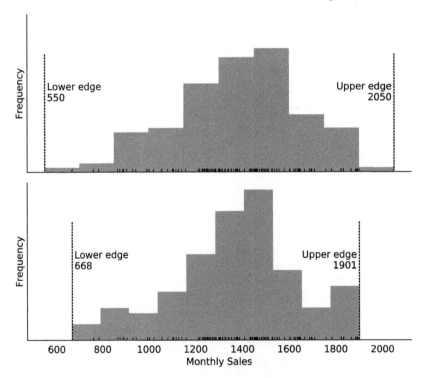

Figure 12.2: Demand density based on a histogram with 10 bins.

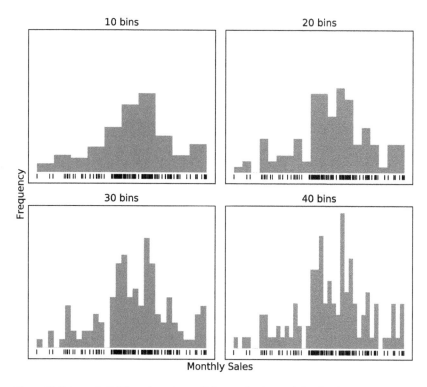

Figure 12.3: Impact of different numbers of bins on the demand distribution.

2. We do not know how many bins we should use. As shown in Figure 12.3, the number of bins will impact the representation we have of the demand distribution.
3. We do not know what the histogram limits should be (left and right edges). Choosing another set of limits will also change the demand distribution representation. For example, the two distributions obtained in Figure 12.2 do not give us the same demand distribution, whereas the only difference is the histogram edges (respectively [550,2050] and [668,1901]).
    To summarize, based on the **arbitrary** choices we make about the number of bins and where they start, we can get a completely different picture of the (demand) distribution.
4. The resulting demand distribution is not continuous (in other words, smooth). As you can see in Figure 12.1 the variation between two consecutive bins can be rather high. For example, we have 23.3% for the demand to be 1525, but only 10.8% to be 1675. This is an abrupt change and it would be more realistic to see a smooth decrease, but obviously (as stated earlier), with only a few possible demand values, a smooth variation is difficult.

DIY

In order to get the dataset we need, we will use the function get_data(car_maker) we defined in Section 9.1. In this chapter, we will use Toyota sales in Norway. Note that we remove the first value (January 2007) that we consider to be an outlier.

```
def get_data(car_maker):
    df = pd.read_csv('norway_new_car_sales_by_make.csv')
    df['Date'] = pd.to_datetime(df['Year'].astype(str)+df['Month'
        ].astype(str),format='%Y%m')
    df = (df.loc[df['Make'] == car_maker,['Date','Quantity']]
        .rename(columns={'Quantity':'Sales'}).set_index('Date'))
    return df
df = get_data('Toyota')
df = df.iloc[1:] #Remove one outlier
```

You can then plot a histogram (see Section 9.1.1 for more details) using the .plot() function.

```
df['Sales'].plot(kind='hist', density=False, bins=30, range=(
    left,right))
```

Let's review some parameters:
- density can be set to True or False to plot either frequencies or absolute numbers respectively;
- bins will set the number of bins;
- range will set the left and right limits of the histogram (in the example above you will have to define left and right earlier in the code).

12.2 Kernel Density Estimation

We can improve our demand distribution estimation by getting rid of the issue of the arbitrary number of bins, and the histogram limits. In order to do so, we will allocate a small density probability around each demand observation thanks to a **kernel** function.[2]

---

[2] See Trapero et al. (2019) for an application of kernel density estimation to safety stock computation. It is available on the blog of Nikos Kourentzes (professor at Lancaster University): kourentzes.com/forecasting/wp-content/uploads/2018/06/Trapero_empirical-safety-stock.pdf

> **Kernel**
>
> A distribution probability function used to determine the density distribution around each observation.

This should be more accurate than a histogram where each observation is allocated to the closest bin. Now each observation will get its **own** bin.

Let's see a first simple example to understand how it works.[3]

12.2.1 Squared Kernel

As a first test, we will use a squared (or box) kernel. In other words, we will allocate a density around each observation by drawing a square around it as shown in Figure 12.4 (here with a **bandwidth** of 20). The overall (demand) density is then the sum of density around each point. In other words, if the kernels (represented by the dotted squares) around neighboring points overlap, we simply map the resulting density as the sum of these kernels. The resulting demand distribution is then the *normalized*[4] sum of the distribution around each and every demand point.

> **Bandwidth**
>
> In kernel density estimators, the bandwidth is the **width** of the kernel.

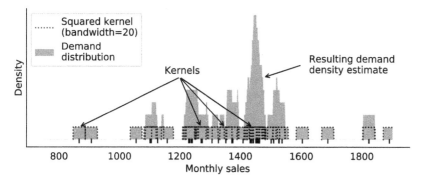

Figure 12.4: Demand distribution based on squared kernels (bandwidth = 20).

3 See the online resources VanderPlas (2013), Duong (2001), Lerner (2013) for complementary explanations and examples. See VanderPlas (2016) for a detailed analysis of various implementation in Python.
4 *Normalized* means that the sum of the total distribution is 1. You can normalize the distribution by dividing it by its own sum.

12.2.2 Limitations

We solved two issues of the histogram—we don't have to determine arbitrarily the number of bins nor the edges of our distribution—but we still face other limitations:

1. The resulting distribution is not smooth because we have used a discontinuous kernel as our building block. This will result in abrupt changes in the demand density estimation.
2. We do not know what the bandwidth of our kernel should be. In other words, what the ideal width is for each square.

As you can see in Figure 12.5 (with a bandwidth of 40), depending on the bandwidth we use for the squares, we get a different demand estimation (even a different overall interpretation of its distribution).

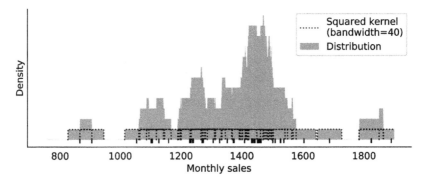

Figure 12.5: Demand distribution based on squared kernels (bandwidth = 40).

12.2.3 Gaussian Kernel

In order to get a smooth demand distribution, we should use a continuous, smooth kernel function. The usual way is to use a normal distribution as a kernel, instead of squares. Note that we could use any other distribution instead of the normal one, but we choose to use it because it is simple, well-known, centered around its mean and smooth.

As for the squared kernel, depending on the kernel bandwidth (i. e., the standard deviation of the normal distribution around each data point) we get a different picture (compare Figures 12.6 and 12.7) with a more or less extreme representation of the demand distribution.

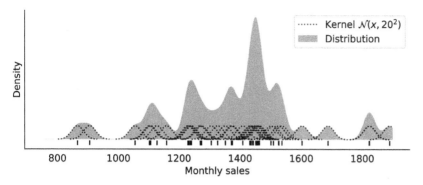

Figure 12.6: Gaussian kernel with $\sigma = 20$.

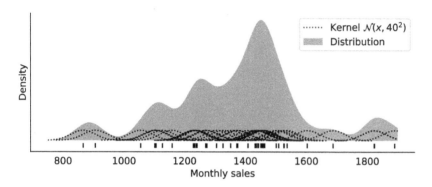

Figure 12.7: Gaussian kernel with $\sigma = 40$.

Kernel Optimization

We have one last issue to solve: how to optimize the bandwidth of our kernel. In other words, how **wide** should the normal distributions we draw around each datapoint be?

Usually, academics use the Silverman or Scott rule of thumbs to optimize the kernel bandwidth.[5] Both rules of thumbs compute the bandwidth in a (very) similar fashion:

$$\textbf{Scott: bandwidth} = \sigma_d \frac{1}{n^{1/5}} \tag{12.1}$$

$$\textbf{Silverman: bandwidth} = \sigma_d \frac{1}{\left(\frac{3}{4}n\right)^{1/5}}$$

where n is the number of demand observations in the dataset and σ_d is the standard deviation estimated from the observations.

---

5 See Silverman (1986), Scott (1992).

You can see in Figure 12.8 multiple demand density estimations with various bandwidths. The demand density estimations go beyond the minimum and maximum values actually observed. This makes sense. Our kernel density estimation is smart enough to understand that it is not because we never saw a demand above 1901 units before that we should estimate that a probability for the demand of 1902 is 0%.

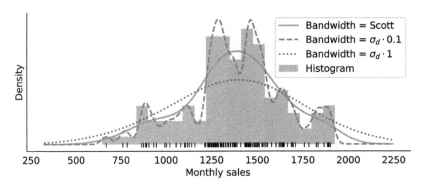

Figure 12.8: Kernel optimization.

Based on practical experience, it seems that Scott's rule of thumbs tends to underfit the true underlying distribution.[6] In other words, as you can see in Figure 12.8, the resulting distribution will be too smooth (loose). Setting the bandwidth at 90% of Scott's rule might then be a more appropriate choice (the resulting distribution will be less smooth based on a lower bandwidth).

> **Important Point**
>
> If some of observed demand is close to 0, the KDE will often result in a probability for negative demand. We will deal with this case later in Section 12.3.

> **DIY**
>
> We will use our function get_data('Toyota') (defined in Section 9.1) to extract Toyota sales.
>
> ```
> df = get_data('Toyota')
> df = df.iloc[1:] #Remove one outlier
> ```

---

6 See the online resource Ciortan (2018). It is available here: github.com/ciortanmadalina/modality_tests/blob/master/kernel_density.ipynb

You can create a Gaussian kernel density estimation (KDE) thanks to the function gaussian_kde from SciPy:[a]

```
from scipy.stats import gaussian_kde
kde_dist = gaussian_kde(df['Sales'], bw_method='scott')
```

The parameter bw_method will set the bandwidth. It can receive two different types of values.
- 'scott' or 'silverman' will use the Scott or Silverman method;
- And a number will set the bandwidth as this number times the dataset standard deviation (bandwidth = multiplicative factor $\cdot \sigma_d$).

The object returned by gaussian_kde() is a distribution. Just as for scipy.stats.norm() or scipy.stats.gamma().

You can also use your own bandwidth (such as 90% of Scott's rule of thumb, see eq. 12.1).

```
scott_bw = 1/(df['Sales'].count()**(1/5))
bw = 0.9*scott_bw
kde_dist = gaussian_kde(df['Sales'],bw_method=bw)
```

You can then plot the results to confirm that it worked. See Section 9.3.1 for a reminder about the function np.linspace(min,max,n).

```
x = np.linspace(df['Sales'].min()*0.9,df['Sales'].max()
    *1.1,1000)
y_kde = kde_dist.pdf(x)
plt.plot(x, y_kde)
```

Using the regular Scott's rule, you should obtain something similar to Figure 12.8.

Cumulative Distribution Function

Unfortunately SciPy does not deliver a full implementation of its Gaussian KDE function (at least compared to the other statistical distributions). In order to get the KDE CDF, we will first have to do a bit of work ourselves. Despite the fact that the object returned by gaussian_kde() is similar to those returned by scipy.stats.norm() and scipy.stats.gamma(), we cannot access its CDF directly via the function .ppf(x). Instead, we have to use .integrate_box_1d(-np.inf,x) (remember that the cumulative distribution function evaluated at x is, by definition, the integral from minus infinity to x of the probability distribution function).

```
print(kde_dist.integrate_box_1d(-np.inf, 1250))
>> 0.297
```

This works fine for one value, but there is another limitation. This function can only take a single value as input (i. e., x cannot be an array). In order to easily compute the CDF of our distribution, we have to create our own function.

```
def kde_cdf(kde_dist,x):
    cdf = [ ]
    for value in x:
        cdf.append(kde_dist.integrate_box_1d(-np.inf,value))
    return cdf
plt.plot(x,kde_cdf(kde_dist,x))
```

The code below will show in Figure 12.9, the demand histogram and its kernel density estimation PDF and CDF. Unfortunately, creating a graph with two y-axes is difficult with matplotlib. We will need to use twinx() to create the second axis. The legend is also particularly complex to create (and beyond the scope of this book).

```
import matplotlib.patches as mpatches
fig, ax = plt.subplots()
df = get_data('Toyota').iloc[1:]
df['Sales'].plot(ax=ax,kind='hist',density=True,bins=30,alpha
    =0.6)
patch = mpatches.Patch(color='C0',alpha=0.6,label='Sales')
x = np.linspace(df['Sales'].min()*0.9,df['Sales'].max()
    *1.1,1000)
y_kde = kde_dist.pdf(x)
plot2 = ax.plot(x,y_kde,lw=1.5)
ax.set_xlabel('Monthly sales')
ax1 = ax.twinx()
ax1.set_ylabel('Frequency')
plot3 = ax1.plot(x,kde_cdf(kde_dist,x),ls='--',color='C2',lw
    =1.5)
ax.legend([patch]+plot2+plot3,['Sales','KDE pdf','KDE cdf'],loc=
    'upper left')
plt.show()
```

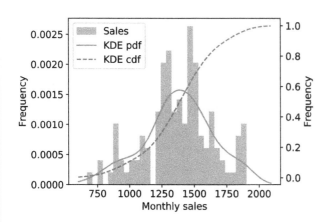

Figure 12.9: Demand kernel density estimation.

---

a See KDE function: docs.scipy.org/doc/scipy/reference/generated/scipy.stats.gaussian_kde.html

Going Further

Instead of optimizing the kernel via the Scott or Silverman rules (which tend to underfit the true underlying distribution[a]), you can also use a grid or random search (together with a cross-validation) to find the best bandwidth. This technique would be closer to data science than to statistics. It will then take more time to get a proper bandwidth but might result in a better estimation. See my previous book *Data Science for Supply Chain Forecasting* for an in-depth discussion about data science, grid search, random search, cross-validation and underfitting.

---

a See the online resource Ciortan (2018). It is available here: github.com/ciortanmadalina/modality_tests/blob/master/kernel_density.ipynb

12.3 From Gaussian Kernels to Discrete Distributions

We just used a Gaussian kernel density estimation to determine a custom continuous demand distribution based on a set of demand observations. The objective of this Part is to build a discrete simulation optimization (we will create the optimization engine in Chapter 13), therefore we now have to transform this distribution from a continuous PDF to a discrete PMF. For each possible (integer) demand value within the range of our demand distribution, we want to estimate its probability to occur.

12.3.1 How to Define a Set of Possible Values

The continuous distribution we created so far is giving us a probability for an infinite range of possible demand values. Mathematicians say that the **domain** of the distribution goes from $-\infty$ to ∞.

> **Domain**
>
> Set of values for which a function is defined.

When we transfer this continuous distribution to a discrete one, it will not be feasible to compute the probability for an infinite number of possible demand values. Especially as we know that the probability for the demand to be *extremely* high (or low) is (virtually) zero.

This means that we have to define a **reasonable** range of possible demand values. In practice, this means setting a **lower** and an **upper bound** to the demand distribution. A simple way to do that is to set these arbitrarily. But we risk cutting the distribution too thin (resulting in losing some possible values) or too wide (resulting in a slower simulation).

We can use a smarter technique: we can set these bounds based on the lowest and the highest demand observations, respectively, subtracted or added to an arbitrary multiple of the bandwidth.

As shown in Figure 12.10, the lower bound can, for example, be set as the lowest observation minus 3 times the bandwidth.

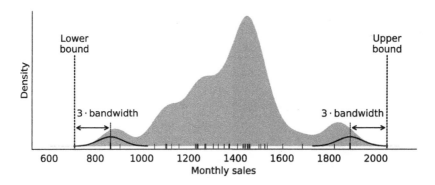

Figure 12.10: Lower and higher bounds for a demand distribution estimation via KDE.

As $\Phi(-3) = 0.13$, it means that there is a probability of only 0.13% for an occurrence of the normal kernel around the lowest observation to be even lower.[7] Moreover, as

---

7 You can compute it in Excel with =NORM.S.DIST(-3,TRUE), or in Python with norm.cdf(-3).

the overall distribution contains n kernels, the probability for an occurrence of the demand distribution to be below this threshold is $\frac{0.13}{n}$% (assuming that the probability for an occurrence of any other kernel is lower than the lowest bound is 0). You can then set your own safety factor to arbitrarily reduce this probability. Nevertheless, a factor such as 3 or 4 should be enough.

Finally, as we want to define our discrete distribution for round numbers, we have to round the lower and upper bounds to an integer value. As a final conservative measure, we can round them to the lower and upper integer respectively.

DIY

We compute the bandwidth based on Scott's rule of thumb (see eq. 12.1 in Section 12.2.3).

```
bandwidth = df['Sales'].std() / (df['Sales'].count()**(1/5))
```

The lower and upper bound are computed based on a safety factor (here 3) times the bandwidth.

Note that we use np.floor() and np.ceil() to round the upper and lower bounds to the higher and lower integer respectively.

```
lower = np.floor(df['Sales'].min() - 3 * bandwidth)
upper = np.ceil(df['Sales'].max() + 3 * bandwidth)
```

We will then use the function np.arange(lower,upper,step=1) to return an array from lower to upper with a step of 1.

```
x = np.arange(lower,upper,step=1)
```

We mention step=1 for the sake of clarity, as 1 is the default value.

One way to (approximately) get the PMF for each possible demand value is to estimate the KDE PDF at each value in this range:

```
pmf = kde_dist.pdf(x)
pmf = pmf/sum(pmf)
```

Note that, in order to normalize the PMF (i. e., the sum of the PMF equals 1), we divide it by its own sum.

Plot   You can plot the resulting PMF with:

```
plt.plot(x,pmf)
```

Random Values   You can create a random set of values out of this PMF thanks to the function np.random.choice(). This function takes a few parameters:
- The first parameter is the pool of possible values to choose from.
- p is the PMF of these values.
- size is the size you want for the output (this allows you to get multiple random values at once).

```
random_values = np.random.choice(x, size=10000, p=pmf)
```

Negative Values   If the PMF allows probabilities for negative demand values (this will happen if some demand observations are close to 0), you can sum them to 0. The following code will clean the PMF in such a case.

```
zero = x == 0
negative = x < 0
#Update the PMF at 0
pmf[zero] = pmf[zero] + pmf[negative].sum()
#Remove negative values
zero_arg = np.argmax(x==0)
pmf = pmf[zero_arg:]
x = x[zero_arg:].astype(int)
```

12.3.2 Demand Attributes

Now that we have defined a custom demand distribution (PMF) over a domain (x), we can compute the demand distribution mean as:

$$\mu_d = \sum_i pmf_i \cdot x_i$$

where x is the demand domain.

And the demand variance (Var_d) and standard deviation as:

$$\text{Var}_d = \sum_i x_i^2 \cdot pmf_i - \sum_i (x_i \cdot pmf_i)^2$$

$$\sigma_d = \sqrt{\text{Var}_d}$$

DIY

We define a function in Python that takes a PMF and its domain and returns the variable attributes.

```
def attributes(pmf,x):
    mu = sum(pmf*x)
    std = np.sqrt(sum(x**2*pmf) - sum(pmf*x)**2)
    return mu, std
d_mu, d_std = attributes(pmf,x)
```

Going Further

As mentioned in Syntetos et al. (2012), *"a distinction needs to be made between the goodness-of-fit on demand-per-period data and the validity of a distributional assumption for representing lead-time demand."* In other words, we can find a very good approximation of what can happen during one period, but the demand over multiple periods might still be different. Remember, we always assume that the demand is independently distributed in each period (see Section 4.3.3). But this assumption can be wrong. If the demand is highly auto-correlated (e. g., a high period is often followed by another high period; or a high period is often followed by a low period), you should directly simulate the demand over the risk-period rather than per period.

12.4 Recap

As shown in Figure 12.11, we can estimate a demand probability distribution thanks to a kernel distribution estimation (KDE). We do this in two steps:
1. Drawing a kernel (i. e., a distribution function) around each demand observation
2. Estimating the demand distribution as the (normalized) sum of the kernels

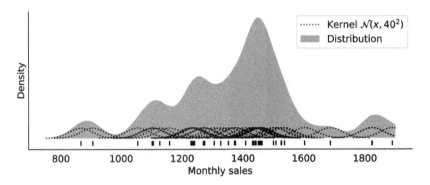

Figure 12.11: Gaussian kernel with $\sigma = 40$.

We saw that using a normal distribution as the kernel was a meaningful choice because it would result in a smooth demand estimation.

The kernel bandwidth (i. e., the standard deviation of the normal distribution around each demand observation) can be estimated by Scott's rule of thumb:

$$\text{Bandwidth} = \sigma_d \cdot \frac{1}{n^{1/5}} \quad \text{(see eq. 12.1 in Section 12.2.3)}$$

where n is the number of demand observations.

A probability mass function (PMF) can then easily be estimated as the normalized PDF for each integer value.

13 Simulation Optimization

As early as 1979, Nahmias noted that, *"Research has tended to focus on providing rigorous analyses of optimal policies for relatively simple problems rather than developing workable solutions to realistic problems."*[1] Indeed, the models we've seen so far rely on restrictive assumptions such as normally distributed demand and lead times, or the fact that all excess demand would result in backorders.

Is this realistic? Most likely not.

Let's review some of the assumptions we made:
- We assumed that all excess demand would result in backorders. What if **part** of them would result in lost sales? What if items staying in the backlog for too long would result in lost sales as clients cancel their orders if they wait too long?
- We assumed the demand to be either normally or gamma-distributed. What if it follows a unique distribution (as presented in Chapter 12)?
- We assumed that our goods do not deteriorate over time. But, in reality, many products will suffer from some kind of deterioration (or even perish over a short timeframe).

It will be extremely difficult (impossible?) to solve these cases using mathematical models. This is where simulation optimization (or simply *sim-opt*) will shine. Instead of creating a mathematical model, in order to optimize a supply chain, we will run (many) simulations, each time with different inventory policies, and pick the one that resulted in the lowest cost.

13.1 Safety Stock Optimization

Let's create a first simulation optimization (*sim-opt*) model to optimize the amount of safety stock we need in a complex setting.

13.1.1 The Case

Let's imagine that we have a supply chain with:
- A demand distribution as determined in Chapter 12, "Discrete Probabilistic Demand."
- A lead time that follows a probability mass distribution (PMF) as shown in Table 13.1.

---

[1] See Nahmias (1979).

https://doi.org/10.1515/9783110673944-013

Table 13.1: Lead time probabilities.

Lead time	3	4	5
Probability	0.1	0.7	0.2

– A **backlog cost** denoted b_τ, i.e., *a cost per unit in the backlog per period* (rather than a fixed backorder cost b that is a cost per unit short as in Chapter 8). In other words, we pay a penalty based on *how long* clients have to wait for their goods to be delivered (rather than a single penalty for not having the goods immediately).

We want to find an inventory policy that minimizes the costs of our supply chain. This would be difficult to do with the mathematical models we've seen so far. Therefore, we will use sim-opt.

We will do this in 3 steps:

1. Model the demand and the lead time.
2. Create a simulation that returns an expected cost based on a given safety stock.
3. Run a search algorithm that will loop through simulations until it finds a proper safety stock level.

13.1.2 Demand and Lead time Estimation

Let's start by extracting the demand PMF and its attributes.

> **DIY**
>
> First, we need to extract the demand based on the function `get_data()` that we created earlier (see Section 9.1).
>
> ```
> df = get_data('Toyota')
> df = df.iloc[1:] #Remove one outlier
> ```
>
> We can then estimate the demand PMF (as we did in Section 12.3.1).
>
> ```
> bandwidth = df['Sales'].std() / (df['Sales'].count()**(1/5))
> lower = np.floor(df['Sales'].min() - 3 * bandwidth)
> upper = np.ceil(df['Sales'].max() + 3 * bandwidth)
> x = np.arange(lower,upper)
> kde_dist = gaussian_kde(df['Sales'],bw_method='scott')
> pmf = kde_dist.pdf(x)
> pmf = pmf/sum(pmf)
> ```

We get the demand attributes (μ_d and σ_d) based on the function `attributes(pmf,` `x)` that we defined in Section 12.3.2.

```
def attributes(pmf,x):
    mu = sum(pmf*x)
    std = np.sqrt(sum(x**2*pmf) - sum(pmf*x)**2)
    return mu, std
d_mu, d_std = attributes(pmf,x)
```

We can then work on the lead time.

DIY

We will define a lead time PMF `L_pmf` and its domain `L_x`. As for the demand, we can use `attributes(pmf,x)` to get μ_L and σ_L.

```
L_x = np.array([3,4,5])
L_pmf = np.array([0.1,0.7,0.2])
L_mu, L_std = attributes(L_pmf,L_x)
L_median = 4
L_max = 5
```

We will need `L_median` and `L_max` later in our simulation.

13.1.3 Simulation Function

We continue by creating a simulation function that takes a safety stock as input and returns a (simulated) average cost per period.

DIY

Let's first set some constants. We will use the same costs that we used in the simulation from Section 8.4.

```
k = 1000 #Fixed cost per transaction
h = 1.25 #Holding cost per unit per period
b = 25 #Backlog cost per unit per period
time = 20000 #Number of timesteps in the simulation
```

Only the backorder cost changed: we now use a backlog cost per unit **per period**, and we set it to 25. Note that we will define the number of timesteps in our simulation (time) as a general variable (and not via a simulation parameter).

We can now create our simulation function simulation(R,Ss)! It takes two inputs: a review period R and a safety stock level Ss; and returns a few KPI (cost, cycle service level, fill rate, safety stock).

Note that (see highlighted rows in the code),

- We set the shape of the array transit based on the maximum possible lead time (L_max).
- For each new order, we pick a random lead time with np.random.choice(L_x, 1, p=L_pmf) (see Section 12.3.1 for a refresher about np.random.choice()).
- The backlog costs are computed, at each timestep, as the current backlog times the backlog unit cost (b*max(0,-hand[t])).

```python
def simulation(R,Ss):

    S = round(d_mu * (R+L_mu) + round(Ss)).astype(int)

    hand = np.zeros(time,dtype=int)
    transit = np.zeros((time,L_max+1),dtype=int)
    unit_shorts = np.zeros(time,dtype=int)

    stockout_period = np.full(time,False,dtype=bool)
    stockout_cycle = []

    hand[0] = S - d[0]
    transit[1,L_median] = d[0]

    p = np.zeros(time) #Physical stock
    p[0] = S - d[0]/2
    c_k = k #Transaction costs
    c_h = h*p[0] #Holding costs
    c_b = 0 #Backlog costs assuming no backlog during the first
        period

    for t in range(1,time):
        if transit[t-1,0]>0:
            stockout_cycle.append(stockout_period[t-1])
```

```
    unit_shorts[t] = max(0,d[t] - max(0,hand[t-1] + transit[t
        -1,0]))
    hand[t] = hand[t-1] - d[t] + transit[t-1,0]
    stockout_period[t] = hand[t] < 0
    transit[t,:-1] = transit[t-1,1:]
    if t%R==0:
        actual_L = np.random.choice(L_x, 1, p=L_pmf)
        net = hand[t] + transit[t].sum()
        transit[t,actual_L] = S - net
        c_k += k
    if hand[t] > 0: #there is enough stock by the end of the
        period
        p[t] = (hand[t-1] + transit[t-1,0] + hand[t])/2
    else: #there is not
        p[t] = max(hand[t-1] + transit[t-1,0],0)**2/max(d[t
            ],1)/2
    c_h += h*p[t]
    c_b += b*max(0,-hand[t]) #backlog cost times the total
        backlog

SL_alpha = 1-sum(stockout_cycle)/len(stockout_cycle)
fill_rate = 1-unit_shorts.sum()/sum(d)
cost = (c_h+c_b+c_k)/time

return cost, SL_alpha, fill_rate, Ss
```

Now that we have a simulation function, we can work on a search algorithm that will find a proper safety stock level based on the simulated results.

Important Point

In this section, we discuss safety stock optimization. Instead, we could optimize directly the policy order up-to level.

Once you have the safety stock, you can compute the order up-to level as:

$$S = S_s + \mu_d(\mu_L + R)$$

In Python, we have S = Ss + d_mu*(R+L_mu). Note that practitioners often confuse the expected average lead time (L_mu) with the "most common" lead time.

13.1.4 Optimization Algorithm

We will discuss two search algorithms to find a *good* level of safety stock. As usual, we will start with a simple method and then improve it.

Method #1 – Start at 0 and Increase

This method is simple:

1. Start by simulating a first policy with a safety stock of 0.
2. Increase the level of safety stock by a **step-size** (we will discuss this in the following pages).

$$S_S = S_S + \text{step-size}$$

3. Run a new simulation and analyze the resulting cost:
   - If it is smaller than the (current) optimal cost, we update the optimal cost as the new one:

$$\text{if cost} < \text{cost}^* \Rightarrow \text{cost}^* = \text{cost}$$

   then,
   - If the ratio between the returned cost and the optimal cost is higher than a **threshold**, we stop our search algorithm:

$$\text{if } \frac{\text{cost}}{\text{cost}^*} > \text{threshold} \Rightarrow \text{Stop}$$

otherwise we perform steps 2 and 3 again.

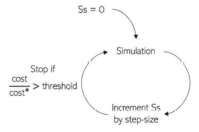

Figure 13.1 shows typical results for this first simple method (applied to the case described earlier).

As we can see, starting with a safety stock level of 0 is not the smartest choice since the cost in this region is particularly high. We will discuss a smarter technique later in this section.

Let's discuss two important parameters of our search algorithm: the step-size and the threshold.

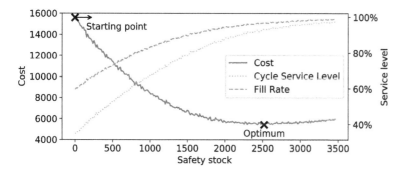

Figure 13.1: Method #1 – start at 0 and increase. Sim-opt with 248 iterations and a step-size of 14.

Calibrating the Step-size

Using a small step-size will make our algorithm slow. But it should allow us to find a better inventory level thanks to a more detailed searching grid. Typically, the step-size can be set as an arbitrary percentage of the mean demand (1 to 5%). It can also be based on practical limitations: if you are required to buy a product in batches of 100 pieces, a step-size of 100 seems a good choice.

Calibrating the Threshold

The threshold defines the ratio (between the latest simulated cost and the current optimal cost) determining when we stop the search algorithm.

$$\text{if } \frac{\text{cost}}{\text{cost}^*} > \text{threshold} \Rightarrow \text{Stop}$$

A high threshold will allow us to search in a larger area, at the expense of a longer running time. Due to the simulation output variability (as you can see in Figure 13.1), a too small threshold might stop the simulation too early just because one simulation-step might return a skewed result. The more complex your supply chain is (i. e., complex lead time, customer behavior), the more variable the simulation result might be, and so you might want to increase the threshold. Another way to decrease the variability is to increase the number of timesteps in the simulation, which, unfortunately, will increase the running time.

DIY

Let's implement our first method into a function `find_best_Ss`. It takes three parameters:
- `step_size=1` is the step-size.
- `start=0` defines the safety stock level at which the algorithm starts.
- `threshold=1.1` is the ratio between the latest simulated cost and the optimal cost. When it is reached, the algorithm will stop and returns the optimal safety stock level found so far.

```
def find_best_Ss(step_size=1, start=0, threshold=1.1):
    results = [ ]
    Ss_opt = start
    results.append(simulation(R,Ss_opt))
    cost_opt = results[-1][0]
    Ss_new = step_size + start
    results.append(simulation(R,Ss_new))
    cost_new = results[-1][0]
    while cost_new < cost_opt*threshold :
        if cost_new < cost_opt:
            cost_opt = cost_new
            Ss_opt = Ss_new
            print('New Ss_opt:',Ss_opt)
        Ss_new += step_size
        results.append(simulation(R,Ss_new))
        cost_new = results[-1][0]
    print('Best found:',Ss_opt,cost_opt)
    return results
```

We can then use our new function to find the optimal safety stock level.

```
time = 20000
R = 1
#We start at Ss = 0 and we increase Ss as long as cost decreases
step_size = int(max(1,round(d_mu/100)))
results = find_best_Ss(step_size=step_size, start=0)
```

We can define a small function to print the sim-opt results.

```
def print_results(results).
    df = pd.DataFrame(results)
    df.columns = ['Cost','Cycle Service Level','Fill Rate','
        Safety Stocks']
    df = df.set_index('Safety Stocks').sort_index()
    df.plot(secondary_y=['Cycle Service Level','Fill Rate'])
print_results(results)
```

This will give you a figure similar to Figure 13.1.

Method #2 – Smart Start and Double Runs

We saw in Figure 13.1 that starting the search with an initial safety stock of 0 is not the smartest starting position: the simulated cost in this region is really high. A smarter starting position would have been around 1500 to 2500 pieces.

Instead of starting at 0 and increasing the safety stock level at each step, we can choose a smarter starting position and search the optimal safety stock level by performing a search in **two** directions. In other words (as shown in Figure 13.2), we will perform two searches: one with a positive step-size, and a second search with a negative step-size (we *decrease* the safety stock to see if it results in lower costs).

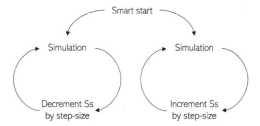

Figure 13.2: Method #2 – Smart Start and Double Runs.

Naturally, we do not know the optimal amount of safety stock, since this is the reason why we are doing simulations. So how can we find a good starting position? We will use **heuristics** to find a good starting position and start searching for the optimal policy from there.

> **Heuristic**
>
> A simple method to find an approximately correct solution to a complex problem. Fancy word for rule of thumb.

Heuristic for (R, S) Policy

Let's assume that the demand and the lead time are normally distributed. Based on this assumption, we know the optimal service level (see eq. 8.3 in Section 8.2.1) and we know how much safety stock will be needed to achieve this cycle service level (see eq. 6.5 in Section 6.3.3):

$$\alpha = 1 - \frac{hR}{b}$$
$$S_s = z_\alpha \sqrt{(\mu_L + R)\sigma_d^2 + \sigma_L^2 \mu_d^2}$$

We can then start our search algorithm at this level of safety stock.

DIY

Let's use this heuristic in Python to compute our starting point Ss.

In our example, since we face backlog costs b_τ (costs per unit in the backlog per period) instead of simply backorder costs b (one time cost per backordered unit), we can increase b a bit in our heuristic (as this formula assumes backorder costs). So, as a quick approximation, we will increase b by 10% in the optimal service level function (simply assuming that some units will stay longer in the backlog).

```
alpha_opt = 1 - h*R/(b*1.1)
x_std = np.sqrt((L_mu+R)*d_std**2 + L_std**2*d_mu**2)
Ss = x_std*norm.ppf(alpha_opt)
Ss = int(round(Ss))
```

As you can see in Figure 13.3, if we use this heuristic as a starting point for our simulation optimization, we end up performing fewer iterations to find the *optimal*[2] policy.

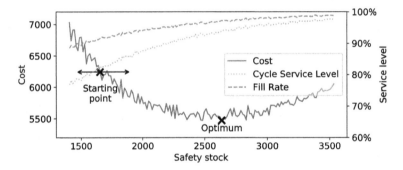

Figure 13.3: Method #2 – smart start and increase/decrease. Sim-opt with 153 iterations and a step-size of 14 (against 248 iterations with Method #1)

DIY

We can use our new algorithm simply by calling twice find_best_Ss(), once with a positive step-size and once with a negative step-size.

```
#Increase
step_size = int(max(1,round(d_mu/100)))
```

---

2 We abuse the language here by calling it the *optimal* policy. Whereas, due to the stochastic behavior of the system, we should only say that this is a *proper* policy.

```
results_increase = find_best_Ss(step_size=step_size, start=Ss)

#Decrease
step_size = int(max(1,round(d_mu/100)))
results_decrease = find_best_Ss(step_size=-step_size, start=Ss-
    step_size)
```

We can then plot our new results.

```
print_results(results_increase+results_decrease)
```

You should obtain something similar to Figure 13.3.

Improving the Sim-Opt Further

The two methods presented here are of course simple ones. They only serve as an introduction to simulation optimization. Here are a few ideas on how to achieve a faster optimization algorithm. Feel free to test your own.

Faster simulation The code presented throughout this chapter is, as discussed in the introduction, not optimized for speed. It seems feasible to make each simulation loop 10x faster (and even more).

Two loops The idea here is to do a search in two loops. The first loop with a wide grid (i. e., a big step-size); and a second one, starting at the optimum of the first, with a much more detailed grid (i. e., small step-size). In other words, we first look quickly to find the general area where the optimum might be; then we look in closer detail to find where it actually is.

Smoothing results As you saw in Figure 13.3, the simulated costs can be noisy. You could reduce this variability by running each simulation during more timesteps, but this will be (very) expensive (i. e., it will take time). Another way to reduce the result variability is to *smooth* the results—for example, by replacing each result by the average of the 3 closest observations.

Variable step-size Instead of performing fixed steps in the search algorithm, you could make them bigger (or smaller) based on the slope of the cost decrease.

Approximation function After a few cost observations, you can fit a (polynomial) function to them, and then look for this function's minimum. Machine learning could even be used here to approximate the cost function.

13.2 Complex Policies Optimization

It works in practice, but does it work in theory?

So far we've analyzed sim-opt techniques with one parameter (the safety stock in our case), but what if we want to optimize more complex policies with multiple parameters at once?

13.2.1 (R, S) Policy Optimization

If we want to optimize both the review period and the safety stock of an (R, S) policy, we can look at a method similar to the one we used in Chapter 8 (see Section 8.2.1):
1. Set a *good* starting review period (based on heuristics, for example, the power-of-2 rule, see Section 3.2.1).
2. Find the optimal safety stock for this review period (based on the methods explained in Section 13.1).
3. Compute the optimal safety stock (and cost) for a shorter and longer review period.
4. If one provides a better result, look for an even longer or shorter period.
5. Repeat step 4 until a good combination of review period and safety stock is found.

In other words, we use our double search method for the review period R; and for each possible review period we use the same method to optimize the safety stock.

13.2.2 (R, s, Q) Policy Optimization

Let's imagine now that we want to follow an (R, s, Q) policy. Remember that, with this policy,[3] we check every review period R if the inventory reached s. If so, we order Q units (or a multiple of Q if this is not enough to bring the inventory level back to s).

This policy is rather difficult to optimize mathematically, even when you assume normal or gamma-distributed demand with fixed lead times.[4] Therefore, when we have a custom PMF for the demand and for the lead time, together with a backlog cost, we should revert to a simulation to optimize our policy.

Review Period Optimization

In an (R, s, Q) policy, the ordering cost is usually optimized with Q. As we saw in Chapter 2, "How Much Should I Order?" the higher the order quantity is, the lower the ordering costs are; but also the higher the holding costs are. We usually assume that

---

3 See Chapters 1 and 5, specifically Section 1.3 and Figure 5.5.
4 See Tempelmeier (2011) for mathematical expressions.

simply checking the inventory (once per review period) does not incur any cost. If this is indeed the case, you want R to be as small as possible. On the other hand, if simply checking the inventory position is already a cost—this can be the case if you need to physically count the inventory—you might want to try multiple values for R following a similar method to the one we just discussed for the (R, S) policy.

Setting of Initial Parameters

Before we discuss optimization techniques, let's find a heuristic to pick reasonably good R, s and Q. In order to do so, we will have to master the art of approximation.

Cycle Service Level α

In Chapter 8, "Cost and Service Level Optimization," we discussed two sets of equations to determine the optimal service level. One for an (R, S) policy (eq. 8.3 in Section 8.2.1) and one for an (s, Q) policy (eq. 8.4 in Section 8.3.1):

$$(R, S) \quad \alpha^* = 1 - \frac{hR}{b}$$

$$(s, Q) \quad \alpha^* = 1 - \frac{hQ}{bD}$$

None of these perfectly match the (R, s, Q) policy. Nevertheless, we have to find a heuristic to find a good starting position. When hesitating between two estimations, a good approximation is to take the average of the two. This is an application of the *wisdom of the crowd*.[5] Our starting service level could then be:

$$\alpha = \frac{1}{2}\left(1 - \frac{hR}{b} + 1 - \frac{hQ}{bD}\right)$$

Reorder-point s

We can use the usual equation of the (s, Q) policy in order to compute the required safety stock. But the lead time L alone is not a good estimation of the risk-period x_τ in an (R, s, Q) policy. Instead, we could use $L + R$ as the risk-period length—as for an (R, S) policy—but as shown by Tempelmeier,[6] this might be too much. We will then choose an in-between solution and set the risk-period x_τ as $L + R/2$. In other words, we assume that the risk-period is around $L + R/2$ periods long in an (R, s, Q) policy. We then have:

$$S_s = z\sigma_d \sqrt{L + R/2}$$

$$s = d_L + d_{R/2} + S_s$$

---

5 As explained in my previous book *Data Science for Supply Chain Forecasting*, the *wisdom of the crowd* concept states that the average opinion of a group of people is going to be more precise, on average, that the opinion of a single member of the group. So it is better to ask the opinion of everyone and average them.

6 See Tempelmeier (2011).

Order Quantity Q

We can simply use the EOQ formula (see eq. 2.2 in Section 2.2.2):

$$Q^* = \sqrt{\frac{2kD}{h}}$$

or use a generalized expression of the stochastic EOQ formula (see eq. 8.5 in Section 8.3.1) that includes the expected backorders per cycle:

$$Q^* = \sqrt{\frac{2(k + b\,U_s)D}{h}}$$

Using this equation is trickier: we do not know the expected backorders per cycle U_s. On top of that, we use in our example a backlog cost b_r rather than a backorder cost b. Nevertheless, even by using rough approximations (such as $U_s = 0.02 \cdot Q$ and $b = 1.1 \cdot b_r$) you might get a better starting position (as we will see in the following pages).

Now that we have a set of initial values for our parameters, rather than create our own search algorithm, we will use one of the optimization functions available in Python.[7]

DIY

We will create a new simulation function `simulation_RsQ(x)` that is mostly the same as the previous function from Section 13.1.3. We can simplify it a bit since we only need to return the cost and no extra information (such as service levels). The few changes are highlighted below. You can remove the `print()` function if you don't want to see what the optimization function is working on.

An important technical point (due to the optimization function we will use) is that the function can only take one variable as input. So we pack s and Q in this variable x and unpack it in the function.

Note that we also need to round s and Q, as the optimization algorithm will try non integer values

```
def simulation_RsQ(x):
    s, Q = int(round(x[0])), int(round(x[1]))
    hand = np.zeros(time,dtype=int)
    transit = np.zeros((time,L_max),dtype=int)
    hand[0] = s + Q - d[0]
    transit[1,L_median] = d[0]
```

---

7 We will treat this optimization function as a *black box* since its optimization algorithm is out-of-scope of this book.

```
p = np.zeros(time)
p[0] = s + Q - d[0]/2
c_k, c_h, c_k = k, h*p[0], 0
for t in range(1,time):
    hand[t] = hand[t-1] - d[t] + transit[t-1,0]
    if t < time-1:
        transit[t+1,:-1] = transit[t,1:]
        if t%R==0:
            net = hand[t] + transit[t].sum()
            if net <= s:
                actual_L = np.random.choice(L_x, 1, p=L_pmf)
                transit[t+1,actual_L-1] = (1+ (s-net)//Q)*Q
                c_k += k
    if hand[t] > 0:
        p[t] = (hand[t-1] + transit[t-1,0] + hand[t])/2
    else:
        p[t] = max(hand[t-1] + transit[t-1,0],0)**2/max(d[t
            ],1)/2
    c_h += h*p[t]
    c_b += b*max(0,-hand[t])
cost = (c_h+c_b+c_k)/time
print('\ts, Q, Cost:',s,Q,round(cost,0).astype(int))
return cost
```

We can now define the starting values (based on heuristics). Remember, we use in our example a backlog cost b_r instead of a backorder cost b. So we increase b by 10% in the equation below to reflect that some backorders will stay multiple periods in the backlog.

```
Q = np.sqrt(2*(k+Q*0.02*b*1.1)*d_mu/h)
alpha_opt1 = 1 - h*R/(b*1.1)
alpha_opt2 = 1 - h*Q/(b*1.1*d_mu)
alpha_opt = (alpha_opt1+alpha_opt2)/2
x_std = np.sqrt((L_mu+R+1/2)*d_std**2 + L_std**2*d_mu**2)
Ss = x_std*norm.ppf(alpha_opt)
s = Ss + (L_mu+1/2)*d_mu
```

Finally, we can use an optimization function. We will use the method Nelder-Mead from scipy.optimize.[a]

```
import scipy.optimize
print('Nelder-Mead')
res = scipy.optimize.minimize(fun=simulation_RsQ, x0=np.array([s
    ,Q]),
    method='Nelder-Mead', options={'maxiter':50})
```

Let's quickly discuss a few parameters:
- x0=np.array([s,Q]) we need to pack the starting parameters as one variable and pass them via x0 (and pass them as a NumPy array).
- options={'maxiter':50} we want the algorithm to stop after maximum 50 simulations.

Once it has run, the optimal cost can be accessed on res.fun and the best parameters on res.x.

```
print('values:',res.x)
>> values: [8249 2445]
print('results:', res.fun)
>> 4719
```

The solution provided should be *around*[b] $s = 8249$ and $Q = 2445$ for an expected cost per period of 4719.

Note that the stochastic EOQ approximation

$$Q^* = \sqrt{\frac{2(k + 1.1\,b_\tau \cdot 0.02\,Q)D}{h}} \simeq 2001$$

provided a (much) better starting position than the deterministic EOQ formula:

$$Q^* = \sqrt{\frac{2kD}{h}} \simeq 1485$$

Our initial value guess for s was 7927, which is really close to the one found by the solver (8249).

---

a https://docs.scipy.org/doc/scipy/reference/optimize.minimize-neldermead.html
b But this is a random process you might get another set of results. As we will see, you can fix the variability issue.

13.3 Stability

Simulation optimizations have one (quite significant) issue: the results are random. If you run the *same* sim-opt twice, you will most likely get different results. This is explained by the fact that simulations are based on random events, so their ultimate cost estimation is random as well. Two consecutive sim-opts will often recommend two very similar—but different—policies that will achieve similar results. But you can also end up with *very* different policies that still achieve similar outcomes!

Nevertheless, even small inventory policy variations will make supply chain planners nervous (potentially causing a *bullwhip effect*[8] with your suppliers). These variations will likely confuse (or worry) any practitioner, ultimately resulting in a lack of confidence in your inventory policies.

Let's discuss 3 ways to make your sim-opt more stable.

13.3.1 #1 – Set a Random Seed

In Python (as with all computer software), all random processes are actually *pseudo-random*. It means that the computer is *simulating* a random process, based on a **random seed**. In NumPy, each time we call a random function it generates a new (pseudo-random) seed and uses it to generate random numbers. If we set this seed to an arbitrary number—instead of letting NumPy pseudo-randomly pick one—all the random functions will always return the exact same numbers.

We can then use this technique to be sure that if we run the same simulation twice, we will get the same results.

Unfortunately this will not be enough: if you change the slightest number (a cost parameter, the demand KDE, and so on) you will still get a different result from the sim-opt, ultimately resulting in a new (slightly different) inventory policy.

> **DIY**
>
> Setting a random seed in NumPy is easy: simply add this to your script.
>
> ```
> np.random.seed(0)
> ```

13.3.2 #2 – Increase the Number of Timesteps

One of the main reasons for lack of stability is the fact that the result of a single simulation is highly variable. The only way to reduce this inner variability is to increase

---

8 See Section 10.2.1 for a reminder about the bullwhip effect.

the number of timesteps performed by each simulation (you can simply increase the variable `time` in your Python simulation).

Increasing the number of timesteps is good because it will bring more stable results. Moreover, it will result in a better overall inventory policy since the simulation will be less likely to pick an inventory policy that performed well only by chance on (a few) timesteps. Nevertheless, this comes at a cost: the running time of your sim-opt will be much longer; and it won't prevent you from getting small inventory policy changes at each new sim-opt. We have to find another solution.

13.3.3 #3 – Limit Policy Updates to Significant Changes

Another way to limit variability is to update an inventory policy **only if** it brings a certain added value compared to the current one. For example you might want to update a policy only if the new expected cost is at least 5% lower than that of the current policy. In other words, you have to find the right trade-off between efficiency and stability.

> **Example**
>
> You run a first sim-opt to optimize your policy. You get $(R, s, Q) = (1, 8249, 2445)$ as a recommended policy, with an estimated cost of 4719 per period.
>
> After a few months, you again run a demand kernel density estimation (as in Chapter 12) based on new demand observations, and then a new sim-opt. You obtain $(R, s, Q) = (1, 8224, 2061)$ with an estimated cost of 4650 per period. That's a cost reduction of 1.5% (below your threshold of 5%).
>
> You decide that updating your inventory policy is not worth it.
>
> A few weeks later, you investigate the cost drivers and see that the fixed transaction cost should be updated to $k = 2000$ (and not 1000 as initially thought). You again run the sim-opt and see that the proposed policy is $(1, 7990, 2771)$, with an expected cost of 5165 per period. If you run a simulation with your current policy $(1, 8224, 2061)$ and the new transaction cost estimate ($k = 2000$), you face a cost per period of 5689. This is a 9.2% cost decrease.
>
> Since the new policy will bring a significant cost reduction, you decide to update your inventory policy.

Using this trick will help you to keep consistent inventory policies. On the other hand, it will not help if you need to perform multiple scenario analysis. In such a case, increasing the number of timesteps is the best way to achieve a reliable (and stable) analysis.

13.4 Recap

As we have seen throughout this book, mathematical models can only take us so far to optimize *real* supply chains. This is where simulation optimization (sim-opt) will help by finding (very) good inventory policies without requiring any mathematical model. Nevertheless, this comes at the expense of computation time. Sim-opt should therefore be used when the supply chain at hand is too complex to be properly approximated by mathematical models.

We discussed three sim-opt algorithms:

Simple search We start by simulating a policy with 0 safety stock. We perform new simulations (each time increasing the safety stock by a step-size) until we find an "optimal" amount.

Smart start and double search We start at a better initial position (based on heuristics) and perform two searches: one by increasing the safety stock level and one by decreasing it.

Black box algorithm We can also rely on external black box algorithms (such as those provided by Python's libraries).

In order to find an appropriate initial set of parameters for our search algorithms, we have to use heuristics. These will allow us to perform a quicker search as we start closer to the optimal policy. We can base our heuristics on the previous chapters, especially Chapter 8, "Cost and Service Level Optimization," that gave us equations to optimize (R, S) and (s, Q) policies.

Finally, simulation optimizations face one drawback: they always provide (slightly) different results. We saw that a good practice is to update an inventory policy only if it brings significant improvement. You can also increase the number of timesteps in the sim-opt in order to get more stable results.

Now It Is Your Turn!

We have not succeeded in answering all our problems—indeed we sometimes feel we have not completely answered any of them. The answers we have found have only served to raise a whole set of new questions. In some ways we feel that we are as confused as ever, but we think we are confused on a higher level and about more important things.

Earl C. Kelley

Supply chains are complex.

But that didn't block us from creating sound mathematical models throughout this book to optimize inventory policies. First, in Part I based on the assumption of deterministic demand and supply; then, in Part II we introduced stochastic demand and supply. The breakthrough came in Part III where we computed the fill rate, optimized our policies to minimize the costs, used gamma-distributed demand and finally looked at multi-echelon inventory optimization. Part IV showed you how to optimize virtually any inventory policy using simulations.

Now that you have finished the book, you will probably want to come back to it when you are working on projects. So, I suggest that you create your models step by step (remember, *Vires acquirit eundo – We gather strength as we go*). First use Parts I and II to properly define safety stock targets (based on arbitrary service levels). Then use Part III to optimize your service levels—and maximize your profit. See if your demand is not gamma-distributed (this can be done easily—even in Excel—as explained in Section 9.4); and finally use the risk-period framework to optimize inventory across multi-echelon networks. Always keep track of the assumptions you are making—it is not an issue to take shortcuts, as long as you are aware of them. If needed, you can use simulation optimizations as presented in Part IV to optimize (much) more complex policies.

Lastly, in order to avoid any blind spots, discuss your models, assumptions and ideas with your colleagues—or even on social media. It is always better to have a model that works 95% of the time, and is understood by its users; than a perfect—but too complex—model that is rejected. Keep in mind, inventory optimization is a journey.

Now It Is your turn!

https://doi.org/10.1515/9783110673944-014

A Python

If this is your first time using Python, let's take some time to quickly introduce and discuss the different libraries and data types we are going to use. Of course, the goal of this book is not to give you full training in Python; if you wish an in-depth introduction (or if you are not yet convinced to use Python) please refer to the recommended courses in the introduction.

How to Install Python

There are multiple ways to install Python on your computer. An easy way to do this is to install the Anaconda distribution on www.anaconda.com/download. Anaconda is a well-known platform used by data scientists all over the world. It works on Windows, Mac and Linux. Anaconda will take care of installing all the Python libraries you need to run the different models that we are going to discuss. It will also install Spyder and Jupyter Notebook, two Python-code editors that you can use to type and run your scripts. Feel free to check both and use your favorite.

Lists

The most basic object we will use in Python is a list. In Python, a list is simply an ordered sequence of any number of objects (e. g., strings, numbers, other lists, more complex objects, etc.). You can create a list by encoding these objects between []. Typically, we can define our first time series ts as:

```
ts = [1,2,3,4,5,6]
```

These lists are very efficient at storing and manipulating objects, but are not meant for number computation. For example, if we want to add two different time series, we can't simply ask ts + ts2, as this is what we would get:

```
ts = [1,2,3,4,5,6]
ts2 = [10,20,30,40,50,60]
ts + ts2
Out: [1, 2, 3, 4, 5, 6, 10, 20, 30, 40, 50, 60]
```

Python is returning a new *longer* list. That's not exactly what we wanted.

https://doi.org/10.1515/9783110673944-015

NumPy

This is where the famous **NumPy**[1] library comes to help. Since its initial release in 2006, NumPy has offered us a new data type: a NumPy array. This is similar to a list, as it contains a sequence of different numeric values, but differs in the way that we can easily call any mathematical function on them. You can create one directly from a list like this:

```
import numpy as np
ts = np.array([1,2,3,4,5,6])
```

As you will see, NumPy is most often imported as np.

We can now simply add our array ts to any other array.

```
ts2 = np.array([10,20,30,40,50,60])
ts + ts2
Out: array([11, 22, 33, 44, 55, 66])
```

Note that the result is another NumPy array (and not a simple list).

NumPy most often works very well directly with regular lists because we can use most of the NumPy functions directly on them. Here is an example:

```
alist = [1,2,3]
np.mean(alist)
Out: 2.0
```

You can always look for help on the NumPy official website.[2] As you will see yourself, most of your Google searches about NumPy functions will actually end up directly in their documentation.

Slicing

To select a particular value in a list (or an array), you simply have to indicate between [] the index of its location inside the list (array). The catch—as with many coding languages—is that the index starts at 0 and not at 1; so that the first element in your list will have the index 0, the second element the index 1, and so on.

```
alist = ['cat','dog','mouse']
alist[1]
```

---

1 NumPy for **Num**eric **Py**thon.
2 https://docs.scipy.org/doc/numpy/reference/

```
Out: 'dog'
anarray = np.array([1,2,3])
anarray[0]
Out: 1
```

If you want to select multiple items at once, you can simply indicate a range of index with this format: [start:end]. Note that,
-   If you do not give a start value, Python will assume it is 0.
-   If you do not give an end, it will assume it is the end of the list.

Note that the result will **include** the start element but **exclude** the end element.

```
alist = ['cat','dog','mouse']
alist[1:]
Out: ['dog','mouse']
anarray = np.array([1,2,3])
anarray[:1]
Out: np.array([1])
```

If you give a negative value as the end, Python will start by counting backward from the last element of your list/array (-1 being the last element of your array).

```
alist = ['cat','dog','mouse']
alist[-1]
Out: ['mouse']
alist[:-1]
Out: ['cat','dog']
```

You can slice a multi-dimensional array by separating each dimension with a comma.

```
anarray = np.array([[1,2],[3,4]])
anarray[0,0]
Out: 1
anarray[:,-1]
Out: array([2, 4])
```

Pandas

Pandas is one of the most used libraries in Python (it was created by Wes McKinney in 2008). The name comes from **pan**el **da**ta, because it helps to order data into tables. Think Excel-meets-databases in Python. This library introduces a new data type:

a **DataFrame**. If you're a database person, just think about a DataFrame as an SQL table. If you're an Excel person, just imagine a DataFrame as an Excel table. Actually, a DataFrame is a sort of data table where each column would be a NumPy array with a specific name. That will come in pretty handy because we can select each column of our DataFrame by its name.

There are many ways to create a DataFrame, let's create our first one by using a list of our two time series.

```
import pandas as pd
pd.DataFrame([ts,ts2])
```

```
Out:
      0    1    2    3    4    5
0     1    2    3    4    5    6
1    10   20   30   40   50   60
```

The convention is to import pandas as pd and to call our main DataFrame df. The output we get is a DataFrame where we have 6 columns (named '0','1','2','3','4' and '5') and 2 rows (actually, they also have a name—or index—'0' and '1').

We can easily edit the column names:

```
df = pd.DataFrame([ts,ts2])
df.columns = ['Day1','Day2','Day3','Day4','Day5','Day6']
print(df)
```

```
Out:
      Day1  Day2  Day3  Day4  Day5  Day6
0        1     2     3     4     5     6
1       10    20    30    40    50    60
```

Pandas comes with very simple and helpful official documentation.[3] When in doubt, do not hesitate to look into it. Just as for NumPy, most of your Google searches will end up there.

Slicing DataFrames

There are many different techniques to slice a DataFrame to get the element or the part you want. This might be confusing for beginners, but you'll soon understand that each of these has its uses and advantages. Do not worry if you get confused or overwhelmed: you won't need to apply all of these right now.

---

3 https://pandas.pydata.org/pandas-docs/stable/

- You can select a specific column by passing the name of this column directly to the DataFrame either with df['myColumn'] or even more directly with df.myColumn.
- You can select a row based on its index value by simply typing df[myIndexValue].
- If you want to select an element based on both its row and column, you can call the method .loc on the DataFrame and give it the index value and the column name you want. You can for example type df.loc[myIndexValue,'myColumn']
- You can also use the same slicing method as for lists and arrays based on the position of the element you want to select. You then need to call the method .iloc to the DataFrame. Typically, to select the first element (top left corner), you can type df.iloc[0,0].

As a recap, here are all the techniques you can use to select a column and/or a row:

```
df['myColumn']
df.myColumn
df[myIndexValue]
df.loc[myIndexValue,'myColumn']
df.iloc[0,0]
```

Dictionaries

Another way to create a DataFrame is to construct it based on a dictionary of lists or arrays. A **dictionary** is a collection of elements that links (unique) keys to values. You can create one by including between {} a key and a value (both can be any Python object).

```
dic = {'Small product':ts,'Big product':ts2}
dic
Out:
{'Small product': array([1, 2, 3, 4, 5, 6]),
 'Big product': array([10, 20, 30, 40, 50, 60])}
```

Here the key 'Small product' will give you the value ts, whereas the key 'Big product' will give you ts2.

```
dic['Small product']
Out: array([1, 2, 3, 4, 5, 6])
dic['Small product'] + dic['Big product']
Out: array([11, 22, 33, 44, 55, 66])
```

What is handy is that we can now create a DataFrame directly from this dictionary.

```
df = pd.DataFrame.from_dict(dic)
Out:
   Small product  Big product
0              1           10
1              2           20
2              3           30
3              4           40
4              5           50
5              6           60
```

We now have a DataFrame where each product has its own column and where each row is a separate period.

Other Libraries

We will also use other very well-known Python libraries. There are discussed below. We used the usual import conventions for these libraries throughout the book. For the sake of clarity, we did not show the `import` lines over and over in each code extract.

SciPy is a library used for all kinds of scientific computation, optimization, as well as statistical computation (SciPy stands for **Sci**entific **Py**thon). The documentation is available on docs.scipy.org/doc/scipy/reference but it is unfortunately not always as clear as we would wish it to be. We mainly focus on the statistical tools and only import them as `stats`.

```
import scipy.stats as stats
```

To make our code shorter, we will import some functions directly from `scipy.stats` in our examples. We can import these as such:

```
from scipy.stats import gamma, normal
```

Matplotlib is the library used for plotting graphs. Unfortunately, matplotlib is not the most user-friendly library, and its documentation is only rarely helpful. If we want to make simple graphs we will prefer using the `.plot()` method from pandas.

```
import matplotlib.pyplot as plt
```

Seaborn is another plotting library built on top of matplotlib. It is actually more user-friendly and provides some refreshing visualization compared to matplotlib. You can check the official website seaborn.pydata.org as it provides both clear and inspiring examples.

```
import seaborn as sns
```

We don't use seaborn in this book. Nevertheless, I advise it as a good addition on top of matplotlib.

B Proofs

B.1 Sum of a Random Number of Random Variables

$$A = B \cdot C$$

The expected value of A is simply the expected value of B times the expected value of C.

$$E[A] = E[B] \cdot E[C]$$

Let's compute the variance of A. We will start from the definition of the variance of a random variable X:

$$V[X] = \frac{1}{n} \sum_{x=1}^{n} (x_i - E[X])^2$$

$$= \frac{1}{n} \sum_{x=1}^{n} x_i^2 + \frac{1}{n} \sum_{x=1}^{n} E[X]^2$$

$$V[X] = E[X^2] - E[X]^2 \tag{B.1}$$

So that $V[A] = E[A^2] - E[A]^2$.

As $E[A] = E[B] \cdot E[C]$, we then have,

$$V[A] = E[A^2] - E[B]^2 E[C]^2 \tag{B.2}$$

We know already $E[B]$ and $E[C]$, we have still to estimate $E[A^2]$.

If we fix the value of B as b we have,

$$V[A|b] = E[A^2|b] - b^2 E[C]^2 \tag{B.3}$$

where the conditional operator | means that we estimate a stochastic variable based on the condition that another variable is known. So that $V[A|b]$ is the conditional probability of $V[A]$ knowing that B is b.

Thus, since we fixed B as a constant b, A is now defined as a constant times a distribution:

$$A|b = b \cdot C$$
$$\Rightarrow V[A|b] = b \cdot V[C]$$

We can then simplify B.3 into

$$E[A^2|b] = b \cdot V[C] - b^2 E[C]^2$$

https://doi.org/10.1515/9783110673944-016

We can then solve our eq. B.2.

$$V[A] = E[A^2] - E[B]^2 E[C]^2$$
$$= \sum_b \left(E[A^2|b] \cdot p(B = b) \right) - E[B]^2 E[C]^2$$
$$= \sum_b \left(\left(b \cdot V[C] - b^2 E[C]^2 \right) \cdot p_B(b) \right) - E[B]^2 E[C]^2 \qquad (B.4)$$

Where $p_B(b)$ is the probability that the variable B takes the value b.

Let's simplify B.4 by using these two relationships:

$$\sum_b b \cdot V[C] \cdot p_B(b) = E[B]V[C]$$
$$\sum_b b^2 E[C]^2 \cdot p_B(b) = E[B^2]E[C]^2$$

We obtain now,

$$V[A] = E[B]V[C] + E[B^2]E[C]^2 - E[B]^2 E[C]^2 \qquad (B.5)$$

We can simplify this further as we know from B.1 that $E[B^2] = V[B] + E[B]^2$. So that we can further simplify B.5 as,

$$V[A] = E[B]V[C] + E[B^2]E[C]^2 - E[B]^2 E[C]^2$$
$$= E[B]V[C] + \left(V[B] + E[B]^2 \right) E[C]^2 - E[B]^2 E[C]^2$$
$$= E[B]V[C] + V[B]E[C]^2$$

B.2 Normal Loss function

We want to compute the loss function $\mathcal{L}(x)$ of our demand d that follows a normal distribution $\mathcal{N}(\mu, \sigma^2)$. The loss function is defined as:

$$\mathcal{L}(x) = \int_{d=x}^{\infty} (d - x)f(d)$$

Where $f(d)$ is the probability density function of the (normally distributed) demand. For the sake of clarity, we abuse the PDF notation by using $f(d)$ instead of $f_D(d)$, and the usual integral notation and not finish them by dd, which would be confusing.

We can solve this by decomposing it into two separated integrals Int1 and Int2.

$$\mathcal{L}(x) = \int_{d=x}^{\infty} (d - x)f(d)$$

$$= \int\limits_{d=x}^{\infty} d \cdot f(d) - x \int\limits_{d=x}^{\infty} f(d)$$

$$= \text{Int1} - x \cdot \text{Int2}$$

Let's first solve Int2.

By definition,

$$\int\limits_{-\infty}^{\infty} f(d) = 1 \text{ and } \int\limits_{-\infty}^{d=x} f(d) = F(x)$$

So that,

$$\int\limits_{d=x}^{\infty} f(d) = \int\limits_{-\infty}^{\infty} f(d) - \int\limits_{-\infty}^{d=x} f(d) = 1 - F(x)$$

Let's now solve Int1.

We will use the definition of $f(d)$ for a normal distribution:

$$f(d) = \frac{1}{\sqrt{2\pi\sigma^2}} e^{-\frac{(d-\mu)^2}{2\sigma^2}} \tag{B.6}$$

So that

$$\text{Int2} = \int\limits_{d=x}^{\infty} d \cdot f(d)$$

$$= \int\limits_{d=x}^{\infty} \frac{d}{\sqrt{2\pi\sigma^2}} \cdot \exp\left(-\frac{(d-\mu)^2}{2\sigma^2}\right)$$

$$= \frac{1}{\sqrt{2\pi\sigma^2}} \int\limits_{d=x}^{\infty} d \cdot \exp\left(-\frac{(d-\mu)^2}{2\sigma^2}\right)$$

We will integrate this by defining

$$u = \frac{d-\mu}{\sigma} \;;\; du = \frac{1}{\sigma}dd \iff d = u\sigma + \mu \;;\; dd = \sigma du$$

So that,

$$\int\limits_{d=x}^{\infty} d \cdot \exp\left(-\frac{(d-\mu)^2}{2\sigma^2}\right) = \int\limits_{u=\frac{x-\mu}{\sigma}}^{\infty} \sigma(u\sigma + \mu) \cdot \exp\left(\frac{-(u\sigma)^2}{2\sigma^2}\right)$$

$$= \sigma \int\limits_{u=\frac{x-\mu}{\sigma}}^{\infty} (u\sigma + \mu) \cdot \exp\left(\frac{-u^2}{2}\right)$$

$$= \sigma^2 \int\limits_{u=\frac{x-\mu}{\sigma}}^{\infty} u \cdot exp\left(\frac{-u^2}{2}\right) + \mu\sigma \int\limits_{u=\frac{x-\mu}{\sigma}}^{\infty} \cdot exp\left(\frac{-u^2}{2}\right)$$

$$= \sigma^2 \cdot Int2_1 + \mu \cdot Int2_2$$

Let's solve the left part $Int2_1$,

$$Int2_1 = \int\limits_{u=\frac{x-\mu}{\sigma}}^{\infty} u \cdot exp\left(\frac{-u^2}{2}\right)$$

We will integrate by defining v as

$$v = \frac{-u^2}{2} \; ; dv = -udu \iff u = \sqrt{-2v}$$

The limits of the integral will change as

$$u = \infty \implies v = -\infty \text{ and } u = \frac{x-\mu}{\sigma} \implies v = -\left(\frac{x-\mu}{\sqrt{2}\sigma}\right)^2$$

So that we can transform our integral

$$\int\limits_{v=-\left(\frac{x-\mu}{\sqrt{2}\sigma}\right)^2}^{-\infty} u \cdot exp\left(\frac{-u^2}{2}\right) = - \int\limits_{v=-\left(\frac{x-\mu}{\sqrt{2}\sigma}\right)^2}^{-\infty} e^v$$

$$= -\left(e^{-\infty} - e^{-\left(\frac{x-\mu}{\sqrt{2}\sigma}\right)^2}\right)$$

$$= e^{-\left(\frac{x-\mu}{\sqrt{2}\sigma}\right)^2} \tag{B.7}$$

Thanks to the definition of the normal density function (see eq. B.6), we can transform B.7 into

$$exp\left(-\left(\frac{x-\mu}{\sqrt{2}\sigma}\right)^2\right) = \frac{\sqrt{2\pi\sigma^2}}{\sqrt{2\pi\sigma^2}} \cdot exp\left(-\frac{(x-\mu)^2}{2\sigma^2}\right) = \sqrt{2\pi\sigma^2} \cdot f(x)$$

We finally solve $Int2_1$:

$$Int2_1 = \sqrt{2\pi\sigma^2} \cdot f(x)$$

Let's now solve the right part $Int2_2$,

$$Int2_2 = \sigma \int\limits_{u=\frac{x-\mu}{\sigma}}^{\infty} exp\left(\frac{-u^2}{2}\right)$$

We can revert to d instead of u and we obtain

$$\sigma \int_{d=x}^{\infty} \frac{1}{\sigma} \cdot \exp\left(\frac{-(d-\mu)^2}{\sigma^2}\right) = \int_{d=x}^{\infty} \cdot \exp\left(\frac{-(d-\mu)^2}{\sigma^2}\right) = \sqrt{2\pi\sigma^2}(1 - F(x))$$

So that,

$$Int2_2 = \sqrt{2\pi\sigma^2}(1 - F(x))$$

We can finally solve Int2

$$Int2 = \int_{d=x}^{\infty} d \cdot f(d)$$

$$= \frac{1}{\sqrt{2\pi\sigma^2}} \int_{d=x}^{\infty} d \cdot \exp\left(-\frac{(d-\mu)^2}{2\sigma^2}\right)$$

$$= \frac{1}{\sqrt{2\pi\sigma^2}} \left(\sigma^2 \cdot Int2_1 + \mu \cdot Int2_2\right)$$

$$= \frac{1}{\sqrt{2\pi\sigma^2}} \left(\sigma^2 \cdot \sqrt{2\pi\sigma^2} \cdot f(x) + \mu \cdot \sqrt{2\pi\sigma^2}(1 - F(x))\right)$$

$$= \sigma^2 f(x) + \mu(1 - F(x))$$

We can then solve our initial loss function:

$$\mathcal{L}(x) = \int_{d=x}^{\infty} (d - x)f(d)$$

$$= \int_{d=x}^{\infty} d \cdot f(d) - x \int_{d=x}^{\infty} f(d)$$

$$= Int1 - x \cdot Int2$$

$$= \sigma^2 f(x) + \mu(1 - F(x)) - x(1 - F(x))$$

$$= \sigma^2 f(x) + (\mu - x)(1 - F(x))$$

B.3 Loss Function Derivative

We define the loss function as

$$\mathcal{L}(\iota) = \int_{\iota}^{\infty} (x - \iota)f(x)\, dx$$

We want to compute the derivative of the loss function:

$$\frac{d\mathcal{L}(\iota)}{d\iota} = \frac{d}{d\iota}\left(\int_{\iota}^{\infty}(x-\iota)f(x)\,dx\right)$$

By the Leibniz integral rule, we obtain:

$$\frac{d\mathcal{L}(\iota)}{d\iota} = \int_{\iota}^{\infty}\frac{\partial}{\partial\iota}(x-\iota)f(x)\,dx$$

$$= \int_{\iota}^{\infty}-f(x)\,dx$$

$$= -\left(\int_{\iota}^{\infty}f(x)\,dx\right)$$

$$= -\left(1-\int_{-\infty}^{\iota}f(x)\,dx\right)$$

$$= -(1-F(\iota))$$

$$= F(\iota)-1$$

So that we have the following relationship:

$$\frac{d\mathcal{L}(\iota)}{d\iota} = F(\iota)-1 \tag{B.8}$$

which is independent of the demand distribution (normal, gamma, etc.).

B.4 Cost Optimization

B.4.1 (R, S) Policy

Cost Expression
We compute the cost per period as

$$C_{period} = h(C_s+S_s) + \frac{k}{R} + \frac{bU_s}{R}$$

where h is the period unit holding cost (i. e., the cost of keeping one unit in stock for **one period**). We also know that $C_s = dR/2$. We will express the safety stock S_s based on ι the inventory level at the beginning of the risk-period (i. e., the policy parameter S):

$$S_s = \iota - \mu_x = \iota - d(R+L)$$

So that we can express the costs per period as

$$C = h\left(\frac{dR}{2} + \iota - d(R + L)\right) + \frac{k}{R} + \frac{b \mathcal{L}_x(\iota)}{R}$$

$$C = h(\iota - d(R/2 + L)) + \frac{k}{R} + \frac{b \mathcal{L}_x(\iota)}{R}$$

where $\mathcal{L}_x(\iota)$ is the loss function of the demand over the risk-period computed at ι.

Remember that

$$\frac{\partial \mathcal{L}_x(\iota)}{\partial \iota} = F_x(\iota) - 1$$

as proven in Section B.3.

Cost Optimization

In order to compute the optimal service level, we can simply take the derivative of the cost function based on ι and set it to zero.

$$\frac{\partial C(z)}{\partial z} = h\frac{\partial(\iota - d(R/2 + L))}{\partial \iota} + \frac{b}{R}\frac{\partial \mathcal{L}_x(\iota)}{\partial \iota} = 0$$

$$hR + b\left(F_x(\iota) - 1\right) = 0$$

$$\frac{hR}{b} + F_x(\iota) - 1 = 0$$

$$F_x(\iota) = 1 - \frac{hR}{b}$$

Because $F_x(\iota) = \alpha$, we conclude that:

$$\text{Optimal cycle service cycle} = \alpha^* = 1 - \frac{hR}{b}$$

and

$$\iota^* = F_x^{-1}\left(1 - \frac{hR}{b}\right)$$

B.4.2 (s, Q) Policy

Cost Expression

We compute the cost per year as

$$C_{\text{year}} = h(C_s + S_s) + k\frac{D}{Q} + b U_s\frac{D}{Q}$$

where h is the yearly unit holding cost (i. e., the cost of keeping one unit in stock for **one year**). We also know that $C_s = Q/2$. We will express the safety stock S_s based on ι the inventory level at the beginning of the risk-period (i. e., the policy parameter S):

$$S_s = \iota - \mu_x = \iota - dL$$

So that we can express the costs as

$$C = h(Q/2 + \iota - dL) + k\frac{D}{Q} + b\,\mathcal{L}_x(\iota)\frac{D}{Q}$$

$$C = h(Q/2 + \iota - dL) + k\frac{D}{Q} + b\,\mathcal{L}_x(\iota)\frac{D}{Q}$$

where $\mathcal{L}_x(\iota)$ is the loss function of the demand over the risk-period computed at ι.
Remember that

$$\frac{\partial\mathcal{L}_x(\iota)}{\partial\iota} = F_x(\iota) - 1$$

as proven in Section B.3.

Cost Optimization

In order to compute the optimal service level, we can simply take the derivative of the cost function based on ι and set it to zero.

$$\frac{\partial C(z)}{\partial z} = h\frac{\partial(Q/2 + \iota - dL)}{\partial\iota} + \frac{Db}{Q}\frac{\partial\mathcal{L}_x(\iota)}{\partial\iota} = 0$$

$$h + \frac{bD}{Q}(F_x(\iota) - 1) = 0$$

$$h + \frac{bD}{Q}F_x(\iota) - \frac{bD}{Q} = 0$$

$$hQ + bD\,F_x(\iota) - bD = 0$$

$$F_x(\iota) = 1 - \frac{hQ}{bD}$$

Because $F_x(\iota) = \alpha$, we conclude that:

$$\text{Optimal cycle service cycle} = \alpha^* = 1 - \frac{hQ}{bD}$$

and

$$\iota^* = F_x^{-1}\left(1 - \frac{hQ}{bD}\right)$$

B.5 Discrete Newsvendor Optimization

In the newsvendor model, the general expression of the cost C as a function of the order quantity Q is expressed as:

$$C(Q) = c_o \sum_{d=0}^{Q} p(d)(Q - d) + c_u \sum_{d=Q}^{\infty} p(d)(d - Q) \tag{B.9}$$

where c_o and c_u are the overage and underage costs (c_u includes the profits as the lost opportunity costs), $p(d)$ is the demand probability mass function in d.

As $C(Q)$ is a concave function (i. e., it has a minimum) we want to increase the order quantity Q until the expected cost of ordering one more unit $C(Q + 1)$ is higher than the expected cost of ordering Q units: $C(Q)$. In other words, we want to increase Q until we have (as shown in Figure B.1):

$$C(Q) \le C(Q + 1)$$
$$C(Q) - C(Q + 1) \le 0$$

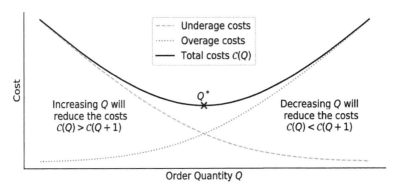

Figure B.1: Optimal order quantity for the newsvendor model based on profits.

Let's replace the expressions of $C(Q)$ and $C(Q + 1)$ by using eq. B.9.

$$c_o \sum_{d=0}^{Q} p(d)(Q - d) + c_u \sum_{d=Q}^{\infty} p(d)(d - Q) - c_o \sum_{d=0}^{Q+1} p(d)(Q + 1 - d) - c_u \sum_{d=Q+1}^{\infty} p(d)(d - Q - 1) \le 0$$

$$c_o \left(\sum_{d=0}^{Q} p(d)(Q - d) - \sum_{d=0}^{Q+1} p(d)(Q + 1 - d) \right) + c_u \left(\sum_{d=Q}^{\infty} p(d)(d - Q) - \sum_{d=Q+1}^{\infty} p(d)(d - Q - 1) \right) \le 0$$

$$(B.10)$$

We will use 2 similar tricks to simplify eq. B.10:

$$\sum_{d=0}^{Q+1} p(d)(Q + 1 - d) = \sum_{d=0}^{Q} p(d)(Q + 1 - d) + p(d = Q + 1) \underbrace{(Q + 1 - (Q + 1))}_{=0}$$

$$= \sum_{d=0}^{Q} p(d)(Q + 1 - d)$$

and,

$$\sum_{d=Q}^{\infty} p(d)(d - Q) = \sum_{d=Q+1}^{\infty} p(d)(d - Q) + p(d = Q) \underbrace{(Q - Q)}_{=0}$$

$$= \sum_{d=Q+1}^{\infty} p(d)(d - Q)$$

So that we have B.10 is equal to:

$$c_o \left(\sum_{d=0}^{Q} p(d)(Q - d) - \sum_{d=0}^{Q} p(d)(Q + 1 - d) \right) + c_u \left(\sum_{d=Q+1}^{\infty} p(d)(d - Q) - \sum_{d=Q+1}^{\infty} p(d)(d - Q - 1) \right) \le 0$$

$$c_o \left(\sum_{d=0}^{Q} p(d)\big((Q - d) - (Q + 1 - d)\big) \right) + c_u \left(\sum_{d=Q+1}^{\infty} p(d)\big((d - Q) - (d - Q - 1)\big) \right) \le 0$$

$$c_o \left(\sum_{d=0}^{Q} p(d)(-1) \right) + c_u \left(\sum_{d=Q+1}^{\infty} p(d)(1) \right) \le 0$$

$$c_o \left(-P(D \le Q) \right) + c_u \left(P(D > Q) \right) \le 0$$

We know that $P(D > Q) = 1 - P(D \le Q)$, so that,

$$-c_o P(D \le Q) + c_u (1 - P(D \le Q)) \le 0$$

$$-\frac{c_o}{c_u} P(D \le Q) + 1 - P(D \le Q) \le 0$$

$$-\frac{c_o}{c_u} P(D \le Q) - P(D \le Q) \le -1$$

$$\frac{c_o}{c_u} P(D \le Q) + P(D \le Q) \ge 1$$

$$P(D \le Q) \left(\frac{c_o}{c_u} + 1 \right) \ge 1$$

$$P(D \le Q) \left(\frac{c_u + c_o}{c_u} \right) \ge 1$$

And finally we show that:

$$P(D \le Q) \ge \frac{c_u}{c_u + c_o}$$

Remember, this means that if $P(D \le Q) \ge (c_u)/(c_u + c_o)$ then $\mathcal{C}(Q) \le \mathcal{C}(Q + 1)$. In other words, it means that ordering one more unit will increase the total costs as of when $P(D \le Q) \ge (c_u)/(c_u + c_o)$. Since the cost function is concave, we conclude that, in order to have the optimal Q^*, we have to pick the **smallest** order quantity Q that satisfies:

$$P(D \le Q) \ge \frac{c_u}{c_u + c_o}$$

Bibliography

Aberdeen (2012). Inventory optimization – impact of a multi-echelon approach. Technical report, Aberdeen.

Andrade, A. and Sikorski, C. (2016). Numerical approximation of the inverse standardized loss function for inventory control subject to uncertain demand. Paper presented at the Canadian Operations Research Society Conference, Banff, Alberta.

Andriolo, A., Battini, D., Grubbström, R. W., Persona, A., and Sgarbossa, F. (2014). A century of evolution from Harris's basic lot size model: survey and research agenda. *International Journal of Production Economics*, 155:16–38.

Axsäter, S. (2015). *Inventory Control (International Series in Operations Research & Management Science Book 225)*. Springer.

Billington, C., Callioni, G., Crane, B., Ruark, J. D., Rapp, J. U., White, T., and Willems, S. P. (2004). Accelerating the profitability of Hewlett-Packard's supply chains. *INFORMS Journal on Applied Analytics*, 34(1):59–72.

Burgin, T. A. (1972). Inventory control with normal demand and gamma lead times. *Operational Research Quarterly (1970–1977)*, 23(1):73–80.

Burgin, T. A. (1975). The gamma distribution and inventory control. *Journal of the Operational Research Society*, 26(3):507–525.

Burgin, T. A. and Wild, A. R. (1967). Stock control—experience and usable theory. *Journal of the Operational Research Society*, 18(1):35–52.

Cachon, G. (2018). *Matching supply with demand: an introduction to operations management*. McGraw-Hill Education, New York, NY.

Ciortan, M. (2018). Kernel density. https://github.com/ciortanmadalina/modality_tests/blob/master/kernel_density.ipynb. Online; accessed 05-September-2019.

Clark, A. J. and Scarf, H. (1960). Optimal policies for a multi-echelon inventory problem. *Management Science*, 6(4):475–490.

Cobb, B. R., Rumí, R., and Salmerón, A. (2013). Inventory management with log-normal demand per unit time. *Computers & Operations Research*, 40(7):1842–1851.

Cooper, W. L., Homem-de Mello, T., and Kleywegt, A. J. (2006). Models of the spiral-down effect in revenue management. *Operations Research*, 54(5):968–987.

de Kok, T. (1991). *Basics of inventory management (Part 2): The (R,S)-model*, volume FEW 521 of *Research Memorandum FEW*. Faculteit der Economische Wetenschappen.

de Kok, T. (2018). Inventory Management: Modeling Real-life Supply Chains and Empirical Validity. *Foundations and Trends(R) in Technology, Information and Operations Management*, 11(2):343–437.

De Smet, N., Aghezzaf, E.-H., and Desmet, B. (2018). Optimising installation (R,Q) policies in distribution networks with stochastic lead times: a comparative analysis of guaranteed- and stochastic service models. *International Journal of Production Research*, pages 1–18.

Duong, T. (2001). An introduction to kernel density estimation. http://www.mvstat.net/tduong/research/seminars/seminar-2001-05/. Online; accessed 05-September-2019.

Edgeworth, F. (1888). The mathematical theory of banking. *Journal of the Royal Statistical Society*, pages 113–127.

Ehrhardt, R. (1979). The power approximation for computing (s, S) inventory policies. *Management Science*, 25(8):777–786.

Ellenberg, J. (2014). *How not to be wrong: the power of mathematical thinking*. The Penguin Press, New York.

Erlenkotter, D. (1990). Ford Whitman Harris and the economic order quantity model. *Operations Research*, 38(6):937–946.

https://doi.org/10.1515/9783110673944-017

Eruguz, A. S. (2014). *Contributions to the multi-echelon inventory optimisation problem using the guaranteed-service model approach*. Theses, Ecole Centrale Paris.

Eruguz, A. S., Sahin, E., Jemai, Z., and Dallery, Y. (2016). A comprehensive survey of guaranteed-service models for multi-echelon inventory optimization. *International Journal of Production Economics*, 172:110–125.

Graves, S. C. and Willems, S. P. (2000). Optimizing strategic safety stock placement in supply chains. *Manufacturing & Service Operations Management*, 2(1):68–83.

Graves, S. C. and Willems, S. P. (2003). Supply chain design: Safety stock placement and supply chain configuration. In *Supply Chain Management: Design, Coordination and Operation*, volume 11 of *Handbooks in Operations Research and Management Science*, pages 95–132. Elsevier.

Grubbström, R. W. and Erdem, A. (1999). The EOQ with backlogging derived without derivatives. *International Journal of Production Economics*, 59(1):529–530.

Hadley, G. and Whitin, T. M. (1963). *Analysis of inventory systems*. Prentice-Hall.

Harris, F. W. (1913a). How many parts to make at once. *Factory, The Magazine of Management*, 10:135–136, 152.

Harris, F. W. (1913b). How much stock to keep at hand. *Factory, The Magazine of Management*, 10:240–241, 281–284.

Hill, A. (2017). The newsvendor problem. www.clamshellbeachpress.com/downloads/newsvendor_problem.pdf. Online; accessed 24-April-2020.

Inderfurth, K. (1991). Safety stock optimization in multi-stage inventory systems. *International Journal of Production Economics*, 24(1):103–113.

Johansen, S. G. and Hill, R. M. (2000). The (r,Q) control of a periodic-review inventory system with continuous demand and lost sales. *International Journal of Production Economics*, 68(3):279–286.

Kenneth, J. A., Harris, T., and Marschak, J. (1951). Optimal inventory policy. *Econometrica*, 19(3):250–272.

Kimball, G. (1988). General principles of inventory control. *Journal of Manufacturing and Operations Management*, 1:119–130.

Klosterhalfen, S. and Minner, S. (2010). Safety stock optimisation in distribution systems: a comparison of two competing approaches. *International Journal of Logistics Research and Applications*, 13(2):99–120.

Lee, H. L., Padmanabhan, V., and Whang, S. (1997). The bullwhip effect in supply chains. *Sloan management review*, 38:93–102.

Lerner, M. (2019). Histograms and kernel density estimation kde 2. https://mglerner.github. io/posts/histograms-and-kernel-density-estimation-kde-2.html. Online; accessed 05-September-2019.

Li, P. (2013). *Optimization of (R, Q) policies for multi-echelon inventory systems with guaranteed service*. PhD thesis, Université de Technologie de Troyes.

Maister, D. H. (1976). Centralisation of inventories and the "square root law". *International Journal of Physical Distribution*, 6(3):124–134.

Maxwell, W. L. and Muckstadt, J. A. (1985). Establishing consistent and realistic reorder intervals in production-distribution systems. *Operations Research*, 33(6):1316–1341.

Moncayo-Martínez, L. A. and Ramirez, A. (2016). A tutorial to set safety stock under guaranteed-service time by dynamic programming. *International Journal of Industrial and Systems Engineering*, 24:490–509.

Murphy, R. A. (1975). Inventory control with gamma demand and gamma lead times. *International Journal of System Science*, 6:81–85.

Nahmias, S. (1979). Simple approximations for a variety of dynamic leadtime lost-sales inventory models. *Operations Research*, 27(5):904–924.

Nahmias, S. (1994). Demand estimation in lost sales inventory systems. *Naval Research Logistics (NRL)*, 41:739–757.

Nahmias, S. (2015). *Production and operations analysis: strategy, quality, analytics, application.* Waveland Press, Inc., Long Grove, Illinois.

Oroojlooyjadid, A., Snyder, L. V., and Takáč, M. (2020). Applying deep learning to the newsvendor problem. *IISE Transactions*, 52(4):444–463.

Qin, Y., Wang, R., Vakharia, A. J., Chen, Y., and Seref, M. M. (2011). The newsvendor problem: Review and directions for future research. *European Journal of Operational Research*, 213(2):361–374.

Robert, R., Gino, K., and Peter, C. (2004). The EOQ and EPQ models with shortages derived without derivatives. *International Journal of Production Economics*, 92:197–200.

Scott, D. W. (1992). *Multivariate Density Estimation: Theory, Practice, and Visualization.* Wiley.

Silver, E. A., Pyke, D. F., and Thomas, D. J. (2016). *Inventory and production management in supply chains.* CRC Press, Taylor & Francis Group, Boca Raton.

Silverman, B. W. (1986). *Density estimation for statistics and data analysis.* Chapman and Hall, London, New York.

Simpson, K. F. (1958). In-process inventories. *Operations Research*, 6(6):863–873.

Snyder, R. (1984). Inventory control with the gamma probability distribution. *European Journal of Operational Research*, 17(3):373–381.

Sterman, J. (1992). Teaching takes off: Flight simulators for management education. *OR/MS Today*, 19:40–44.

Strijbosch, L. and Moors, J. (1999). Simple expressions for safety factors in inventory control. Workingpaper, Econometrics.

Syntetos, A., Babai, M., and Altay, N. (2012). On the demand distributions of spare parts. *International Journal of Production Research*, 50(8):2101–2117.

Taft, E. W. (1918). The most economical production lot. *Iron Age*, 101:1410–1412.

Tayur, S. (2007). Supply & demand chain executive. *Supply & Demand Chain Executive*.

Tempelmeier, H. (2011). *Inventory Management in Supply Networks.* Norderstedt.

Thonemann, U. W. (2011). Benefits of multi-stage inventory planning in process industries. https://api.semanticscholar.org/CorpusID:12077335. Online; accessed 24-April-2020.

Tijms, H. C. (1994). *Stochastic models: an algorithmic approach.* Wiley, Chichester, New York.

Tijms, H. C. and Groenevelt, H. (1984). Simple approximations for the reorder point in periodic and continuous review (s, S) inventory systems with service level constraints. *European Journal of Operational Research*, 17(2):175–190.

Trapero, J. R., Cardós, M., and Kourentzes, N. (2019). Empirical safety stock estimation based on kernel and garch models. *Omega*, 84:199–211.

Trietsch, D. (1995). Revisiting ROQ: EOQ for company-wide ROI maximization. *Journal of the Operational Research Society*, 46(4):507–515.

Turrini, L. and Meissner, J. (2019). Spare parts inventory management: New evidence from distribution fitting. *European Journal of Operational Research*, 273(1):118–130.

Tyworth, J., Guo, Y., and Ganeshan, R. (1996). Inventory control under gamma demand and random lead time. *Journal of Business Logistics*, 17:291–304.

U.S. Census Bureau (2019). 2019 census, business and industry, manufacturing & trade inventories & sales.

Vandeput, N. (2021). *Data Science for Supply Chain Forecasting.* De Gruyter.

VanderPlas, J. (2013). Kernel density estimation in Python. https://jakevdp.github.io/blog/2013/12/01/kernel-density-estimation/. Online; accessed 05-September-2019.

VanderPlas, J. (2016). In-depth: Kernel density estimation. https://jakevdp.github.io/
PythonDataScienceHandbook/05.13-kernel-density-estimation.html. Online; accessed
05-September-2019.

Veinott, A. F. and Wagner, H. M. (1965). Computing optimal (s, S) inventory policies. *Management Science*, 11(5):525–552.

Vermorel, J. (2018). The quantitative supply chain. https://www.blurb.com/b/8517792-the-
quantitative-supply-chain. Online; accessed 24-April-2020.

Wang, P., Zinn, W., and Croxton, K. L. (2010). Sizing inventory when lead time and demand are
correlated. *Production and Operations Management*, 19(4):480–484.

Wanke, P. (2009). Consolidation effects and inventory portfolios. *Transportation Research Part E:
Logistics and Transportation Review*, 45:107–124.

Wanke, P., Ewbank, H., Leiva, V., and Rojas, F. (2016). Inventory management for new products with
triangularly distributed demand and lead-time. *Computers & Operations Research*, 69:97–108.

Ward, J., Oca, A., Zimmerman, M., Acar, K., Sonthalia, B., and Sun, Y. (2019). 30th Annual Council of
Supply Chain Management Professionals (CSCMP) State of Logistics Report. Technical report,
ATKearny.

Whitin, T. M. (1953). *The Theory of Inventory Management*. Princeton University Press.

Wilson, R. H. (1934). A scientific routine for stock control. *Harvard Business Review*, 13:116–128.

Glossary

array Data structure defined in NumPy. It is a list or a matrix of numeric values. *See page* 262

backorders Backlog of orders that are not yet fulfilled. This happens when you do not have enough on-hand inventory to fulfill the orders directly and when the orders are not lost. *See page* 3

coefficient of variation (CV) Expresses the relative dispersion of a dataset compared to its mean, $CV = \sigma/\mu$. *See page* 59

correlation (ρ) Measures the dependence between two variables. It varies between -1 (straight negative correlation) and 1 (straight positive correlation). A correlation of 0 means no linear correlation. *See page* 62

cumulative distribution function ($F_{\mathcal{X}}(z)$) Is the probability that an occurrence of a random distribution $\mathcal{X}$ is lower than or equal to a threshold z. We note $\Phi(z)$ the CDF of a standard normal distribution. *See page* 51

cycle service level (α) Probability of not having a stock-out during an order cycle. In other words, the probability that the inventory at the beginning of an order cycle will be higher (or equal) than the demand during this cycle. Often called the "Type 1 service level." *See page* 46

cycle stock C_s Stock dedicated to the normal demand (or forecast) consumption. *See page* 12

DataFrame Table of data as defined by the pandas library. It is similar to a table in Excel or an SQL database. *See page* 264

EOQ (EOQ) Economical order quantity that optimizes the supply chain costs. Also called the optimal order quantity. *See page* 19

excess demand Demand that cannot be served directly from the on-hand inventory. *See page* 76

fill rate (β) Over the long term, the fraction of demand that is supplied directly from on-hand inventory. Often called the "Type 2 service level," we note it β. *See page* 47

Gaussian See *standard normal distribution*. *See page* 50

goodwill (g) In inventory models, any extra cost associated with the risk of losing a client. We note it g. *See page* 214

holding costs Costs related to storing (or simply possessing) products. We note h the yearly holding costs for one single product (generally expressed as a % of the product cost). *See page* 13

in-transit inventory (I_s) Inventory that is currently ordered from a supplier but not yet available in our warehouse. *See page* 35

net inventory Inventory level including: available on-hand inventory and in-transit inventory, minus backorders, orders not yet shipped, etc. *See page* 3

https://doi.org/10.1515/9783110673944-018

NumPy One of the most famous Python libraries. It is focused on numeric computation. The basic data structure in NumPy is an array. *See page* 262

on-hand inventory Inventory available right away (*"on-hand"*) for a client to buy. *See page* 3

order cycle Time elapsed between two orders. In periodic replenishment policies the order cycle is R, in continuous policies it is Q/D. *See page* 12

pandas Python library specializing in data formatting and manipulation. Allows the use of DataFrames to store data in tables. *See page* 263

period service level (α_p) Probability of not having a stock-out during one demand period (e. g., day, week). This can be similar or different than the cycle service level depending on the length of an order cycle. *See page* 46

probability density function $(f_{\mathcal{X}}(z))$ The higher the probability density function (PDF) of random distribution $\mathcal{X}$ is around a value x, the higher the probability that an occurrence of this distribution is close to this value x. In other words, if the PDF of a distribution is high around 1, it is likely that an occurrence of this distribution would fall close to 1. The PDF of a standard normal distribution is noted $\varphi(x)$. *See page* 50

probability mass function $(p(x))$ The probability that a discrete probability function is exactly the integer x. It is the discrete equivalent to the probability density function. *See page* 208

risk-period (x_τ) Maximum amount of time you need to wait to receive an order (from your supplier). During this period your inventory is at risk of being depleted. *See page* 66

Root Mean Square Error $RMSE = \sqrt{\frac{1}{n}\sum e_t^2}$ *See page* 157

salvage value (s_v) Either the discounted price at which a product is sold when the inventory needs to be cleared. Or the cost a company incurs to clear its inventory (e. g., recycling, waste disposal). *See page* 213

service level factor (z) A value that multiplies the demand deviation in order to compute the needed safety stock for a certain service level. *See page* 56

skewness (γ_1) Measure of a distribution asymmetry. It is expressed by a number—just as the mean or the standard deviation. A positive one means a right skew, and a negative one means a left skew. *See page* 149

SKU A stock keeping unit refers to a specific material kept in a specific location. Two different pieces of the same SKU are indistinguishable. *See page* 38

standard normal distribution A standard normal distribution with a variance of 1 and a mean of 0: $\mathcal{N}(0,1)$. It is also known as a Gaussian distribution. *See page* 50

transaction costs (k) Costs triggered by an order (or a transaction). *See page* 15

undershoot (U) In an (R,s,Q) policy, the expected level of inventory below the reorder point s that is reached at the review period R when an order is made. *See page* 70

unit short (U_s) Number of units missed to entirely fulfill the demand. Equal to the excess demand. *See page* 100

vendor managed inventory (VMI) A business model where the supplier of a product takes the ownership of the stock that its client holds. In practice, it means that the supplier is managing and responsible for its client's inventory policy. In some cases the supplier can also own the inventory held at its client's premises, we call this consignment. *See page* 176

work-in-progress Unfinished piece of inventory currently in the production process or waiting between two consecutive steps of the production process. Also known as WIP and work-in-process. *See page* 84

List of Symbols

Statistics

μ_X	Mean of variable X
σ_X	Standard deviation of variable X
$\rho_{X,Y}$	Correlation between X and Y
$E[x]$	Expectation of variable x
$V[x]$	Variance of variable x
$f_{\mathcal{X}}(x)$	Probability density function of distribution $\mathcal{X}$ evaluated at threshold x
$F_{\mathcal{X}}(x)$	Cumulative distribution function of distribution $\mathcal{X}$ evaluated at threshold x
$p(x)$	Probability for a discrete random variable to be equal to x
$P(\mathcal{X} \leq x)$	Probability for random discrete variable $\mathcal{X}$ to be smaller than or equal to x. Equivalent of $F_{\mathcal{X}}(x)$ for a continuous distribution.
$F_{\mathcal{X}}^{-1}(\alpha)$	Inverse cumulative distribution function of distribution $\mathcal{X}$ evaluated at probability α
$\mathcal{L}_{\mathcal{X}}(z)$	Loss Function of distribution $\mathcal{X}$ evaluated at threshold z
$\mathcal{L}_{\mathcal{X}}^{-1}(x)$	Inverse loss function of distribution $\mathcal{X}$ evaluated at probability x

Statistics – Normal distribution

$\mathcal{N}(\mu, \sigma^2)$	Normal distribution with mean μ and standard deviation σ
$f_{\mathcal{N}}(x; \mu, \sigma)$	Probability density function of the normal distribution $\mathcal{N}(\mu, \sigma^2)$ evaluated at x
$\varphi(x)$	Standard normal probability density function evaluated at x
$F_{\mathcal{N}}(x; \mu, \sigma)$	Cumulative distribution function of the normal distribution $\mathcal{N}(\mu, \sigma^2)$ evaluated at threshold x
$\Phi(x)$	Standard normal cumulative distribution function evaluated at threshold x
$F_{\mathcal{N}}^{-1}(\alpha; \mu, \sigma)$	Inverse cumulative distribution function of the normal distribution $\mathcal{N}(\mu, \sigma^2)$ evaluated at probability α
$\Phi^{-1}(\alpha)$	Inverse standard normal cumulative distribution function evaluated at probability α
$\mathcal{L}_{\mathcal{N}}(z; \mu, \sigma)$	Loss function of the normal distribution $\mathcal{N}(\mu, \sigma^2)$ evaluated at threshold z
$\mathcal{L}_N(z)$	Standard loss function evaluated at threshold z

https://doi.org/10.1515/9783110673944-019

$\mathcal{L}_{\mathcal{N}}^{-1}(x;\mu,\sigma)$ Inverse loss function of the normal distribution $\mathcal{N}(\mu,\sigma^2)$ evaluated at probability x

$\mathcal{L}_{N}^{-1}(x)$ Inverse standard loss function evaluated at probability x

Statistics – Gamma distribution

$\Gamma(k,\theta)$ Gamma distribution with shape k and scale θ

$f_{\Gamma}(x;k,\theta)$ Probability density function of the gamma distribution $\Gamma(k,\theta)$ evaluated at x

$F_{\Gamma}(x;k,\theta)$ Cumulative distribution function of the gamma distribution $\Gamma(k,\theta)$ evaluated at threshold x

$F_{\Gamma}^{-1}(\alpha;k,\theta)$ Inverse cumulative distribution function of the gamma distribution $\Gamma(k,\theta)$ evaluated at probability α

$\mathcal{L}_{\Gamma}(x;k,\theta)$ Loss function of the gamma distribution $\Gamma(k,\theta)$ evaluated at threshold x

$\mathcal{L}_{\Gamma}^{-1}(x;k,\theta)$ Gamma inverse loss function of the gamma distribution $\Gamma(k,\theta)$ evaluated at probability x

Inventory Policies

Q Order quantity

R Review period

s Reorder point

S Order up-to level

Deterministic Models

D Yearly demand

d Demand per period

d_L Demand over the lead time

d_R Demand over the review period

k Fixed transaction costs per transaction

c_T Variable transaction costs per unit

h Holding costs per unit per period

Q Order quantity

$C(Q)$ Total (holding and transactions) costs with regard to Q

Q^* Optimal order quantity (or EOQ)

C^* Optimal total costs

Q_B^* Optimal order quantity with backorders B

B	Maximal amount of backorders
b_τ	Backlog cost (cost per unit in the backlog per unit of time)
r	Production throughput per period
ρ	Throughput ratio ($\rho = 1 - d/r$)
Q_ρ^*	Optimal order quantity with production throughput ratio ρ
T	Time between two consecutive orders
T^*	Optimal time between two consecutive orders

Stochastic Models

C_s	Cycle stock
I_s	In-transit stock
S_s	Safety stock
U_s	Units short
α	Cycle service level
α_p	Period service level
β	Fill rate
z	Service level factor
z_α	Service level factor for cycle service level α
z_β	Service level factor for fill rate β
d_c	Expected demand over an order cycle
x_τ	Length of the risk-period
d_x	Demand distribution over the risk-period
μ_x	Expected demand over the risk-period
σ_x	Demand deviation over the risk-period
b	Backorder cost (cost per unit backordered)
b_τ	Backlog cost (cost per unit in the backlog per unit of time)

Multi-echelon Models

S_s^i	Safety stock held at node i
S^i	Order up-to level at node i
x_τ^i	Risk-period covered by node i
gs_τ^i	Guaranteed-service time at node i
h_i	Holding cost at node i
L_i	(Incoming) Lead time at node i
$d(\tau)$	Demand over τ periods
$\hat{d}(\tau)$	Demand bound over τ periods

Newsvendor

c_o	Overage cost
c_u	Underage cost
c	(Purchasing) Cost
p	(Sales) Price
s_v	Salvage value
g	Goodwill
h	Holding cost
$\mathcal{C}(Q, D)$	Expected (total) costs based on Q and D
$\mathcal{P}(Q, D)$	Expected profits based on Q and D

Index